RUSSIAN WRITERS

THEIR LIVES AND LITERATURE

by

JANKO LAVRIN

D. VAN NOSTRAND COMPANY, INC.

TORONTO   NEW YORK   LONDON

NEW YORK
D. Van Nostrand Company, Inc., 250 Fourth Avenue, New York 3

TORONTO
D. Van Nostrand Company (Canada), Ltd., 25 Hollinger Rd., Toronto

LONDON
Macmillan & Company, Ltd., St. Martin's Street, London, W.C. 2

Preface

The scope of the present book is indicated by its title. The author's intention is to present in a brief, suggestive manner the growth and the character of Russian literature in its entirety, as far as is possible in a book of this size. The stress is of course on the nineteenth century when Russian literature, having assimilated western methods and influences, asserted its own originality and became one of the leading literatures in the world, in fact a literary great power. But, instead of the usual systematic exposition, the author has preferred to dwell on a series of striking personalities and their work. These are shown against their historical and cultural background partly with the wish to stimulate readers to further research.

A number of chapters are actually abbreviated lectures given to University students. Some of them have appeared earlier (1948) in my book, *From Pushkin to Mayakovsky,* published by the Sylvan Press (London) to whom my sincere thanks are due. The poems and passages in the present book have been taken from several editions which are mentioned in each case separately. I express my thanks and acknowledgment to the translators and publishers of the works concerned.

J. L.

Contents

CHAPTER ONE

"The Lay of Igor's Campaign"

I.

Russian civilization began towards the end of the 10th century in Kiev, with the baptism of Prince Vladimir in 988. It was not for religious but for political reasons that this ruler imposed overnight, so to speak, Christianity upon his subjects as an accomplished fact which was not to be argued about, let alone resisted. As Kiev was in those days a kind of central citadel guarding the trade route "from the Varangians to the Greeks," it was natural that Christianity should have come to the Kievan Russians not from Rome but from the "Greeks," that is from Constantinople. Such, at any rate, was one of the earliest reasons for that gap between Russia and the West which was destined to affect eventually the history of Europe. At the time when Russia became Christian, Byzantium was passing through its third period—the "silver age"—of its artistic and cultural revival, and the new converts showed an amazing assimilative power. Byzantine church architecture and painting were first imported wholesale, but it did not take long before the Russians imbued both with a refreshingly original flavor and "accent" of their own.

As a general commercial-feudal center of the far-flung Russian tribes and principalities Kiev soon became a promising focus of culture. The beauty of the city, too, was so great that

a German traveler of that period (Adam of Bremen) compared it favorably even with Constantinople. Nor was there a
lack of political and other contacts between Kiev and the rest
of Europe. Prince Yaroslav the Wise, who was responsible for
the building of the magnificent St. Sophia church at Kiev
(1037), married one of his daughters to the King of France,
another to the King of Hungary, and a third to the King of
Norway. He was also a great lover of books and read them—
so the chronicle says—"continually day and night." One of his
successors, Vladimir Monomakh (he became Grand Prince in
1115), even took the trouble to learn five foreign languages.

No wonder that literature there was given a good start. The
more so because the Russians did not adopt the Greek language
for ecclesiastical purposes but obtained their first religious
books from the Balkan Slavs whose language was similar to
their own. It should be borne in mind that during that early
period of Russian Christianity the Bulgarians in particular had
already developed a rich literature in the Slavonic vernacular.
The old-Bulgarian language was taken over, with certain modifications, by the Russian Church, and since in those days literature was mainly in the service of religion, this "Church-
Slavonic" language was used (although not exclusively) for
literary purposes well until the second half of the 17th century,
or even until the reforms of Peter the Great. The magnificent
oral literature of Russia—its folk-tales, legends, epic sagas or
byliny, ritual and lyrical songs, proverbs, etc.—thus developed
parallel with, and independently of, written literature.

Having severed herself from Byzantium linguistically, Kiev
Russia had no direct contact with the literary heritage of
Greece. The stimulus which Latin literature, with its worldly
impact, exercised on Western Christianity and Western learning had no equivalent in Kievan Russia. This means that for a

long time the religious-monastic ideal prevailed to the exclusion of everything secular. Its asceticism tended towards unusual severity for the very reason that the chaotic vitality of a young barbaric race could have been tamed, up to a point, only by a ruthless repression of the flesh. This ideal saw its embodiment in the founding of numerous monasteries. It also provided the principal characteristics of Kievan literature which was almost entirely in the hands of the ecclesiastics and in the service of the Church. In addition to liturgical books proper, there was an early crop of pious legends, apocrypha, lives of the saints, patristic writings, parables, and some magnificent sermons—especially those by the Kiev Metropolitan Hilarion and Cyril the Bishop of Turov. The manuscript of the oldest Gospel, the so-called *Ostromir Gospel,* dates from the middle of the 11th century. The copious translations from the Byzantine even include a very free late 11th century version of Josephus Flavius's *De bello judaico,* with a few unique passages about Christ and Pilate, the character and the authenticity of which have recently aroused international controversy. Among the early original works of Kievan literature Prior Daniel's simply but beautifully written *Pilgrimage to the Holy Land* (1106-08) can be mentioned. Another gem is the so-called *Primary Chronicle* or *The Tale of By-gone Years.* Modelled on the Byzantine type of Chronicle, notably on that by Hamartolas, it brings the early history of Russia up to 1113 and abounds in delightful anecdotic material. The two manuscripts—the Laurentian and Hypatian—in which it has come down to us were copied in the 14th and the 15th centuries respectively. The work as a whole can be compared with the finest medieval chronicles in any language. In sheer literary brilliance it is superseded, though, by another masterpiece of old Russian-literature: the brief heroic epic, *The Lay of Igor's Campaign (Slovo o polku*

Igoreve), now known to the world mainly through Borodin's famous opera, *Prince Igor*.

2.

The main feature of this epic is its poetical as well as documentary value. Written largely in the spoken language of the period, it stands at the height of literary excellence. At the same time it reflects the conditions of the country when Kiev had already lost its control over other principalities whose rulers were now constantly wrangling with each other despite the threat of Mongol invasions.

There were, on the whole, three successive waves of Asiatic invaders intent on plundering the Russian territory. The Pechenegs were the first to come. Then, in the middle of the 11th century, there appeared the Polovtsians or the Koumans, but they were driven by the Russians beyond the Don region whence they continued to make frequent raids, especially in the second half of the 12th century—the period of Igor's campaign. Finally, the Polovtsians were replaced by the Tartars who in 1238-40 invaded practically all the Russian lands and held them in subjection for some two hundred and forty years. The Polovtsians had failed to take Kiev, but they disturbed the commerce with Constantinople and succeeded in closing the trade route from Dvina to the Sea of Azov. In this manner they cut off the Kiev Russians from their distant but important commercial city of Tmutarakan on the Caucasian side of the Taman peninsula (between the Sea of Azov and the Black Sea).

Harassed by them, Prince Svyatoslav of Kiev made a coalition with some other princes against the Polovtsians and was at first successful. But personal ambitions, feuds, and jealousies among the lesser rulers kept undermining that unity which was essential for warding off the nomadic hordes. In 1185 Svyato-slav was preparing a joint expedition against the enemy who seemed to have been most restive at the time. Yet spurred on by the vision of personal glory, the young Prince Igor of Novgorod-Seversk (in the Chernigov area) decided to make a raid on the Polovtsian territory on his own. With the help of his brother Vsevolod, his son Vladimir, and his nephew Svyatoslav Olgo-vich, he actually turned the whole of it into a kind of family affair and even scored a victory at first. He was, however, de-feated and taken prisoner, while the victorious Polovtsians ravaged the land of Russia. In the autumn of the same year Igor escaped from his captors and arrived—via Chernigov—in Kiev where he was received with joy. The finale thus has a symbolic touch, since Prince Svyatoslav was a champion of unity and of a common action against the Mongols. Such is the gist of this epic, which is supposed to have been written by a professional bard belonging to the Prince's retinue (*druzhina*). The poet does not unfold the account logically in all its phases but con-centrates on a series of dramatic-lyrical episodes. These are pre-ceded by an introduction in which he hints at the existence of other bards, naming a certain Boyan who, evidently, must have been something of a *vates*.

"Might it not befit us, brethren, to begin in ancient style the heroic tale of the raid of Igor, of Igor son of Svyatoslav?

"Then let this song rather begin according to the events of our time, and not after Boyan's invention.

"For when Boyan the seer wished to make someone a song, he would fly in fancy over the trees, like a grey wolf across the land, like a blue-grey eagle beneath the clouds.

"For recalling, quoth he, the fights of olden times, it was his wont to loose ten falcons on a flock of swans: whichever swan was overtaken was the first to sing a song.

"But indeed Boyan did not loose ten falcons on a flock of swans, my brethren, but laid his own magic fingers upon the living strings, and they would of themselves sound forth the glory of the princes—

"Let us then, brethren, forego this tale from Vladimir of old to Igor of our days, who proved his mind with firmness and sharpened his heart with valor.

"Filled with martial spirit, he led his brave hosts against the Polovtsian land in defence of the land of Rus."

This opening redolent of the folk-style, leads to the actual account. There follows—after several ill omens—a condensed description of the march of the warriors who are inspired by the knightly ideal of honor for themselves and glory for their princes. The poem is pervaded by a Christian spirit, but with a strong admixture of pagan elements. Even the names of the Slavic pagan gods crop up time and again. Still, the initial victory of the Russians is regarded as a gift of God, whereas their subsequent defeat is looked upon as a punishment for their sins. The defeat itself is rendered with an imagery full of poetic parallelisms, epithets and similes, nature symbols, effective refrains, and repetitions.

"Already ahead of his misfortune the birds hide in the oaks; wolves in the ravine howl in the storm; eagles with their cries summon beasts to the bones; foxes bark at the scarlet shields.

"One day they fought, they fought another, and on the third, towards midday, the banners of Igor fell!

"Then the two brothers parted on the banks of the river Kayali.

"Then the bloody wine ran dry.

"Then the bold sons of Rus finished the feast: they gave the wedding guests to drink, and themselves they lay down for the Russian land.

"The grass bends in sorrow, and the tree is bowed down to earth by woe."

In spite of Igor's defeat, after which "anguish flooded the Russian land," the princes continued their mutual feuds. But they are severely rebuked and condemned by the bard. And so the poem turns from the battlefield to Svyatoslav—the champion of unity. Svyatoslav has in Kiev a dream full of evil forebodings. The dream is followed by an outburst against his two nephews Igor and Vsevolod, and by a patriotic harangue against the princes on account of their quarrels and egoism. Each of the ruling princes is given a brief but trenchant characterization. Then the scene suddenly shifts to Putivl where on the city ramparts Yaroslavna—the beautiful wife of Igor—bewails her fate "like a cuckoo singing without tidings at morn" in the manner of the Russian folk-songs.

"Yaroslavna weeps at morn at Putivl on the city wall, wailing:

' "Wind, O Wind! Wherefore, Lord, blowest thou so fiercely?

' "Wherefore carriest thou the Huns' arrows upon thy carefree wings against the warriors of my beloved?

' "Is it not enough for thee to blow on high, beneath the clouds, rocking ships upon the blue sea?

' "Wherefore, Lord, hast thou scattered my joy over the grass of the plains?'

"Yaroslavna weeps at morn in Putivl upon the city wall, wailing:

' "O bright and thrice-bright Sun! Towards all art thou
warm and fair.

' "Wherefore, Lord, hast thou shed thy scorching rays on
the warriors of my beloved and wherefore in the waterless
plain hast thou parched their bows with thirst, locked their
quivers with weariness."

After Yaroslavna's complaint there follows the escape of Igor
who, with the help of God, speeds towards the bank of the
Donetz. He is pursued by two Polovtsian chiefs, but nature
itself is on Igor's side. Along the whole of his road birds are
either silent so as not to give him away, or else they indicate to
him the direction which he ought to take.

"Then crows croaked not, daws grew silent, magpies did
not chatter.

"Woodpeckers climbed upon the willows: with their
knocking they show the way to the river; and lo! nightingales announce the dawn by gay songs."

Finally, all ends well, and there is jubilation in Kiev.

"The sun shines in heaven: Igor the Prince is in the
Russian land! . . . The countries are glad, the cities re-
joice."

And then a suitable conclusion:

"Hail Princes and retinue, fighting for the Christendom
against the infidel hosts!

"Glory unto the Princes and to their retinue honor!" *

3.

Like *La Chanson de Roland,* or the Jugoslav cycle of the Kosovo
ballads, *The Lay of Igor's Campaign* sings of a defeat. And like

* Translated by S. H. Cross in *La Geste du Prince Igor* (École Libre des Hautes Etudes,
N. Y., and Université Libre, Bruxelles), 1948.

AN ILLUSTRATION TO "A POEM ABOUT THE IGOR BATTLE"
BY THE PALEKH ARTIST, IVAN GOLIKOV

The Battle of Malden, it was written soon after the event by a man who evidently had taken part in it. The epic which must have been finished not later than in the spring of 1187, i.e. some two years after the campaign, bears witness not only to the author's poetic gift but to his familiarity with Byzantine and Russian writings, as well as with the folk-songs. His imagery shows a certain resemblance to the one used in the Russian paraphrase of *The Judaic War.* Yet the bond between man and nature, in a true animistic spirit, is always there. So is, surprisingly enough, the poet's ardent advocacy of national unity as the only hope of a successful resistance against the Asiatics. National consciousness at the end of the 12th century is surely something of a phenomenon! The reproaches hurled at the quarrelling princes who have destroyed the unity that prevailed under former rulers, show a rare political and civic sense.

> "Victory over the infidels is gone, for now brother said to brother: 'This is mine, and that is mine also', and the princes began to say of little things, 'Lo! this is a great matter,' and to forge discord against themselves.
>
> "And on all sides the infidels were victoriously invading the Russian land."

Unfortunately, at the time this poem was written the edifice of Kievan Rus was already cracking. The Polovtsians were followed by the mightier and better organized Tartar hordes who were soon to sack Kiev (1238) and to become masters of Russia —just as the bard of this epic predicted. An "iron curtain" fell between Russia and the West, cutting off practically all cultural contacts between the two. And when at the end of the 15th century the "curtain" was lifted, the gap was already too great to be bridged on the terms of parity.

4.

The only manuscript of *The Lay of Igor's Campaign* (an early 16th century copy) was discovered by Count A. I. Musin-Push-kin in a monastery-library at Yaroslavl in 1795. Its first printed edition appeared in 1800. In the conflagration of Moscow dur-ing Napoleon's invasion in 1812 the original manuscript per-ished. What survived, though, was a copy which had been made for Catherine II. Considering the fact that paleographic art was in those days still in its infancy, we must not be surprised that there are a number of obscure words and passages in the copy preserved.

The discovery of this masterpiece caused a great sensation in Russia and later also abroad. Remembering McPherson's *Ossian* and Chatterton, some scholars began to question its authenti-city. In 1832 Professor Kachenovsky held at Moscow University an open dispute with the poet Alexander Pushkin, trying to prove that the epic was a literary fake. Pushkin, however, was adamant in his opinion to the contrary.

The controversy continued, but competent admirers never doubted the genuineness of the Lay.* The studies and explora-tions written about this work during the last hundred and fifty years would fill a library. Recently (1940) Professor André Mazon made in his *Le Slovo d'Igor* a new onslaught on it. The cudgels were taken up by a number of scholars. The results were not in favor of Prof. Mazon's theory. An adequate, indeed decisive, answer came from Prof. Roman Jakobson and Prof. George Vernadsky (both of whom are now active in America)

---

* It may be of some interest that the Czech romantic poet and philologist Vàclav Hanka (1791-1861) "discovered" the faked manuscripts of "old-Czech" poems (the Kraledvorský and Zelenohorský manuscript) partly under the influence of *The Lay of Igor's Campaign*.

in *La Geste du Prince Igor*. A great deal of research has also been done in Soviet Russia. Among the more recent works on the subject those by V. N. Perets, S. K. Shambinago, A. S. Orlov, and N. Gudziy may be mentioned. Anyway, authoritative opinion has fully vindicated the authenticity of this masterpiece of old-Russian literature.

CHAPTER TWO

Avvakum

I.

The great promise of Kievan literature and culture was under-mined by the Tartar yoke. As the Tartars were mainly after tribute, they let the native Russian princes collect it. And since the Moscow princes were by far the shrewdest diplomats, they gained ascendancy over their rivals and turned Moscow into the new political, cultural, and religious center of the Russians. Protected by forests and rivers, Moscow was certainly in a better position to assert its power than Kiev had once been. It was in fact the Moscow Prince Dimitry (Dimitry Donskoy) who in 1380 dealt the first smashing blow to the Tartars in the field of Kulikovo—a prelude to the liberation of Russia in 1480. Ivan III compelled most Russian principalities to recognize him as their over-lord. His grandson Ivan IV (Ivan the "Terri-ble") was thus able to proclaim himself—in 1547—the Tsar of "all Russias," and to start that expansionist policy which was so typical of the Moscow period. This period lasted, roughly, from 1480 until the foundation of Petersburg in 1703 by Peter I. It added to the actual Russian territory the enormous spaces reach-ing as far as Astrakhan on the one hand, and the shores of the Pacific (1639) on the other. In the West, a large portion of the Ukrainian population rebelled against the Poles and accepted (in 1654) the suzerainty of Russia. Through the Ukrainians again Western influences began to penetrate into Russia, although this process was hampered by certain factors whose roots were both historical and psychological.

To begin with, Ivan III, who had married the niece of the last Byzantine emperor, regarded the Muscovite Russia as the rightful heir to Byzantium after Constantinople had fallen to the Turks in 1453. Under his son and successor Vasily III Moscow was actually proclaimed the "Third Rome" and the only repository of true Christianity. Several narratives were written to propagate this particular idea which took root at once. In 1589 the Russian Church, moreover, set up her own Patriarch who was independent of the Greek patriarchate at Constantinople. This self-assertion and infallibility in matters of Christian doctrine made Muscovy look with suspicion upon the "heretical" West, even though her trade-relations with Europe were now on the increase.

Autocratic centralization of the State and of the Church thus became one of the main themes in Russian literature at a time when Western Europe had already reached the height of her Renaissance culture. Polemical and religious writings were the order of the day, not to mention all sorts of compilations supporting the historical pretensions of Moscow. The most imposing product was the *Chetyi Minei* or *The Saints Calendar* (1562), compiled by the Metropolitan Makary according to the days of each month. Rigid regulations for the Church were collected in *Stoglav* ("A Book of Hundred Chapters"), while the even more rigid "patriarchal" rules for home and family were laid out in *Domostroy* ("Home Builder"). In his anxiety to consolidate the State, Ivan IV made far-reaching social changes by smashing the power of the princely boyars and distributing the bulk of their lands among the more amenable "serving nobility"—from now on the backbone of the country. In spite of his achievements, his death in 1584 was followed by a "troubled period" (1595-1613), with False Dimitry and the Poles in Moscow, while the whole of Russia was on the verge of anarchy and ruin. This critical period was ably recorded by three contemporary witnesses: Palitsyn, Katyryov, and Timofeyev.

The election of Michael Romanov to the throne in 1613 improved the situation. It also opened up the country to further influences from the West. Moscow herself had developed by then a large foreign or "German" quarter whose style of life was entirely European. She even emulated the westernized Theological College of Kiev by instituting a Slavo-Graeco-Latin School of higher theological learning in which some of the principal monk-teachers were invited from Kiev. One of them was the prolific but hardly gifted poet Simeon Polotsky (1629-80), who even wrote two biblical plays based on the Jesuitic school-drama. The belated Western motifs of *Gesta Romanorum, Speculum magnum,* even of *Decameron* and the *Fabliaux,* trickled into Russia mainly via Poland and the Ukraine, and found a soil ready to absorb them. Yet while all sorts of influences (forestalling the gradual divorce between church and culture) were active, the opposite tendency to remain entrenched in the "infallible" Muscovite traditions was not silenced. It flared up strongly indeed and soon produced among its defenders such a dynamic figure as the archpriest Avvakum whose autobiographic *Life* is a unique personal and literary document of the period.

2.

Avvakum Petrovich was born into a priest's family in 1620 or 1621 in Grigorovo, a village in the Nizhni Novgorod district. He became a village priest at the age of twenty-two and was raised some eight years later to the rank of a *protopop* or archpriest. During all that time he distinguished himself by his stubborn independence, his blunt honesty, and by a kind of ruthless puritanism which made him as severe to others as he was to himself. This brief but typical extract from his autobiography shows what his morality must have cost him at times, since he too was a man of flesh and blood.

"And in these days of my ministry a young woman came to confess to me, burdened with many sins, guilty of fornication and of all the sins of the flesh, and, weeping she began to acquaint me with them all, leaving nothing out, standing before the Gospels. And I, thrice accursed, though a leech, fell sick myself. I inwardly burned with a lecherous fire, and that hour was bitter to me. I lit three candles and fixed them on the lectern and placed my right hand in the flame, and held it there till the evil passion was burned out and, when I had dismissed the young woman and laid away my vestments, I prayed and went to my house, grievously humbled in spirit."

No less typical is the incident which occurred when he found his wife and her maid-servant in so violent a quarrel that, in a fit of anger, he beat them both. But no sooner had the beating been administered than he began to repent of his un-Christian action. In order to atone for it he lay down and ordered that all those who were in the parlor should beat him forthwith with a scourge upon his back. "There were twenty people. And my wife and my children and all of them, weeping, did beat me. And I spake and said, 'If there be any man that doth not beat me, let him have no part with me in the kingdom of heaven. And they beat me, against their will, and weeping; and I, at every blow, said a prayer. And when they had all beaten me and I was stood up, I pronounced forgiveness before them all."

Such was the man who was destined to become the leader of

that group of the conservative community which eventually broke off from the official church and remained in opposition to it until the present day. The misunderstanding began innocently enough. What happened was that the Moscow Patriarch Joseph (1642-52), anxious to restore the ancient Russian piety, made some slight improvements in the corrupt liturgical texts. His successor, the Patriarch Nikon (1652-58), encouraged by Tsar Alexey Mikhailovich and his circle who were anxious to centralize the Church, went much further. He not only wanted to correct the Church-Slavonic books by going back to the Greek originals, but ordered that some religious rites, such as crossing oneself with three fingers instead of two, ought to be taken over from the Greeks. The more conservative portion of the Russians, who regarded their own rites and formulae as hallowed signs of spiritual realities, naturally raised a protest. And the man who seemed to have been cut out for the leadership of such an opposition was Avvakum.

He certainly had the virtues marking him out as a leader: integrity, ruthless courage, the gift of words, and even a great literary talent. His numerous polemics, epistles, admonitions, and above all his *Life* are all written in the vigorous and racy spoken language, aptly sprinkled with Biblical or Church-Slavonic phrases. Avvakum's autobiography was in fact the first Russian masterpiece in prose deliberately written in the people's tongue. But it had a personal touch as well. The author not only showered in it homely idioms and similes, but made effective use of his sardonic wit, his "folky" sense of realism and of humor. Infinitely tender towards his friends, he could be savage towards his opponents for whom no epithet was vile enough. He presented things very simply, because he himself saw them only in terms of black and white. For him a thing was either true or false, so there was no compromise between the two. As

AVVAKUM

Nikon and the Nikonites were on the side of error, they
were the instruments of the devil and deserved to be pun-
ished accordingly. "We would begin by quartering the devil
Nikon and afterwards all the Nikonites," he once wrote to the
Tsar. And he meant it.

The only trouble was that the Nikonites, being in power,
were able to use, and eventually did use, the same charitable
method towards Avvakum himself. They remained in power
even after 1658, when Nikon—defeated in his ambitious bid to
subdue the State to the Church—had to give up the high office
of Patriarch. Having sized up their opponent, they tried again
and again to win Avvakum to their own side, or at least to
make him silent, but it was all in vain. The formidable archpriest would make no concession. In one of his epistles he
actually urged his followers to suffer death at the stake rather
than think of any compromise. "Your burning will not last
long—only a moment—and then your soul will be free." A
kind of collective spiritual masochism, with a lust for martyr-
dom, or else for self-immolation, spread among those "old believers" who took his injunctions literally. The first collective
self-immolation of an entire religious community, which refused to submit to the official Church, took place in 1675.* But
Avvakum was not spared either. Nor did he want to be spared.
He not only underwent all sorts of trials and tortures for the
sake of his faith, but actually revelled in them as we can gather
from his *Life* which was above all a confession he wrote at the
request of his spiritual father, the Elder Epiphanius, so that the
"word of God should not be given to forgetfulness." Such was

---

* All quotations in this chapter are taken from *The Life of the Archpriest Avvakum
   by Himself,* translated by Jane Harrison and Hope Mirrless. L. & V. Woolf.
   London, 1924.
* The last act of Moussorgsky's opera *Khovanshchina* gives an example of such a
   voluntary collective auto-da-fè.

the origin of this strange literary, inhumanly human, and even historical document of the Moscow period.

3.

Avvakum's trials and wanderings were almost incredible. And so was his heroic endurance. They take us to his Siberian exile in Tobolsk (1653), in the Lena district, in the unexplored Trans-Baikal region—one worse than the other. After having nearly perished with his wife and children in the wilds of Transbaikalia, where he had undergone the greatest humiliations at the hands of the Cossack leader Pashkov, he was suddenly recalled to Moscow in 1662. Here he was received with great pomp by the Tsar, the boyars, and the official clergy, all of whom were hoping he would be more amenable after his lessons in Siberia. Honors and riches were showered upon him, but he continued to preach what he regarded as right.

Soon he was exiled, together with his family, once again; this time to Mezen in the inhospitable Archangel region. In 1667 the dissenters were condemned by the Oecumenic Church Assembly in Moscow, and from now on the schism between the Orthodox and the "old believers" or *raskolniki* became complete. Avvakum, more stubborn than ever, was unfrocked and then imprisoned in a dismal place called Pustozersk in the Arctic circle. It was here that he wrote, between 1672 and 1675, his *Life* or *Zhitie* as he called it. It was from here, too, that he continued to send to his followers all sorts of polemics, commentaries, letters, petitions, and admonitions. Finally, he and some of his principal companions were burned at the stake on April 14th, 1682. The events which led to such a climax are described in his autobiography, the straightforward realism of which can best be illustrated by a few quotations.

"And I, too, while I was celebrating vespers, was arrested by Boris Neledinsky and his musketeers, and together with me they arrested nigh on sixty souls and took them off to prison, and me they fastened with a chain for the night in the Patriarch's court. And when the Sabbath dawned they placed me in a cart and stretched out my arms and drove me from the Patriarch's court to the monastery of Andronicus, and there they put chains on me and flung me into a black dungeon, dug into the earth, and there I lay for three days, and I had nothing to eat or to drink in the darkness, as I sat there bowing myself to the earth against my chains, though I knew not, as I made my obeisances, which was east and which was west. No one came to me but mice and black beetles, and the crickets chirped, and of fleas there was abundance."

The man's vitality was proved, however, during his long years in the Siberian wastes, where he was at the mercy of the sadistic Cossack commander Pashkov. While dragging on through unchartered regions, scores of people were dying of cold and starvation. But Avvakum survived and told the tale.

"Then he [Pashkov] roared like a wild beast, and struck me a great blow first on one cheek and then on the other, and then again on the head, and knocked me off my feet; and seizing his leather sword-strap struck me, where I lay, thrice on my back, and then, tearing off my shirt, gave me seventy-two strokes on my naked back with the knout . . . And after that they brought me to the fortress Bratsky, and flung me into a dungeon, and gave me straw to lie upon. And there I lay till Advent in a freezing tower."

Or take the hardships he shared with those early pioneers in Siberia with whom he was compelled to wander about. "And in winter we would live on fir-cones, and sometimes we found the bones of stinking carcasses of wild beasts left by the wolves, and what had not been eaten up by the wolves that did we eat; and some would eat frozen wolves and foxes—in truth, any filth that they could lay their hands on. A mare foaled, and, in secret the starving folk devoured the foal together with the caul. And Pashkov got wind of it, and he flogged them with his knout to the point of death. And another mare died, and desperation seized them all, inasmuch as they had pulled the foal out of her stealing a march on nature. When naught but the head had as yet emerged from the womb, they tore it out, yea, and they began to eat the blood that came away with it. Ah, me! What a time! And two of my little sons died from these sore straits, and roaming the hills and the sharp rocks with my children that survived, naked and barefoot, living on grass and roots, what did I not endure?"

The most surprising thing was the stoicism with which his wife and children bore all the hardships together with him for the sake of a strange ideal in which they believed. They even encouraged him in his intransigence. While on his long trail from Siberia back to Moscow, Avvakum had a moment of doubt as to whether he should—for the sake of his family—be silent or else continue to preach with the same unconcern as before. Knowing what the second course might lead to, he revealed his thoughts to his wife. And this was her answer:

' "I and the children give you our blessing, continue the preaching of the Word of God as heretofore, and take no thought for us until such time as shall seem good to God; when that time comes, remember us in your prayers; Christ is strong and He will not abandon us. Get thee gone, get thee gone to church, Petrovich! Unmask the whore of heresy!' and I bowed myself to the earth before her [he continues] and shook myself free from the blindness of a troubled mind and began once more to preach and teach God's Word in the towns and in all places until such time as I could boldly tear the mask from the heresy of Nikon."

4.

So much for the man's undaunted spirit pervading the whole of this book. It was not only the piety of the old Russia but also her intolerant conservatism that flared up in Avvakum at a time when her unavoidable contact with the West could not but foster certain innovations in all fields, Church and religion included. The patriarchal Muscovite mentality could hardly have found a more heroic and at the same time fanatically narrow-minded representative than Avvakum. And however Christian he may have been at heart, there was no charity in him towards those with whom he disagreed. "Filthy dogs," "fat-bellies," "fornicators"—such were the usual epithets with which he tried to brand the Nikonites.

The roots of the conflict were yet deeper than the pretexts provided by Nikon's innovations. They showed an *instinctive* revulsion of the self-complacent medieval Russia to that secularization of culture which could no longer be barred by any obstacles and whose logical climax were the reforms of Peter the Great. Whereas Peter's reforms opened wide the gates to European influences, the spirit of Avvakum was only repressed but not destroyed. So it continued to crop up, periodically and in most unexpected forms, until the problem of Russia and Europe, of East and West, assumed (in our own days) global dimensions. The problem is not only one of politics or ideology —it is also one of psychology. And its psychological aspects are perhaps the most difficult of all. Avvakum's literary masterpiece has the merit of providing at least some clue to that Russian mentality which continues to puzzle the more soberly and skeptically attuned West.

CHAPTER THREE

Fonvizin

I.

The foundation of Petersburg in 1703 by Peter I marked the beginning of a new period in Russian history and culture—the "Petersburg period," which lasted from Peter's accession to the throne in 1794 until the revolution of 1917. The trite phrase that Petersburg was a "window into Europe" is an understatement. The new Russian capital was more than that: an open dam through which Europeanization kept rushing in at an accelerated pace and often quite regardless of whether it would find there a propitious soil or not. The process was neither simple nor easy. Yet the fermentation resulting from it was full of new dilemmas the very conflicts and clashes of which proved in the end stimulating. At any rate, it helped the Russian consciousness to make a shortcut as it were and to pass in less than two hundred years through an evolution which normally would have taken twice or three times longer. Moreover, what is usually known to the outside world as Russian literature proper coincided with the second half of the Petersburg period.

For convenience's sake it is perhaps best to divide it into three phases. The first of these comprised practically the whole of the 18th century which was one of apprenticeship and imitation. Europe was the teacher and Russia was her zealous pupil. A mixture of the two was typical of that period. The second phase began after Russia's victory over Napoleon in 1812 and ended with the unsuccessful revolution of 1905. It is marked by a process of groping for a creative synthesis between the Russian and the Western elements—a process which resulted in the monumental Russian realism, Russian music, as well as in some important features of Russia's social, political, and religious-philosophic thought. One of its characteristics was the formation of the intelligentsia which, from the 1840's onwards, became the guardian of Russian culture. The third and rather brief phase between the revolutions of 1905 and 1917, was one of general blind-alley and bewilderment, accompanied by a bankruptcy of practically all the values which the intelligentsia had stood for. Its mental climate consisted of despair, cynicism, and of vague apocalyptic moods which found an appropriate finale in the downfall of the old regime in 1917. Out of the ensuing chaos the Soviet period of Russian history and culture was born. The capital of Russia was transferred—symbolically enough—back to Moscow, thus turning a new page in Russia's relations with Europe as well as with the rest of the world.

2.

Needless to say Russian 18th century literature, "Westernized" by the reforms of Peter I, had very little to do with the Church-Slavonic language. Its medium was now the spoken tongue which was first standardized for such a purpose by that remarkable scientist, literary theoretician, grammarian, and poet in one—Mikhail Lomonosov (1711-65). Towards the end of the century Nikolai Karamzin (1766-1826), the leader of the sentimental trend in poetry and prose, modified Lomonosov by raising the speech of the gentry to the status of a literary language.

It was during the span of time between Lomonosov and
Karamzin, and especially under the rule of Catherine II
(1762-96), that Russia made her greatest efforts to assimilate the
Western literary forms and methods, with the latent hope of
creating eventually a national literature of her own. The influences up to Karamzin were those of the French pseudo-
classicism. The Russians were not slow in manufacturing odes,
epics, satires, tragedies, comedies, and didactic tales or novels of
their own—creditable up to a point, but mostly second-hand.
Catherine II, in spite of her German extraction, not only encouraged these efforts but herself became a prolific if smartly
superficial Russian authoress. The peak of that period was
reached in the poetry of Gavrila Derzhavin (1743-1816) whose
colorful "Tartar genius" was robust enough to defy any literary
conventions. Nikolai Novikov (1744-1818), who was a free-
mason, publisher, and liberal philanthropist, founded a number
of satirical journals at a rather high level. The stilted pseudo-
classic tragedians Sumarokov, Ozerov, and Knyazhnin failed to
create anything remarkable, yet one of the fashionable 18th
century genres—the fable—found in Ivan Krylov (1768-1844)
its belated and perhaps greatest exponent after Lafontaine. In
spite of the fact that he preserved the imported pseudo-classic
pattern of the fable, he remained very Russian and national in
the true sense of this word. Chronologically, however, he no
longer belonged to the 18th century. His equally witty and
stinging counterpart, the playwright Denis Fonvizin, on the
other hand, was entirely of that century and cannot be dissociated either from its historical or its literary background.

DENIS IVANOVICH FONVIZIN (1745-1792), FAMOUS RUSSIAN DRAMATIST

3.

Denis Ivanovich Fonvizin (1745-92) was born into a fairly
well-to-do family of the landed gentry. After his graduation at
the newly established (1755) University of Moscow he entered
the army, then became associated with the director of the
theatres Elagin, and finally, in 1769, joined the Ministry of
Foreign Affairs as secretary to the progressive-minded minister
Count Nikita Panin. His literary activities began at the end of
the 1760's and in the early 1770's when, with a number of other
young liberals, he became a contributor to Nikolai Novikov's
satirical journals, *The Drone, The Tatler,* and *The Painter.* In
1777-78 he accompanied his chief on a journey to Paris. Judging
by the letters he wrote home, his impressions of France and of
her *après nous le déluge* moods were most painful, and he took
a certain pride in his being a Russian. Although a liberal mind,
he stood much nearer to the Russian freemasons of the Novikov brand than to the French encyclopaedists who—for reasons
of their own—kept on shamelessly flattering the "enlightened"
façade of Catherine's rule. What was behind that façade was a
different matter.

It is true that the early and the middle years of Catherine's II
regime were full of fashionable slogans and tendencies—as long
as these did not encroach upon the prerogatives of the serf-
owning nobility. When in 1766-68 the commission designed to
regulate the relations between the landed nobility and the serfs
was at work, the Novikov circle favored the rights of the serfs,
but with hardly any success. The serfs were left in the same
position as before. In order to diminish the influence of
Novikov's periodical *The Drone,* Catherine II founded her own
mildly liberal and mildly satirical journal *Pell Mell.* She her-

self wrote diatribes against Novikov's periodicals to the effect
that everything was all right under her own wise rule. The
armed peasant rising of 1773-75 in the Urals and on the lower
Volga, under the leadership of Pugachov, gave a more sobering
answer. But Pugachov was defeated, and his defeat was a
further triumph for the landed serf-owners. One of the reasons
which made these insist with such tenacity on their rights was
their aristocratic blood. They regarded their superiority over
the "villains" almost as a law of nature. Shocked by it all,
Fonvizin decided to debunk and expose this would-be superiority as mercilessly as he could. Which he did in his two satirical
comedies, *The Brigadir* and *The Young Hopeful* *—the first
truly realistic masterpieces of the Russian repertory.

It seemed as if Fonvizin's turn of mind was made for satire.
His early works consisted of fables, epistles, imaginary letters—
all of them written with his tongue in his cheek. He did also a
lot of translating, notably from Holberg and from some fashionable French authors. Yet his version of Voltaire's *Azire* and
his adaptation of Gresset's *Sidney* (Fonvizin gave it the title of
Korion) were only exercises for his own independent plays to
come. The first of these was *The Brigadir*, written probably in
1768-69.

As the Russian literary historian Alexey Veselovsky pointed
out, in writing this work Fonvizin must have taken a great deal
from the well-known 18th century comedy *Jean de France* by
the "Danish Molière" Ludwig Holberg. And since Holberg
himself had written it under the partial influence of Wycher-
ley's *The Gentleman Dancing Master,* the first Russian comedy
is thus linked also to the English Drama. But whatever Fonvizin's borrowings and influences, he assimilated them to perfection and made them typical of the manners and conditions

---

* The Russian title *Nedorosl* is frequently translated as *The Minor*.

he saw among the provincial gentry at the time of Catherine II. He did this so well that his play fully deserved the success it had earned on the stage and otherwise.

The plot of *The Brigadir* is not rich in external action—the stress is on the characters, the dialogue, and the general picture of life in the remote corners of Russia. The method still conforms to Molière's tradition, with the three unities preserved, yet the realistic sense which pervades it is entirely Fonvizin's. The Brigadir* and his wife are paying a visit to Sophia's parents in order to woo their pretty daughter for their son Ivanushka (Johnny) who is with them. Like the hero of Holberg's *Jean de France,* Ivanushka is infected with Franco-mania so fashionable among the young snobs of that period. He is as silly, vulgar, and depraved as are his parents or, for that matter, the parents of Sophia. Sophia's father—the Councillor—begins to run after the Brigadir's wife, while both the Brigadir and his son become rivals for the Councillor's wife's favors. There is an irresponsible erotic mix-up quite in the style of the 18th century, but with a strong provincial accent. Sophia and her secret sweetheart—the only decent characters in the comedy—thus have their own way, while the dastardliness and the uncouth vulgarity of the others are shown up during the denouement. Fonvizin's laughter was here strong enough to augur well for some later satirists. It was a debunking of the "blue blood" unparalleled in the Russian literature of that time. Yet he gave an even more cruel indictment of the same kind in *The Young Hopeful.*

4.

Fonvizin worked at this comedy of manners for a number of years and finished it in 1781-82. Published in 1783, it showed

* A rank which was between a colonel and a general.

even better characterization and also a greater variety of motifs than *The Brigadir*. For it contains at least three converging motifs, the bestiality of the provincial gentry being one of them. Then there is the humanitarian motif: the demoralizing influence of serfdom upon the serf-owners. And finally, interwoven with all this is the motif of a "gentleman's" education in those days—presented in all its appalling grotesqueness.

Also this time the action takes place in the provinces, on the estate of the Prostakovs (Mr. and Mrs. Simpleton). The character of the ignorant, tyrannical, stupid, and greedy Mme. Prostakova is most convincing in its realism. No less vivid is the portrait of her worthy brother Skotinin (Mr. Beastley) who, needless to say, does full justice to his name. Mme. Prostakova's sixteen-year-old son, the "young hopeful" Mitrofan (a kind of Russian Tony Lumpkin) is typical of the atmosphere in which he has been brought up. As the snobbery in those days demanded that at least one teacher in a squire's house, where there were children to educate, should be either French or German, the "young hopeful's" education kept to this rule. But towards the end it transpired that his German mentor was an ex-coachman who found the post of a tutor in a Russian nobleman's family much more profitable than his former occupation. Lastly, there is the conventional secret love between Sophia and Milon which provides the structural backbone of the play. But there are two other wooers of Sophia as well, or rather of her sudden fortune: the "young hopeful" and his uncle Skotinin. On hearing of the financial prospects in store for Sophia, Mme. Prostakova does all she can to secure her hand for Mitrofan, but her intrigues are foiled. The comedy has a happy ending for the two secret lovers, but a catastrophic one for Mme. Prostakova and her beloved offspring.

Such is the scaffolding of the play which serves as a pretext for all sorts of invectives and indictments. The very first scenes illustrate through Mme. Prostakova's behavior the subhuman treatment meted out to serfs. Her brother Skotinin is of course no better in this respect. Nor is the "young hopeful." As a contrast Fonvizin puts forward two positive types—noblemen whom he wants to show as being really noble. Unfortunately, his Pravdin (Mr. True) and Starodum (Mr. Oldsense) are both *raisonneurs* as well as the author's mouthpieces. Starodum's didactic tirades (in the 18th century style) have been made rather heavy by the subsequent addition of sententious passages found among the author's papers. On the other hand, it was through these two characters, or rather types, that the author vented his contempt for Catherine and her collection of richly rewarded male prostitutes—one more despicable than the last. Starodum, who had to leave the court because he was both unwilling and unable to adapt himself to it, mentions this fact to his friend Pravdin who reacts as follows:

> *Pravdin* Men with a moral code like yours should not be dismissed from the court, rather they should be asked to enter that career.
>
> *Starodum* To enter it? And what for?
>
> *Pravdin* What for? Why is a physician necessary for a sick man?
>
> *Starodum* My friend, you are mistaken! It is no use to call in a doctor to an incurable patient. In this case a physician can do no good—he may even contract the disease himself.*

* Translated by George Y. Patrick and George Rapall Noyes in *Masterpieces of Russian Drama*, Appleton, 1933.

5.

It required courage to be outspoken about the court even in those "enlightened" days. Fonvizin knew, of course, what he was doing. His association with Novikov enabled him to exercise his satirical and critical gift also outside his plays, no matter whether the court liked it or not. But the Empress was not a fool either. In the company of Princess Dashkov she began to edit, in 1783, a periodical—*The Interlocutor*—with the object of grouping around it all the best authors of that period in order to make them subservient to her own whims and wishes. Fonvizin did not mind writing for it, but only on his own terms. One of his contributions was a set of twenty questions which must have made the Empress wince. He even concocted for it a satirical *Court Grammar* indicting Catherine and her favorites but, needless to say, it was not printed.

In 1788 Fonvizin intended to publish a liberal journal of his own under the well-meaning title of *Honest People's Friend*. The periodical was never allowed to appear. What soon made things worse was the panic which took hold of Catherine II after the French Revolution. Banking on her "enlightenment," one of the remarkable men of that generation, A. V. Radishchev (1749-1802), dared to publish in 1790 his *Journey from Petersburg to Moscow,* containing the most outspoken attacks on autocracy and serfdom. The author's political radicalism can best be gathered from his *Ode to Liberty* (included in the book) which contains these lines addressed to Cromwell:

"Ay, thou wert cruel and perfidious, a bigot and a hypocrite, thou hast profaned things sacred; thou wert the greatest villain in the world; for, possessed by the plenitude of power, thou hast abolished every manifestation of freedom in thy people. And yet thou art a great man, because thou wert the first to dare show a beneficent example to the people by executing, in accordance with the people's judgment, your King Charles; thou hast taught mankind how to avenge itself on its oppressors."

The book was immediately confiscated and burned, while the author himself was sentenced to death. The death sentence was commuted to exile in Siberia whence he returned only after Catherine's death in 1796. Radishchev's case had to be mentioned as an illustration of what happened once the Empress had shed her would-be liberalism. Novikov, too, was imprisoned. As for Fonvizin, he remained silent. Besides, during the last years of his life he had had a stroke after which he became an invalid, with fits of religious and mystical moods into the bargain. He died in 1792.

6.

Fonvizin was not a prolific playwright. Apart from the two mentioned comedies, he wrote a third one, *The Choice of a Tutor,* which remained unfinished. Yet of all the Russian 18th century dramatists he is the only one who still belongs to the repertory of his country. Moreover, Fonvizin anticipated Gogol's "laughter through tears," as well as the castigating indignation of other critical realists from Griboyedov to Saltykov-Shchedrin. Of his two comedies the first was written in an exclusively critical spirit, whereas the second—though even more critical—was to be constructive as well. The didactic element, introduced into it by Pravdin and Starodum, is rather top-heavy and not fully integrated with the rest of this work; but even so both plays gave a good start to the Russian comedy of manners.

There was yet another trait in Fonvizin which seemed to be a pointer to the finest Russian type after Peter I. A liberal at heart he was yet fully aware of those Western-European features which he regarded as negative. His ideal was a blend of the constructive European elements with what was best and truly promising in the Rusisan spirit as he understood it. This is why he wrote from Paris during his stay in France (1777-78): "The people here had started to live before us, but we who are now beginning to live can at least choose a form of existence suitable to ourselves and thus avoid those evils and errors which have taken root here."

At the time of Fonvizin's death there were already enough signs that Russia's literary apprenticeship was coming to an end. In poetry in particular she had made great strides. The vigorous if somewhat splashy Muse of Derzhavin was followed, towards the end of the century, by the gentle and "genteel" sentimental trend, represented by N. N. Karamzin and his school. But Vasily A. Zhukovsky, who made his debut in 1802 with an excellent translation of Gray's *Elegy,* already marked a step further towards romanticism. He, himself, was a dreamy romantic, with all the attributes of a *schoene Seele* (a "beautiful soul"). Endowed with a wonderful virtuosity of language, he enlarged the area of Russian poetry also by his matchless translations from English and German. Together with his contemporary, the neo-classicist K. N. Batyushkov, he heralded, as it were, the rise of that national literature in Russia which received its mightiest impetus from the genius of Alexander Pushkin.

CHAPTER FOUR

Alexander Pushkin

I.

Alexander Sergeyeivich Pushkin (1799-1837) is a strange and in some respects unique phenomenon. Under one of the most tyrannical regime in Europe, he knew how to preserve his creative freedom and, in spite of all the obstacles, to crystallize the irrepressible vitality and *joie de vivre* of a belated Renaissance figure into works of imperishable harmony and beauty. A Russian to his very core, he yet absorbed organically the literary and cultural heritage—in fact, the entire humanistic tradition—of the West and grafted it upon his native country as part and parcel of its own inner life. In addition to being the greatest national poet of Russia, he thus became the principal link between the literature of his own country and the literatures of Europe, notably that of England. He not only provided a brilliant conclusion to the period which preceded him in Russia, but indicated, in his own creations, that kind of synthesis between Russia and Europe which could serve as a pointer to the future. In spite of that, Pushkin is probably the only first-rate genius whose reputation outside Russia rests on credit rather than on actual acquaintance with his work. The fact that he is a great poet and, in a way, the founder of modern Russian literature is taken of course for granted. Nevertheless, a foreigner ignorant of the Russian language

33

and culture can hardly understand what the name of Pushkin means to a Russian and what his name stands for.

This drawback is further increased by a lack of adequate translations. And Pushkin still remains one of the most difficult poets to translate—difficult mainly on account of his uncanny ease, obviousness (he is perhaps the greatest genius of the obvious), and simplicity. Equally uncanny was his flair for the *mot juste,* for the right inflection, as well as for that orchestration of sounds, rhymes and rhythms the harmony of which he always worked out with matchless clarity and precision. Few poets indeed have known how to extract the full value out of words with that Hellenic instinct for art that conceals art which is one of Pushkin's primary qualities. In his poems each word, each image, seems to be born out of another with that inevitability which excludes anything artificial, forced and labored. And the more perfect and disciplined the result, the stronger is the impression of spontaneity. The texture of his verse, too, is so individual that it is impossible to confuse it with that of anybody else. He may and often does use several parallel themes in one and the same poem, yet he organizes them in such a balanced polyphonic manner as to make the content utterly indivisible from its rhythmical and verbal pattern. The economy and the sparkling lucidity which as a boy Pushkin had learned from the French poets (including Voltaire and Parny), he later combined with his own realistic sense, as well as with that broad perception of life which made him compare his work in one of his lyrics, with the echoes, reproducing all the sounds and vibrations around even if the echoes themselves remain unanswered.

> When cries of beasts the forests fill,
> The thunder rolls, the trumpets shrill,
> A maiden sings behind the hill,

> To every sound
> Responsive, sudden echoes thrill
> The air around.
> They hear the thunder's roaring glee,
> The stormy sobbing of the sea,
> The shouts of shepherds on the lea,
> And answers find,
> Themselves unanswered.—How like thee,
> Poetic mind.*

Intensely human and all of this world, Pushkin "echoed" everything in terms of visual images and symbols, that is, of concrete reality. However intimate his personal experiences, he knew how to sublimate them, especially in his matchless love-lyrics, by means of his "shorthand" realism into things of beauty the purport of which is far above the merely personal. It becomes universal, that is applicable to all whose imagination can respond to analogous experiences. This deeply moving avowal may be quoted as a proof:

> I loved you. Even now I may confess
> Some embers of my love their fire retain.
> But do not let it bring you more distress—
> I do not want to sadden you again.
> Hopeless and tongue-tied, yet I loved you dearly,
> With pangs the jealous and the timid know.
> So tenderly I loved you, so sincerly,
> I pray God grant another love you so.

One of Pushkin's most haunting lyrics, *Remembrance,* may serve as another example.

> When trade and traffic and all the noise of town
> Is dimmed, and on the streets and squares

* Translated by Walter Morison. The theme of this exquisite lyric was inspired by an English poem, *The Sea-Shore Echo,* by Barry Cornwall.

The filmy curtain of the night sinks down
With sleep, the recompense of cares,
To me the darkness brings nor sleep nor rest.
A pageant of the torturing hours
Drags its slow course, and writhing in my breast,
A fanged snake my heart devours.
My fears take form, and on the wearied brain
Grief comes in waves that overflow,
And Memory turns a scroll to tell again
A legend that too well I know.
Reading the past with horror, shame, and dread,
I tremble and I curse,
But the repentant tears, the bitter tears I shed,
Will not wash out a single verse.*

Poems like the ones just quoted speak for themselves. Their
emotional and artistic integrity is beyond any doubt or question. Furthermore, in Pushkin's lyrics there is no gap between
the physical and the spiritual planes, between "soul" and
"body." Instead of being hostile, the two are mutually complementary and, in fact, inseparable. No matter how impulsive,
passionate, even turbulently passionate he may have been as
a man, as a poet he remained to the end one of the most
balanced geniuses in world literature—in some respects even
more balanced than Goethe. His was not a static, but a
dynamic balance which made him experience life as an *élan
vital* and perpetual movement. Feeling at home in this world,
he adopted that affirmative attitude which accepts all life—
whether "happy" or "unhappy"—provided it is really intense.
What he hated was sham-life, camouflaged by all sorts of
respectable labels. It was for this reason that he affirmed life
in its entirety, with its joys and sorrows, even the most tragic

* This and the previous poem were translated by R. M. Hewitt.

sorrows. Such acceptance is perhaps best expressed in his well-known *Elegy*, full of readiness to face any adversities without saying *no* to existence.

> The frenzied merriment of misspent years
> Like wakening from wine my spirit sears:
> Like wine, the poignant imprints of past pain
> Grow stronger in me as in years they gain.
> My path is sombre; fraught with toil and sorrow
> The storm-encompassed ocean of tomorrow.
>
> And yet, my friends, I do not ask for death;
> Life I desire, for pain and contemplation.
> I know I shall be stirred by pleasure's breath
> 'Mid all my grief, and care, and agitation.
> Again at times with melody I'll throb,
> My fancy's fruit again will make me sob;
> And maybe, as my last sad days decline,
> Love with a farewell smile on me will shine.*

2.

Pushkin's appetite for life was so strong indeed that on a purely human plane and amidst ordinary circumstances he was, despite his sense of measure, often swayed by excesses and vagaries the causes of which may, perhaps, be traced to his exotic ancestry. Whereas on his father's side he came of an aristocratic Russian stock six hundred years old, his maternal great-grandfather had been an Abyssinian princeling, bought in the slave market at Constantinople and sent as a present to Peter the Great, who took good care of his education and his subsequent career. Pushkin's own parents were rather

---

* This lyric and the verses quoted in sections 2 and 3 have been translated by Walter Morison.

commonplace, without any particular talents or distinctions. Besides, he saw little of them, and the only person for whom he felt genuine attachment in his childhood was his old nurse Arina. That lovable peasant-woman was actually destined to form something of a bridge between the poet and the people. As a boy of twelve he was sent to the newly opened *Lycée* or privileged boarding school at Tsarskoye Selo (now called Pushkin), where the atmosphere was so much to his liking that, years afterwards, he always commemorated in verse the opening day—October 19th. One of these poems, *October 19th, 1825,* ranks among his finest and best-known creations. Its first two stanzas may serve as an example of what the whole of it (written in exile) is like:

> The autumn wood casts off its crimson gown,
> The faded field is silvered o'er with frost,
> The sun peers forth, a sad, reluctant ghost,
> And hurriedly behind the hill goes down.
> Burn brightly, pine-logs, in my lonely cell;
> And thou, O wine-cup, that in autumn rains
> Dost comfort so, in my sad heart instil
> A brief oblivion of bitter pains.
>
> How sad I am, no friend to comfort me,
> With whom my sorrows I might solve in drink,
> Whose trusty hand in my hand I might link
> And wish him all his days felicity.
> I drink alone; in vain my fancy calls
> To visit me the friends of former years;
> No pleasure I await; no footstep falls
> With sweet familiar ring upon my ears.

The five or six years of Pushkin's schooling at the *Lycée* were responsible for the enduring friendships which he alludes to in the two verses quoted. But those were also the years which coincided with one of the most eventful and promising eras in modern Russian history. The younger generation, which had witnessed Russia's victory over Napoleon in 1812, could not but expect a better future for their country. The two basic evils of Russia—serfdom and autocracy—weighed heavily on all those who hoped for the eventual triumph of justice and freedom; but as the years passed things only became worse under the jackboot of reaction. Still, the ideas bequeathed by the French Revolution could not be entirely suppressed even in Russia, where a considerable portion of the young aristocrats aimed at reforms corresponding to the more liberal spirit of the age. Disappointed in their hopes, these liberals found an outlet in secret societies. Finally, on December 14th, 1825, an open revolt broke out against the new Tsar Nicholas I, the brother of the deceased Alexander I. It was engineered chiefly by the officers of the Guards—all of them sincere patriots, anxious to turn Russia into a free constitutional country. Unfortunately, their organization was so bad that the venture ended in a *débâcle*. Five of the most prominent "Decembrists" (as they were called henceforth) were hanged. The rest, one hundred and twenty in all, were sent to Siberia. Yet in spite of its failure, this revolt from above became a landmark in the social history of Russia and a source of inspiration for all the subsequent fighters for freedom.

Pushkin, who belonged to the same class of landed gentry, had a number of friends among the "Decembrists" and was in fact their favorite bard. Quite a few of his earlier verses were saturated with the spirit of rebellion. One of them, *The Dagger,* he dedicated to the German student Sand, who in 1819 stabbed to death the notorious reactionary and spy (in the Russian service) Kotzebue, otherwise known as the most popular German playwright of that period. Sand's in-

strument of revenge, the dagger—a "secret punisher of Freedom's rape"—is addressed by Pushkin in terms such as these:

> Like dart from Hell, or bolt by gods released,
> Thy silent blade gleams in the tyrant's eyes;
>   He trembles, as around he spies
>   For death amidst the feast.
>
> Where'er he be, thy point seeks out his sin:
> On land, on sea, in temple, in the field,
>   On passion's couch, among his kin,
>   By secret locks concealed.

After the total defeat of the rebels, Pushkin's revolutionary
zeal was temporarily cooled down, yet his allegiance to the
cause of freedom never faltered. In the very heyday of the
"leaden regime," imposed upon Russia by Nicholas I, he
wrote his revolutionary *Message to Siberia* (addressed to his
"Decembrists" friends), which ends with the promise that
eventually—

>   will the heavy fetters fall,
> The prison crumble; freedom's words
> Will greet you by the dungeon wall.

3.

The tragedy of frustration among those younger intellectuals
of the gentry class, who at the time were the guardians of
Russian culture, can be imagined. Yet by some paradox of
history it was in the years of reaction and oppression that Russia passed through her "golden age" of poetry. The starting
point was the publication of Pushkin's *Ruslan and Ludmila*
(1820), which brought him national fame. Here a fantastically
romantic theme is treated with the classical discipline, detach-

ALEXANDER PUSHKIN (1799-1837)

ment, and wit typical of the eighteenth century. Pushkin's gaily sensuous acceptance of life is equally reminiscent of that easy-going age. But when this sprightly epic appeared its author was already in exile. Because of some biting epigrams he had been ordered, in the spring of the same year, to leave Petersburg for the South of Russia whence he made a journey to the Caucasus and the Crimea. He was then transferred to Kishinev in Bessarabia (where he lived much as he pleased); from there to the more civilized Odessa; and finally, in the summer of 1824, he was ordered to go to his mother's estate, Mikhailovskoye, in the North—not very far from Pskov.

This compulsory absence from Petersburg, apart from having prevented Pushkin from joining the December revolt, gave him enough leisure to deepen his literary interests and to bring his genius to maturity. The products of his exile were amazingly good and varied, however painful his loneliness may have been at times. But in the autumn of 1826 the poet was summoned by the Tsar's special courier to Moscow, where the coronation festivities were in full swing. Nicholas I received Pushkin amiably, pardoned his past "transgressions," and cunningly offered to be the only censor of his future writings.

The Tsar's intention may have been to turn the greatest Russian genius into a glorifier of the reactionary regime. In this he failed, although, beguiled by his assumed friendliness, Pushkin became well-disposed towards him personally—at least for the time being. The poet's entanglements with the Tsar and with the Court, however involuntary on his part, assumed a few years later a character which was bound to interfere with the whole of his existence and even led to his premature death. It all started after his marriage (in 1831) to the beautiful but not over-intelligent Natalia Goncharova.

Natalia was graciously (too graciously) noticed by the Tsar himself. In order to enable her to attend the exclusive court balls Nicholas, in 1834, made her husband a "gentleman of the chamber"—an office suitable for a youth of eighteen, but hardly for a man of thirty-five and a great poet into the bargain. It was obviously an affront, which Pushkin resented but could do nothing about.

Meanwhile, the queue of Natalia's admirers kept on growing, the Tsar himself being at the head of it. The most persistent of these was a certain d'Anthès—a French refugee with a commission in the Guards. Having been "adopted" by the Dutch Ambassador, Baron Heeckeren (notorious as a pervert and intriguer), he was able to cut a society figure. For some reason Heeckeren himself did all he could to bring about a liaison between Natalia and his rather smart "son." Gossip and slander took their usual course. Disgusted with the "gilded rabble," Pushkin thought of escaping from it all to Mikhailovskoye, where he hoped to live in his own way—

> . . . called to render
> Account to no one; free to serve and suit
> Oneself alone; not forced to bend one's neck,
> One's conscience, thoughts to livery and power,
> At liberty to wander here and there
> And savor all the beauty of creation,
> Before the fruits of art and inspiration
> Swoon in a speechless spasm of delight—
> There's happiness indeed, and human right.

But Natalia would have none of it. She was too much fascinated by the noisy glitter of society. Besides, it was made clear to the poet that the Tsar himself would be displeased by such an "ungrateful" move. So Pushkin stayed on—he had to. The intrigues, with all the scandal and gossip, gradually reached such proportions that he found it necessary to defend his wife's honor as well as his own. On January 27th, 1837, a duel between him and d'Anthès took place. Pushkin was mortally wounded and died two days later in his thirty-eighth year.

4.

Despite such a short life, Pushkin left a great literary heritage in verse and in prose. In both he showed a rare capacity for adapting himself to others in order to adapt them to himself. He experienced a number of literary influences, without however succumbing to any of them. Having absorbed them instead, he thereby increased the wide range and also the peculiar originality of his own genius. The strongest influences came from England and were connected with the names of Byron, Shakespeare and Sir Walter Scott respectively. Yet all of them, while acting as powerful stimuli, were remodelled by Pushkin in his own image.

Pushkin's Byronic period came after the earlier spell of French influences and was responsible for his four Byronic tales in verse, all of them written between 1821 and 1824: *The Prisoner of the Caucasus, The Fountain of Bakhchisaray, The Robber Brothers,* and *The Gypsies,* of which only the second one is entirely romantic. The other three, for all their romantic motifs, abound in that terse classical realism which was one of the basic features of Pushkin's genius. True enough, in *The Prisoner of the Caucasus* and in *The Gypsies* he introduced into Russian literature the uprooted Childe Harold type, but even this essentially romantic hero is shown in a realistic setting. Later, in *The Gypsies,* he debunked not only his egotism, but also the fallacy of any Rousseauesque retreat or escape, above all the escape to a more primitive state of consciousness which has already been left behind by history and civilization. Finally, Pushkin debunked the Byronic poseur, fashionable in those days even on the banks of the Neva, in his famous *Evgeny Onegin* (1823-31).

This "novel in verse," as Pushkin himself calls it, is his central and in many respects most typical creation. It was here that he overcame Byron on Byron's own ground. His first intention seems to have been to write a satirical equivalent of Byron's *Don Juan*. But having probably realized that Russian censorship would never allow him to publish a satire after his own heart, he wrote a lyrical "novel" instead, in which such a romantic prig as Onegin was transferred to the Russian countryside in its true setting of the 1820's.

The very contrast between the unsophisticated warmth and simplicity of the countryfolk on the one hand, and the *blasé* child of Petersburg society on the other, was enough to explain why Onegin remained the same poseur in his inherited manor as he had been before in the capital. His cold priggishness had become so much his second nature that he could not divest himself of it even when coming across the profound love on the part of Tatyana—a shy, inexperienced product of the country-house, yet potentially full of strength of character. In her naïve sincerity it was she who first confessed to Onegin her love for him, and this *faux pas* was itself enough to make the Petersburg dandy wince. With a few commonplaces to the effect that he is so disappointed with life as to be unable to love anyone, he returns her the letter she had, with much trepidation, sent to him. After months of boredom and ennui, during which Onegin kills in a stupid duel his only friend, he—like Childe Harold—spends a few years in travelling, and finally returns to the "high life" in Petersburg. There he meets

Tatyana once again; this time a mature married woman, admired by all as one of the most charming and dignified members of that rather exclusive circle. Now it is Onegin who falls in love with her and, in his turn, sends her letters which remain unanswered. When, in a fit of despair, he personally confesses to her his feelings, she acknowledges with firm candor that she still loves him but intends to remain faithful to her husband, and she means it. So in the end a note of frustration creeps into Onegin's fate which, despite his posing as a "Muscovite in Childe Harold's cloak," started a whole series of truly "superfluous men" in Russian fiction. However slender the plot of this "novel in verse," its art remains supreme from the first to the last line. And its realistic background—the life and atmosphere in the 20's—is depicted so well that Pushkin's first great critic, Belinsky, wrote: "In *Onegin* we see a poetic picture of the whole of Rusisan society in one of the most interesting phases of its development. *Onegin* can be called an encyclopaedia of Russian life, and a national work in the highest degree." Written in the special "Onegin" stanzas (in four-footed iambics and consisting of fourteen lines), it lends itself to all sorts of moods, and sparkles like champagne in sunshine.

Some of Pushkin's other narrative poems, such as the humorous *Count Nulin* (its theme is in the style of the eighteenth century *contes*) and *The Little House in Kolomna,* are entirely realistic. The latter is even confined to lower middle-class characters, which was something of an innovation. Different in plane and treatment are, however, *Poltava* and *The Bronze Horseman*. Both of them deal with the larger destinies of Russia, while dwelling at the same time, each in its own way, on the "super-human" aspects of Peter the Great. *Poltava* is a torso of a national epic in the truest sense of this word, and

is magnificent precisely as a torso. It combines two themes:
the conflict between Russia and Sweden—at that time the
most powerful maritime state in the North; and the tragedy
of Maria Kochubey who had fallen in love with the aged
Mazepa, a secret ally of the Swedish King Charles XII. En-
ticed far into Southern Russia, the Swedes and the treacherous
Mazepa were beaten at Poltava (1709)—a victory which made
Russia an indisputable European power. The appearance of
Peter I among his soldiers during the battle of Poltava is one
of the passages illustrating the condensed and dynamic matter-
of-factness of Pushkin's poetry.

>   His eyes
> Dart fire, his face commands surrender,
> His steps are swift. The tempest's splendor
> Alone with Peter's splendor vies.
> He goes. They bring his charger, panting,
> High-strung, yet ready to obey,
> He scents the fire of the fray
> And quivers. The blazing heat bores deeper.
> The battle rests—a tired reaper.
> The Cossack steeds, paraded, shine.
> The regiments fall into line.
> No martial music is redounding,
> And from the hills the hungry roar
> Of the calmed cannons breaks no more.
> And lo! across the plain resounding,
> A deep "Hurrah!" roars from afar:
> The regiments have seen the Tsar.*

The Bronze Horseman, commonly regarded as the greatest
poem ever written in Russian, marks the height of Pushkin's
poetic realism passing into the symbolic. The climax of the

---

* Translated by Babette Deutsch in *The Works of Alexander Pushkin,* edited by
Avrahm Yarmolinsky. Random House, N. Y.; Nonsuch Press, London.

poem is the matchless picture of the flood of Petersburg in 1824. During one of the severest gales the Neva—dammed and driven by the winds back up the gulf—suddenly began to flood the islands in and round the capital. Panic and havoc were in its trail. But instead of subsiding the storm grew worse, while the swelling and roaring river

> . . . like a maddened beast was hurled
> Swift in the city. All things routed
> Fled from its path, and about it
> A sudden space was cleared; the flow
> Dashed in the cellars down below;
> Canals above their border spouted.
> Behold Petropol floating lie
> Like Triton in the deep waist-high!
> A siege! The wicked waves attacking
> Climb thief-like through the windows; backing,
> The boats stern-foremost, smite the glass,
> Trays with their soaking wrappage pass.
> And timbers, roofs, and huts all shattered,   ·
> The wares of thrifty traders scattered,
> And the pale beggar's chattels small,
> Bridges swept beneath the squall,
> Coffins from sodden graveyards—all
> Swim in the street!*

The capital is at the mercy of elements which have no regard for the works of man or for the man himself. The number of victims grows. Yet Evgeny, an insignificant young *déclassé,* saves his life by clinging to the lions on the porch of the Senate House opposite the bronze monument of Peter the Great, the founder of the imperial city. Later he learns that his bride has perished in the disaster. He is so crushed by it that he loses his reason. A deranged vagrant, he wanders in

* Translated by Oliver Elton in *Verses by Pushkin and Others* (Arnold).

the streets for weeks. One night he stops in the Senate Square
before Peter's statue and vaguely recollects all that has happened in the accursed city whose founder now surges there like
a demon on horseback. The madman flings curses at him
and suddenly raises his fists. But here, in his dim mind, the
bronze statue seems to have reared. Frightened, Evgeny begins
to run through the cobbled streets, all the time hearing the
clatter of bronze hoofs behind him. It is not his business to
question whether Peter, in his designs for Russia's destiny, had
any moral right to disregard the happiness of thousands of
little men. Or, perhaps, it is! Pushkin only asks the question;
but he does so with all the artistic power at his disposal.

5.

While retaining the pattern of the Byronic tale in verse, Pushkin transcended Byron and only took from him what he needed
for his own creative purposes. In a similar manner he underwent the influence of Shakespeare, the principal result of
which was his drama, *Boris Godunov*—now known all the
world over because of Moussorgsky's opera under the same title.
Written at Mikhailovskoye in 1825, *Boris Godunov* was the
first Shakespearian play in Russian literature. Pushkin took
the subject matter from the "troubled period" at the end of
the sixteenth and the beginning of the seventeenth centuries,
when the pretender False Dimitry rose (with the help of the
Poles) against the ruler Godunov—the supposed murderer of
the real Tsarevich Dimitry and heir to Ivan the Terrible. He
modelled this work, written in the five-footed iambic and in
blank verse, on "our Father Shakespeare" largely in order to
counteract the sterile pseudo-classic plays which still lingered
on and even dominated the Russian stage. The result was not

so much a play made all of a piece as an ably dramatized chronicle, in which (in spite of its title) the Pretender rather than Boris Godunov is the actual hero. While paying much attention to the "convincingness of situations and naturalness of the dialogue," Pushkin yet displayed a surprising sense of history. Equally surprising was his understanding of the epoch concerned, not to mention his treatment of human characters and the great variety of dramatic scenes, in which he always achieved a maximum of effect by a minimum of means. The play itself was based on the pattern of Shakespeare's "Histories," but its condensed dialogue is Pushkin's.

Boris Godunov was not his only contribution to the dramatic literature of Russia. The four miniature plays, which he finished in the autumn of 1830, are small in size but big in artistic value. And here, too, English stimuli were at work. It was Barry Cornwall's now forgotten *Dramatic Scenes* that suggested to Pushkin the idea of writing his own series of "little tragedies." One of these, *The Feast at the Time of Plague,* was actually taken from John Wilson's *The City of the Plague* (1816) and translated, or rather paraphrased, into a Russian masterpiece in blank verse. Pushkin intended to write at least ten such miniature plays but finished only four. Each of these deals with one of the cardinal human passions: In *Mozart and Salieri* it is envy; in *The Miser Knight*—avarice and will to power; in *The Stone Guest* (Pushkin's own interpretation of the Don Juan motif) it is carnal lust; while the scene taken from *The Feast at the Time of Plague* is worked out so as to stress man's defiance in the very teeth of death.

Knowing well that all these themes had been widely used in European literature before him, Pushkin decided to tackle them not in order to repeat what had been said already, but to show them in a new light and from a new angle, in which

he fully succeeded. But even in these miniature plays he shaped,
again under the influence of Shakespeare, such complex characters as the Hamlet-like Salieri (the supposed poisoner of Mozart
in the first of the four "little tragedies"), or the hero of *The
Miser Knight,* so different from Molière's *Harpagon,* and interesting enough to have inspired, later on, the "idea" of Dostoevsky's novel *A Raw Youth.* He is like a Rothschild in a beggar's
garb, and this makes him the more aware of his paradoxical
power as one can judge by the end of his famous monologue
in the cellar, amidst his coffers stuffed with ducats:

> What does not own my sway? I, like some demon,
> From here can dominate the universe.
> I have but to wish. Palaces rise straightway,
> And through the thickets of my glorious gardens
> Fair nymphs go running in a merry crowd.
> The Muses bring their tribute to my feet.
> Free Genius is my slave and works for me,
> Virtue and Toil, labouring sleeplessly,
> Will humbly wait on me for recompense.
> I shall but whistle and submissively
> Will bloodstained Crime come crawling to my feet,
> Timidly lick my hand, look in my eyes,
> And read in them the signal of my will.
> All shall be subject to me, I to nothing.
> Out-stripping all desires I shall know peace.
> I understand my power; this knowledge
> Will be enough for me*

Pushkin's not entirely finished poetic play *Rusalka* (*The
Water-Fairy*) can only be mentioned in passing. Here the
central idea of retribution is intertwined with Russian folk-lore,
the spirit and the flavor of which he had splendidly rendered

---

* Translated by V. de Sola Finto and W. Marshall.

in his *Fairy-Tales* (*Skazki*) in verse, thus making an important *rapprochement* between literature and folk-lore.

6.

In addition to his poetic activities Pushkin was a pioneer of modern Russian prose. Here, too, as in poetry and the drama, he acted as a creative intermediary between English and Russian literatures. This time it was Sir Walter Scott who served as a stimulus for Pushkin's bigger narratives: *The Negro of Peter the Great* (unfinished), *Dubrovsky*, and *A Captain's Daughter*.

The first of these was to deal with Pushkin's Abyssinian maternal great-grandfather, Hannibal. Pushkin never went beyond the initial five chapters, but even within so small a compass he gave a fine picture of early eighteenth-century manners, as well as a portrait of Peter the Great in his homelier and more human moods. *Dubrovsky* (not quite completed either) is based on a romantic plot, its central figure being a polished young gentleman turned brigand in order to avenge the wrongs done to his father by a feudal neighbor. The agitated incidents, slightly reminiscent at times of *The Bride of Lammermoor*, are set against the background of the uncouth provincial gentry under the reign of Catherine II. Pushkin's principal work in prose, *A Captain's Daughter*, depicts the same period but on a bigger scale. Its subject-matter is the rising of the Ural Cossacks against Catherine II under the leadership of the illiterate peasant Pugachov, who gave himself out for the supposedly escaped Tsar Peter III (Catherine's "liquidated" husband), and threatened for a while a large portion of the central and lower Volga area. The narrative is much shorter than any of the Waverley Novels, and its style, modelled on the clear eighteenth-century prose, is enlivened by Pushkin's inimitable touch and inflection. A similar result might have been expected if one of Scott's novels had been written or re-written, say, by Jane Austen. The whole of it has the character of a "family chronicle" narrated in the first person by a young nobleman whose fate became strangely entangled with that of Pugachov and of his semi-Asiatic *Jacquerie.* Pushkin's research into the events described in this novel are recorded in his excellent *History of Pugachov's Rebellion,* which he began with his studies in the State archives and completed on a journey to the regions concerned.

Among his other writings in prose *The Tales of Belkin* and *The Queen of Spades* enjoy a deservedly high reputation. The five tales supposed to have been told by the "late Ivan Petrovich Belkin"—a simple, pathetic, yet somewhat comic figure —are reduced to their "naked" essentials, while yet skilfully preserving the narrator's tone and manner. One of these tales, *The Posting-Station Master,* exercised a considerable influence upon subsequent narratives (beginning with Gogol's *Greatcoat*) in so far as it definitely sanctioned the insignificant "little man" in Russian fiction. The would-be narrator Belkin himself is such a "little man," and his touching comicality becomes even more pronounced when we meet him, once again, as the compiler of Pushkin's unfinished satire on the serfdom system in *A History of the Village Goryukhino.*

Quite an amazing example of Pushkin's prose is his story *The Queen of Spades,* in which his art of the "naked word" is displayed to even better advantage than in his other prose works. A fantastic Hoffmannesque anecdote about a gambler, who in a mysterious way obtains the secret of winning at cards a large sum of money but loses the whole of it at his last stake and goes mad, is here worked out with incredible economy and detachment. The tale is moreover permeated with the atmosphere of that "irrational" Petersburg which was subsequently taken up and further dealt with by Dostoevsky. Last but not least, Pushkin's prose style scintillates also in his letters—the finest in Russian literature.

7.

When all is said and done, Pushkin seems to refute our current ideas about a "Russian" genius. It would be futile to look in him for any morbid introspection, or even for the passionate inner questing typical of Gogol, Dostoevsky, and Tolstoy. As artist, at any rate, he was so harmonious and balanced that he is frequently referred to as a Hellene of the North. It was the broadness as well as the sanity of his genius that made him so universal. This enabled him to graft his universality of a late humanist upon the literature of Russia which he turned into a creative part of European literature as a whole. Having brought all the previous literary achievements of his country to a conclusion, he also opened up new possibilities, the consequences of which were far-reaching. There is not a single literary *genre* in which he did not excel or produce something memorable. And the number of new themes which he introduced helped to enlarge the area of Russian literature beyond all recognition. It was he, too, who directed it towards that simple yet monumental realism which became one of its most prominent characteristics in the second half of the nineteenth century.

Finally, in spite of his being the climax of the gentry culture in Russia, Pushkin helped to impart to the literature of his country a decidedly democratic, humanistic-democratic, and, in his early period, even revolutionary trend. He was, moreover, the first Russian poet who was read by all strata, from the highest to the lowest. And when Russian literature, in the course of its growth, began to differentiate into a number of currents and "isms," Pushkin was accepted as the standard of literary values and also as a symbol of cultural continuity up to our own day.

"Pushkin is our all," said Apollon Grigoryev—one of the highly intelligent Russian critics in the middle of the last century. And Pushkin's work, far from having aged since then, is still as vital as ever before. He is the most widely read classic in Russian, and the day is perhaps not far distant when he will be read as a universal classic also outside his own country.

CHAPTER FIVE

Nikolai Gogol

I.

When Pushkin died, in 1837, there were quite a few poets left to foster the growth of a literature which now rested on firm foundations of its own. Baratynsky—a prominent member of the Pushkin *pléiade*—wrote some of his best things after 1837, when the vigorous genius of Lermontov too was in the ascendant. Yet the interest in poetry, as well as the high standard of craftsmanship, typical of the Pushkin era, from the 'forties onwards was on the decline. As a compensation, a mighty wave of prose set in, and the leadership in Russian letters now fell upon the shoulders of the greatest prose-writer of that period, Nikolai Vasilyevich Gogol (1809-1852), who, in almost every way, was a strange contrast to Pushkin. Whereas Pushkin marked the apex of the gentry period in Russian culture, Gogol's creative activities coincided with the formation of the intelligentsia, in which the voice of the educated "commoners" asserted itself through the critic Belinsky (1811-48). Mentally and temperamentally, the two men were and remained poles apart. Pushkin, who was a classical realist even in his romantic works, felt at home in this world, however much he may have clashed with some of its aspects. Gogol, on the other hand, was so maladjusted and as though frightened of what he saw that he never felt at ease with the

surrounding reality, and this attitude came out most conspicu-
ously in his peculiar realism. Primititive, archaically primitive
at times, but never simple, he became in fact the first enigmatic
figure in modern Russian literature—a puzzled questioner for
whom writing was a process of self-examination, self-defence,
and catharsis in one. Hence the two alternatives which were
opened to Gogol the artist. One was escapist, and the other
searchingly as well as aggressively realistic. It was with the first
that he started his literary career, but he finished it with the
second. This was however logical, since the two attitudes
can be complementary to each other.

A disappointed and frustrated idealist of Gogol's stamp,
who is haunted by life to such an extent as to be unable to
find a shelter even in escapist romanticism, may in the end
turn art itself into a "realistic" weapon for self-defence. And
the greater his romantic rancor against the reality he is unable either to accept or to alter, the stronger will be his realism
of indictment. His bitter laughter will be a revenge upon
reality which he will try to show up as something ridiculously
vulgar and therefore unworthy of acceptance.

Such an attitude is typical of Gogol's writings and even of
his style. For in contrast to Pushkin's dynamic and disciplined
calm, the style of Gogol is agitated, emphatic, full of superlatives, and always ready to pass from solemn, at times almost
hypnotic exuberance, to a realistic accumulation of details,
especially if these can be twisted and distorted into something
grotesque. His ornate lyrical passages verge on rhetoric, the
pitfalls of which he avoids only thanks to his uncanny sense
of verbal rhythm and music. At the same time his realism of
the *petits faits* and of the grimaces of life is unforgettable
precisely on account of his rancorously comic exaggerations.
All this makes Gogol one of the most puzzling figures be-

NIKOLAI GOGOL (1809-1852)

tween the romantic and the realistic periods in literature—
puzzling both as a writer and as a personality, since, in his
case, it is impossible to separate one from the other. This is
why a few biographical data may be helpful in our approach.

2.

Born in 1809 into an impoverished Ukrainian gentry family
of Cossack stock, Gogol spent his childhood in the idyllic
countryside near Poltava. From 1821 until 1828 he was educated at the Grammar School in Nyezhin and then lived, for
some eight years, in Petersburg, which represented the greatest
possible contrast to his warm and sunny Ukraine. The years
between 1836 and 1848 he spent chiefly in Rome—always dear
to his romantic temperament. In 1849 he returned to Russia
and stayed for the most part in Moscow, where he died in
February, 1852.

Small and not very prepossessing in appearance, Gogol was
rather nervous by disposition. As though under the weight of
a social and moral "inferiority complex," he became morbidly
touchy and was always ready to attack in others the defects
from which he himself suffered or thought he suffered. This
fostered not only his gift of observation (confined to negative
features only), but also that intensely satirical and ridiculing
vein which became so conspicuous in his writings. At the
same time he was anxious to counter, even as a schoolboy,
the feeling of his inferiority by compensatory day-dreams of
future greatness. While still at Nyezhin, he indulged in
visions of a brilliant career waiting for him, and it may have
been with such hopes that, at the age of nineteen, he came
to Petersburg. But it did not take long for a naïve provincial
youth to discover that without money and connections he was

less than a nobody in that cold and inhospitable city. Having tried his luck repeatedly without success, he decided to flee to America. He took a boat to Lübeck, but as the money at his disposal was by then exhausted, he had to return and make new efforts to find a living. This time he obtained a humble underpaid post in one of the Government offices.

A victim of circumstance and disillusionment, Gogol—like so many sons of the impoverished gentry—was in danger of becoming a failure, a social *déclassé*. But chance intervened, and his whole life underwent a sudden and complete change. Having dabbled in literature while still a schoolboy, he now renewed his efforts in this direction chiefly as a means of escape from the dreary reality which preyed upon him. The tales he had once heard from his Cossack grandfather, the picturesque life and folk-lore of the people, the sun-drenched landscape of the south, the banks of the Dnieper, the expanse of the steppe— all this came back to his memory with an alluring halo and shaped itself into a number of stories, published (1831-32) in two volumes under the general title, *Evenings on a Farm near Dikanka,* which were an immediate success. Their appeal was enhanced by their ethnographic flavor, which happened to be the fashion of the day. In spite of certain touches of Tieck and of Hoffmann, Gogol's romanticism, as exemplified here, had all the colorfulness of the Ukrainian countryside. The same holds good of Gogol's boisterous humor. The compositors setting the text were so amused by some of the pages that their laughter interfered with their work. Furthermore, the rhythm and the texture of Gogol's prose brought a new note into Russian fiction, which the readers were by no means slow to appreciate. While dexterously blending romantic themes with the spirit of the folk-lore, Gogol created an agitated and ornate style of his own. His pages were full of verbal embroideries as though he had wanted to lull himself into a trance by the music of his own language. The very first story, *The Fair of Sorochintsy* (turned by Borodin into an opera) opens with a description of a Ukrainian summer day, abounding in so many superlatives and metaphors that, but for its musical quality, it would resemble an oleographic improvisation. The moods and the motifs vary, and after situations full of boisterous fun and gaiety, one comes across such a story as *A Cruel Vengeance,* which is more gruesome than anything Edgar Allan Poe had ever imagined. Constructed in the spirit of a folk-ballad and told in a language redolent of poetry, it is full of a magic of its own, emanating from Gogol's own verbal rhythm and music. It also points to some rather disturbing "complexes" in the writer himself, who thus found at least a temporary relief in his art.

In the whole collection there is only one story, *Ivan Shponka and his Aunty,* in which realistic details prevail. But, significantly enough, Gogol left it unfinished, although here already he clearly showed that grotesque Hogarth-like quality which, in some of his later works, he developed to perfection. Otherwise the humor and the buffoonery of *Evenings* abound in an over-loud gaiety which he probably intended to be both a refuge and a tonic. He himself said a few years later: "The cause of that gaiety which has been noticed in my first works was an inner need. I became a prey to fits of melancholy which were beyond my comprehension. . . . In order to get rid of them I invented funny characters in the funniest situations imaginable."

But the word "invented" is perhaps not right, since Gogol's inventive fancy was much weaker than his imagination, and the latter was predominantly of an intensifying kind. Instead of inventing complicated plots of his own, he organized and intensified those he had heard from other people. And as for his realism, its propensity towards grotesque and satirical distortions is here not yet imbued with that *ressentiment* which became so conspicuous a feature in his works after *Evenings.* Externally, Gogol's "realistic" manner has quite a few features in common with that of Dickens, yet it would be wrong to compare the two in the way this is often done. For one thing, Dickens is devoid of Gogol's incurable rancor with regard to life; so he can afford to be affirmative even when he ridicules. The "realism" of Gogol, on the other hand, is that of a wounded and frustrated romantic. Its inner motivation has certain affinities with the negative realism of Gustave Flaubert or of Thomas Hardy, however different his reactions otherwise may have been. His next collection of four narratives published under the title of *Mirgorod* (1835) can amply repay any further inquiries.

3.

These stories, which at first look like a continuation of *Evenings,* mark the dividing line between the romantic and the realistic manner in Gogol's art. Two of them, *Taras Bulba* and *Viy,* are romantic in the extreme, while the other two, *The Old-World Landowners* and *How the Two Ivans Quarrelled,* are—technically at least—as realistic as can be. *Taras Bulba* is above all a romance of the Cossack past. Although inspired by the Waverley Novels, it is spun out in Gogol's ornate and agitated manner at its best. As in *A Cruel Vengeance,* here, too, the Cossack lore is turned into a gorgeous narrative reminiscent of balladic poetry. The old Cossack leader Taras, the executioner of his own son, who (prompted by his love for a Polish belle) had gone over to the enemy, might have been taken straight from a folk-ballad. Some other figures— the comic Jew Yankel and the swaggering Poles—have much in common with the *vertep* or the traditional Ukrainian puppet show for the people. The whole of it is told with unflagging verve, and some descriptive passages—the night in the steppe, for example, the riotous Cossack life in Syetch, the scenes of starvation in the beleaguered city, the battle episodes—are unforgettable. This work is often referred to, and rightly so, as the Cossack *Iliad*.

A strong romantic flavor of the same creepy variety as in *A Cruel Vengeance* emanates from the story *Viy*. According to Gogol's statement, Viy is the name of a symbolic monster taken from the Ukrainian folk-lore. But the nightmare-like monster as represented here is the projection of certain disturbing fears and phobias, stored up in Gogol's own "racial" unconscious. It is as complex a story as the two realistic narratives, included in the volume, are simple in their subject-matter. In *The Old-World Landowners* there is hardly a plot at all. The whole of it is a genre picture (in the Dutch manner) describing the vegetative existence of an aged couple: a kind of Ukrainian Darby and Joan, whose thoughts never go beyond the fence of their orchard. The principal function of their idyllic life is eating and sleeping, yet both of them are contented and so touchingly attached to each other that when old Pulcheria suddenly dies, her husband is past consolation and follows her soon after. It seems as though Gogol had put into this story his own sentimental-romantic nostalgia for a haven of peace, even vegetative peace, as a contrast to the turmoil of his metropolitan experiences.

The same kind of vegetative existence permeates the opening

chapter of *How the Two Ivans Quarrelled*,* but this time from
a different angle. Nostalgia is here replaced by invective. The
plot is again slender, but even such as it is, Gogol borrowed
it from another Ukrainian—the older writer Narezhny. The
story depicts two bosom friends who for some idiotic reason
quarrelled and started a series of litigations, dragging them on
and on until both of them were ruined. Here, for the first
time, Gogol's comic laughter turned into that proverbial
"laughter through tears" which, from now on, clung to him
with an increasingly sinister ring. His realism à la Hogarth
made him depict the negative features of his characters, as well
as of life in general, with all the indignation of a wounded
romantic. Gloom and sadness which lurk behind this otherwise comic story, protrude quite plainly towards the end, this
description of the author's departure from Mirgorod providing
a final touch: "The lean nags famous in Mirgorod as post-
horses began to stamp their hoofs, which were buried in a
grey mass of mud, with a sound displeasing to the ear. The
rain poured in torrents upon the Jew seated in the box, covered
with a rug. The dampness penetrated to my very bones. The
dreary barrier with a sentry-box in which an old soldier sat
repairing his weapons, was passed slowly by. Once again the
same fields, black in the places where they had been dug up,
and of a greenish hue in others; wet daws and crows; monoto-
nous rain, a tearful sky, without one gleam of light! . . . A
gloomy place—this world, gentlemen!"

4.

"A gloomy place—this world, gentlemen," became from now
on Gogol's motto as well as his basic disposition. But he masked

* The Russian title is *A Story of the Quarrel Between Ivan Ivanovich and Ivan
Nikifirovich*.

it by his laughter in which he found first an escape from life and then a means for revenge upon life. Unable to escape from reality, he tried to fight it by laughing at its ugliness and drabness, which he did with all the vindictiveness at his disposal. It was here that Gogol's romantic temperament often took on a highly realistic garb, notably from his Petersburg stories onwards. Three of these, *A Portrait, The Nevsky Prospect* and *The Diary of a Madman,* appeared in his miscellany, *Arabesques* (1835). *The Nose* was written about the same period, and his famous *Greatcoat* some four or five years later.

The least satisfactory from an artistic standpoint is *A Portrait.* Its romanticism may remind one of E. T. A. Hoffmann's *Die Elexiere des Teufels,* or of Maturin's *Melmoth the Wanderer* (which Gogol had read in a Russian translation). On the other hand, the story contains some of Gogol's own dilemmas and inhibitions, one of them being his belief in the demoniacal agencies inherent in life itself. We find in it also the elements of his subsequent conception of art as the promoter of moral good. Similarly revealing is *The Nevsky Prospect,* which expresses Gogol's wounded idealism perhaps more directly than any other narrative of his. The very antithesis between the two main characters, one of them being a vulgarian and the other an incurable romantic dreamer, only serves to point out the incompatibility of beauty and life as it is.

Apart from his "romantic irony," Gogol introduced here the background of Petersburg in its negative and de-humanizing aspects. These came out even more potently in *The Diary of a Madman* and *The Greatcoat,* depicting the two varieties of one and the same "little man": the humble office drudge, victimized by the big city—a predicament that (but for a lucky chance) might well have been in store for Gogol himself. While working in the Government office, he was able to study this type from personal observations. Hence the detailed concreteness of his portrayals.

However insignificant in life, Poprishchin—the hero of *The Diary of a Madman*—does not entirely surrender to his fate, but entrenches himself behind all sorts of wishful thinking and day-dreams, the object of which is the daughter of his omnipotent chief. He is in love with her, although the pretty girl does not even condescend to be aware of his existence. This plunges him all the more deeply into his compensatory dream-world, duly recorded in his diary. The heavier the blows he has to endure, the stronger is his self-concocted antidote. And when he learns at last that his idol has become betrothed to one of those "social betters" whose hollow glitter is despised—in his opinion—by the very dogs, his imaginary grandeur takes on the size of his defeat: he is no longer a nonentity, an underpaid scribe, but His Majesty Ferdinand VIII, the fugitive King of Spain. His manners assume at once a style worthy of such an exalted position. Even when he is taken to the lunatic asylum, he sees and interprets everything only in this light. During the painful manipulations he is here compelled to undergo, a momentary idea as to his condition flashes through his mind, but the world of madness closes upon him once again and for good.

Akaky, the hero of *The Greatcoat,* is another Poprishchin, but—this time—aged and battered enough to acept his humble place in life without grumbling. The highest ambition he can still rise to is to scrape enough money together to buy a fashionable greatcoat—with marten collar and all. With great difficulties he makes his dream come true, and one morning he appears in the office in a smart greatcoat—a real somebody. General surprise is crowned by his being invited to an evening party, at which he drinks too much and leaves the company rather late at night. While crossing a lonely square, he is knocked down by two individuals and, when he comes to himself, there is no trace left either of the thieves or of his greatcoat. Full of despair Akaky falls ill and dies of grief. Such is the gist of this masterpiece of *Kleinmalerei,* which exercised a strong influence on the development of Russian realism.

Gogol's remaining Petersburg story, *The Nose,* can best be described as a fantasy constructed on the pattern of a dream—something like *Alice in Wonderland,* but probably suggested by the "nosological" passages in *Tristram Shandy* (he knew it from a Russian translation). Devoid of any surface logic, it is yet—like *A Cruel Vengeance* and *Viy*—of great value to anyone interested in the workings of the subconscious mind, and especially in the meeting point between psychoanalysis and literature. Its amusingly grotesque jumble hides what has been called Gogol's castration-complex, as well as a few other peculiarities of his sexual life. In this respect it is connected with certain passages of Poprishchin's gibberish in *The Diary of a Madman,* notably with those describing the earth falling upon the moon.

5.

Further aspects of Gogol's art can be gleaned from his satirical comedy, *The Government Inspector* (1836), and his novel *Dead Souls* (1842), both of which occupy a very high place in Russian literature. The plots even for these two works were not invented by Gogol—they were suggested to him by Pushkin; yet Gogol worked them out into masterpieces in which, among other things, he gave full scope to his "laughter through tears." With *The Government Inspector,* Gogol's laughter assumed, moreover, a deliberately castigating role. He himself acknowledged later in his *An Author's Confession:* "I saw that in my former works I laughed in vain, uselessly, without knowing why. But if we must laugh, why not laugh at what really deserves to be laughed at by us all. In my *Government Inspector* I decided to bring together and to deride all that is bad in Russia, all the evils which are being perpetrated in those places where utmost rectitude is required from man."

Here Gogol's attention was focused on the corrupt bureaucracy, and with so much malice, too, that this comedy rightly belongs to the most biting specimens of its kind. The plot is simple. An irresponsible windbag, Khlestakov by name, who, together with his servant, travels from St. Petersburg to his father's village, loses at cards in a provincial hole all his money and is in danger of being put into jail for his inability to pay the hotel bill. The *gorodnichy* (police governor) of the town expects at that time the incognito arrival of a Government Inspector, the very thought of whom makes him shudder. Nor are the other officials in an elated state of mind, and they know why. Two of the local worthies, who have just seen in the restaurant the starved Khlestakov rather wistfully inspecting other people's meals, come upon the idea that the inquisitive, smartly dressed stranger must be the dreaded incognito. Unanimously, the officials decide to bribe him, and the *gorodnichy*—an expert in these matters—goes personally to the hotel. Frightened at first by the visit and then puzzled by it, Khlestakov soon regains his aplomb and enters into his new rôle with relish. He is fêted, bribed, shown the institutions of the town, and finally even becomes betrothed to the *gorodnichy's* daughter. Fortunately, Khlestakov's sagacious servant guesses that the worthy gentlemen must have taken his master for someone of consequence and urges him to leave the hospitable town before it is too late. So the would-be inspector departs—

his head full of pleasant memories and his pockets bulging
with money. In order to reassure all the nice folk around him,
he promises, of course, to be back in time for the wedding. The
gorodnichy's arrogance is now unbounded. Puffed up by the
dreams of his future greatness under the wing of such a mighty
son-in-law, he bullies the town people more than ever. All the
local "notables" of any importance are so anxious to ingratiate
themselves in turn that they hurry at once, together with their
spouses, to congratulate him. It is a grand and animated
gathering. But suddenly, like a thunderbolt from the blue, the
truth leaks out that the Government Inspector was an impostor.
The local postmaster, always willing to increase his knowledge
by reading other people's letters, could not resist opening the
one Khlestakov had written to a pal in Petersburg, boasting in
the frankest terms possible of all that had befallen him in that
blessed town. As the letter is read to the gathering, its effect can
be imagined. But when the general consternation is at its height,
a gendarme enters with the announcement that the real Government Inspector has just arrived and demands an immediate
interview with the *gorodnichy*. Here the curtain slowly falls.

The Government Inspector is a condensed picture of all the
rottenness, corruption, and stupidity of that bureaucratic Russia
which Gogol hated so much. The portraiture is, once more,
thoroughly Hogarthian. As a satirical comedy of manners, the
play actually continued the tradition which had started with
the eighteenth-century playwright Fonvizin, and reached something of a climax in Griboyedov's *Woe from Wit* (1823). Its
effect was bound to be overwhelming in the "leaden" atmosphere of the Nicholas regime. The first performance, on 19th
March, 1836, took place by a special order of the Tsar himself
who, this time, overruled the official censorship and came personally to see the production. "Everyone has received his due,

and I most of all," Nicholas I is reported to have said after the performance. But the gall contained in the comedy was too much for those concerned. A hue and cry was raised against Gogol and before long assumed such proportions that he preferred to leave Russia altogether. He settled down in Rome where he remained, with various interruptions, until 1848. There he finished two more plays, *Marriage* and *Gamblers*. The first is an uproarious farcical comedy against the background of the old-fashioned merchants whose rich daughters were a bait for government officials and noblemen gone to seed. The second is based on the cleverly worked out theme of cheating the cheat. It has an unexpected but powerful denouement. It was in Rome, too, that he completed his greatest work, *Dead Souls*.

6.

This novel, which by now has conquered its rightful place in the literature of the world, is difficult to classify. Gogol himself called it an epic (*poema*). Like some of his other works, it is devoid of an involved plot and even the love motif, so essential in a novel, is here absent. The chapters follow one another like those of an old-fashioned picaresque narrative, the episodes of which are connected by the central character only— a rogue, a travelling adventurer, or both. The book should really be called *Dead Serfs;* but as serfs were nicknamed "souls" in Russia, its title has a businesslike and a symbolic meaning in one. Chichikov, the hero of the novel, is a travelling businessman and a swindler, but with the stamp of an immaculate gentleman. The aim of his journey is to buy up a number of those serfs who have died so recently that they have not yet been struck off the register and are therefore officially recorded as being still alive. "Now is the time," he reasons, "there has just been an epidemic, peasants have died, thank goodness, in great numbers." Chichikov's intention is to mortgage such fictitious serfs in a bank for a substantial sum of money, after which he would disappear and start a respectable existence in some province sufficiently remote to hide his past. This would not be too difficult, since his manners and appearance are so winning that everybody is charmed by him. In the provincial town, chosen by him as the starting point for his errands, he is simply worshipped, at least during the first few days of his stay. But he has no time for adulation. He means business, and so a visiting tour to those landowners in the district who might be of use to him, cannot be delayed.

His interviews introduce to the reader a number of portraits in Gogol's style at its best. Their characteristics are brought out so intensely that they often verge on grotesque spooks, while yet remaining concrete and real. Manilov; Sobakevich;* the miser Plyushkin; the professional cheat and scandalmonger Nozdryov —they all parade before us like so many caricatures of humanity, seen with the eyes of a Hogarth or a Breughel. What increases the comicality of Chichikov himself is the contrast between the gentlemanliness of his appearance on the one hand, and the criminal nature of his errand on the other. Realizing the delicate task he is engaged in, he broaches the subject with due circumspection, but his maneuvers invariably lead up to the question whether and how many dead "souls" are available —a kind of groping which, apart from its comic touches, is bound to give away the moral level of both Chichikov and his interlocutor. In the end Chichikov's eagerness to get rich outstrips even his caution: he blurts out a word too much where

---

* From the Russian word *sobaka*, the dog. Like Dickens, Gogol was a master at inventing suggestive names, most of which are untranslatable.

silence would be wisdom. As a result the news about his strange
purchases leaks out, and the same town which at first welcomed
him as a paragon of charm, is all at once astir with the wildest
rumors about his doings and even about his identity. Sensible
enough to clear out, Chichikov makes a hasty departure in his
troika (a coach drawn by three horses) at the end of the first
volume—the only one that was finished. Yet quite unexpectedly,
the concluding note of this volume is a personal lyrical digres-
sion on the part of Gogol himself. In contrast to the general
mood of the work, the conclusion strikes (in a major key and
in a manner which can serve as an example of Gogol's tempera-
mental style) a regular paean to the *troika* and the wide open
spaces of Russia. In the same passage, Gogol addresses Russia
with a question which all her great authors have been asking
since—asking in vain. But here is the passage itself:

"Chichikov was fond of fast driving, and as he rocked on the
leather cushion he only smiled at the bumps. And what Russian
does not love fast driving? And how should his soul not love
it? For is he not prone to surrender to the sudden whirl of a
spree? Is he not liable to cast discretion to the winds, saying
'the devil take it all'? And therefore is not fast driving his
delight? How can he not love its magic and incantation? And
is not a galloping troika like a mysterious force that has swept
you away on its wings, so that you find yourself flying along,
and everything else is flying with you? The milestones fly past
to meet you, the merchants in their carts are flying by, on each
side of you forests of dark fir and pine-trees are flying past to
the thump of axes and the croaking of crows, the whole of
the highway is flying on, no one knows where, into the reced-
ing distance; and there is a lurking terror in that glimmer of
objects that keep flashing by rapidly and are gone before they
can be identified; and only the sky overhead, the nimble clouds,

and the emergent moon, appear motionless. Ah, you troika! Bird-like troika, who invented you? Surely you could only have been born among a spirited people—in a land which does not stop at jokes but has taken half the world in the embrace of its smooth plains so that one can go and count the milestones till one's head turns dizzy! Nor does it seem that much cunning was required to fabricate a sledge or carriage drawn by those three horses; it was improvised with the help of an axe and a drill by some handy Yaroslavl peasant. Your driver wears no great top boots of foreign make: he is all beard and mittens, and sits perched on his seat the devil knows how; but when he stands up, cracks his whip and starts up a song, then the horses rush like a hurricane, the spokes of the wheels spin in one smooth disk, and only the road shudders beneath them while some passer-by cries out as he stops in alarm! And the troika is off and away, away! . . . And very soon there is only a swirl of dust on the horizon.

"Russia, are you not speeding along like a fiery and matchless troika? Beneath you the road is smoke, the bridges thunder, and everything is left far behind. At your passage the onlooker stops amazed as by a miracle divine. 'Was that not a flash of lightning?' he asks. What is this surge so full of terror? And what is this force unknown impelling these horses never seen before? Ah, you horses, horses,—what horses! Your manes are whirlwind! And are your veins not tingling like a quick ear? Descending from above you have caught the note of the familiar song; and at once, in unison, you strain your chests of bronze and, with your hoofs barely skimming the earth, you are transformed into arrows, into straight lines winging through the air, and on you rush under divine inspiration! . . . Russia, where are you flying? Answer me. There is no answer. The bells are tinkling and filling the air with their wonderful peal-

ing: the air is rent and thundering as it turns to wind; everything on earth comes flying past and, looking askance at her,
other peoples and States move aside and make way." *

7.

It is hardly necessary to explain the symbolic meaning of the
lines quoted. The enigma of the same endless irrational Russia
crops up similarly in a number of authors, including Alexander
Blok—the finest symbolist poet modern Russia has produced.
But as for Gogol's novel, even such a spirited finale does not
make up for the unpleasant pictures spread over the rest of the
book. Their sharp outlines remain in the reader's mind for
good. They may not contain any direct propaganda against the
serfdom system as such, yet indirectly they did at least draw
attention to the anomaly of its existence. If in *The Government
Inspector* Gogol dealt a blow at the bureaucratic regime of
Nicholas I, in *Dead Souls* he attacked the vulgarity of life as a
whole. The hidden romantic in him now took revenge for his
frustrations by laughing at life more maliciously than in any of
his previous works. And the method he made use of was again
that of realistic *Kleinmalerei*. He once complained that the
critics who "dissected my literary talent were not able to find
the essential traits of my nature. Pushkin alone was able to see
them. He used to say that no other writer was endowed with
my capacity for bringing out all the trivialities of life and for
opening one's eyes on those trifles, which, as a rule, remain
unnoticed."

Vulgarity and drabness, presented in *Dead Souls,* are thus
symbolic in the very intensity of their realism which seems to
imply that something must be wrong with the transcendental

* Translated by George Reavey, in the Novel Library, Hamish Hamilton.

inner core of life, or of what Gogol understood by life. Vulgarity as something immanent in existence became in fact Gogol's *idée fixe* which he added to his habitual moral hypochondria. Conscious of his own defects, he was the more aware of all that was negative and nasty in the world with which he could never come to terms. Hence his restlessness of a man who is impelled to be eternally on the move, as though trying to escape from reality and from himself. After 1836 he lived mostly in Italy, but he travelled also in France, Switzerland, Germany, feeling everywhere an uprooted stranger and a prey to his own ennui. "Before the eyes of all there only grows the gigantic figure of Tedium," he wrote in 1847. "It grows and assumes infinite dimensions day in, day out. O Lord! Empty and terrible is Thy world!"

Gogol's aggressive realism became directed above all against this Tedium. Yet his fight with the defects in the world around was in essence a fight with himself. "While attacking some bad trait of mine," he says, "I presented it in a different rôle and tried to make it appear in my own eyes as a deadly fiend who has injured me terribly. Then I persecuted it with malice and irony, with anything I could. But had anyone seen those monsters which came from under my pen in my first drafts, he would have shivered with fear." The subjective root of his realism is thus obvious. On the other hand, once art had become a weapon of this kind, then a much too conscious moral purpose or even moral mission, bestowed as it were by God Himself, was likely to be one of its dangerous temptations. This was what happened to Gogol's art after he had witnessed the chastising moral effect of *The Government Inspector* and *Dead Souls*. In order to be worthy of his high mission in spite of his "sins," he did all he could to deserve God's grace by rigorous ascetic practices—like the ones described in the second part of *The Portrait*. Unfortunately, this mood coincided with a period when his artistic inspiration was at an ebb. So he increased his didactic propensity and as if anxious to force the grace of God, began to talk as one having authority even concerning things he knew little or nothing about. At a time when the Russian intelligentsia, led by the critic Belinsky, was fighting for a more liberal and progressive system of life, the incurable romantic Gogol continued to look upon such institutions as State, Church, serfdom, autocracy, and education in a bigoted conservative and patriarchal spirit. To make things worse, he decided to enlighten his readers upon these matters. In the hope that the whole of Russia would listen to his "Christian" sermons with the same enthusiasm as she had hitherto welcomed his literary works, he published (in 1847) his *Selected Passages from Correspondence with My Friends*.

This book was responsible for the most painful shock in Gogol's life. Instead of resounding all over Russia like a prophet, he was overwhelmed with attacks, criticism and derision which came not only from the radical-minded intellectuals but even from some of his own friends in the conservative Slavophil camp. The most slashing blow came, however, from his former admirer Belinsky, who in a letter—now famous—called Gogol a preacher of the knout, an apostle of ignorance, a defender of obscurantism and darkest oppression. "You are only bemused and not enlightened, you have understood neither the form nor the spirit of contemporary Christianity. It is not the truth of Christian teaching that your book breathes, but the fear of death, of the devil, and of hell." Which was largely but not entirely true. The violent attacks on *Selected Passages* helped to raise and partly to clear certain problems in the light of which Gogol's own position grew worse and more ridiculous. Unable to parry the blows, he wrote—in July 1847—to his

friend Sergey Aksakov (the author of *A Family Chronicle*):
"Impatience made me publish my book. Seeing that I would
not be able to master my *Dead Souls,* and genuinely grieving
over the colorlessness of modern literature which indulges in
empty discussions, I hurried to say a word or two on the problems I was interested in; the problems which I had wanted to
develop or else to embody in living images and characters." And
this brings us again to his *Dead Souls.*

Gogol had intended to follow up the success of the first
volume of this novel by another two volumes, and to turn the
whole of it into a kind of *Divina Commedia* of Russian life—
with an important "message" attached to it. The first part,
presenting only the negative side of Russia was to be its
Inferno. The second part was planned, like Dante's *Purgatory,*
on a higher level, while the third would deal with Chichikov's
moral rebirth. But such a task required convincing portraits of
positive characters, and these were beyond Gogol's power, since
his sources of inspiration were confined to indictment and
laughter. Thus in the rescued five chapters of the second
volume of *Dead Souls* (on which he labored for eleven years)
the virtuous characters look artificial and stilted, whereas the
negative ones are portrayed with vigor, even if Gogol's former
verve was cooling down—a process by which the author himself was seriously perturbed.

8.

Gogol acknowledged in his letter to Aksakov that he had
hastened to publish *Selected Passages from Correspondence*
partly because he felt he was unable to cope with the creative
task imposed upon him by *Dead Souls,* and therefore wanted
to give Russia at least the benefit of his message. Gogol the

Teacher, severed from his art, had however little to say, and what he did say was neither new nor particularly interesting. The very fact that he published it in such a shape was a proof that he was beginning to doubt his former artistic power. And since he regarded—quite in the spirit of romanticism—his literary genius as a special gift from on high, he was bound to interpret the drying up of his artistic inspiration as being tantamount to a withdrawal of God's grace in punishment for his "sins." Morbidly conscious of certain weaknesses which were partly due to his underdeveloped sex, he considered himself a great sinner. He repented, prayed, mortified his flesh, and even undertook a pilgrimage to Palestine, but it was all to no purpose. Neither the glow of literary creation nor that of religious fervor was now granted to him. What Gogol called his religious feeling was really nothing but atavistic fear of the devil and hell Belinsky had alluded to. Gogol himself wrote in a letter before his departure to Palestine (12th February 1848) as follows: "It even seems to me I have no religion. I confess Christ only because my reason commands me to. I only have the will to believe and, in spite of this, I still dare to go on a pilgrimage to our Saviour's tomb. Oh, do pray for me!"

The cry, "Oh, do pray for me!" became even more frequent after his journey to Jerusalem which had left him inwardly as cold, frightened, and bewildered as ever. His state of mind was aggravated by forebodings of imminent death. Was he ready for it? What answer would he give to the inexorable Judge? While in the throes of such moods and torments, he fell under the spell of an ignorant despotic priest, Father Konstantinovsky, who, playing on Gogol's fears, bullied him into spiritual submission. It was probably due to him that on the night of 11th February 1852, Gogol burned the more or less completed manuscript of the second volume of *Dead Souls*.

In that night he prayed with great contrition, after which he called his boy-servant and wandered through the rooms, in each of them making the sign of the cross. Finally, he took out of the portfolio his manuscript (the second volume of *Dead Souls*), threw it into the fireplace and lit it with the candle. The boy protested, but Gogol's only answer was, "This is not your business—you must pray." When the sheets were burned, he crossed himself, kissed the boy, shuffled to his bedroom, fell upon the divan and began to cry. A few days later, on 21st February, he died—probably from physical exhaustion due to ascetic practices.

9.

Less studied abroad than some other Russian authors, Gogol yet occupies one of the most important places in the fiction of his country. It was the heritage of Pushkin and of Gogol that determined the character as well as the trend of modern Russian literature. Whereas the Apollonian genius of Pushkin bequeathed to it its lucidity, simplicity and plastic power, Gogol was responsible for its disturbing subjectivism, inner quest and vexation of the spirit, in which he anticipated both Dostoevsky and Tolstoy. He, moreover, laid stress on the portraiture of characters at the expense of a well-constructed plot and (following Pushkin) sanctioned the "little man" as a subject worthy of literary treatment—the two features which were adopted by the majority of subsequent Russian authors. The "natural school," championed by Belinsky, took from Gogol above all the realism of ordinary life and of "small facts" as well as that humanitarian note of pity which was stressed in Gogol's *Greatcoat* and assumed, later on, such gigantic proportions in Dos-

toevsky's works.* "We have all come from under Gogol's
Greatcoat," Dostoevsky said of the writers of his generation at
a time when the monumental Russian realism was already at
its height. Akaky certainly had a long literary progeny of the
"insulted and the injured," beginning with Dostoevsky's own
Poor Folk (1846). Even Dostoevsky's "pathological" trend,
from *The Double* onwards, has one of its sources in Gogol's
The Diary of a Madman. His Petersburg stories, on the
other hand, introduced (together with Pushkin's *Queen of
Spades* and *The Bronze Horseman*), that "irrational" atmosphere of the Tsarist metropolis which was later expanded and
deepened by Dostoevsky and, at the beginning of this century,
by Andrey Bely.

What affected, however, a large number of Russian writers
was not Gogol's style, but his peculiar attitude towards life
and the world. His realism of a frustrated (and therefore
rancorous) romantic idealist is conspicuous in the work of such
authors as Pisemsky and Saltykov-Shchedrin. As for the other
elements of his writings, Goncharov took on and continued
Gogol's realism of the minute *petits faits*. In addition, the two
principal characters (Oblomov and Stolz) in Goncharov's
novel *Oblomov,* are obviously a further elaboration of Tentetni-
kov and Konstanzhoglo in the second volume of *Dead Souls*.
Gogols' agitated prose was carried on mainly by Dostoevsky.
Its rhythmical and ornate character was investigated and further developed by the modernist Andrey Bely, who, together

* Overlooking the subjective character of Gogol's art, Belinsky opposed by his own
  theory of the "natural school" the artificial and rhetorical romantic current of
  the period. Yet while championing descriptions of life as it is, he also demanded that the authors should expose the evils of life (such as serfdom, for
  example) in the name of a better existence. His "natural school" thus implied
  both critical realism and the idea that literature should be in the service of life,
  while yet remaining literature. Among foreign influences that of George Sand,
  with her philanthropic bent, was rather prominent at the time.

with Alexey Remizov, was responsible for some of the most interesting recent experiments on similar lines.

Last but not least, it was in Gogol's works and in his "laughter through tears" that literature made a decisive attempt to become also a moral and social force in life—a tendency which was fully endorsed by the authors who came after him: from Nekrasov to Tolstoy, and from Saltykov-Shchedrin to Gorky. All that is vital in Gogol's work has thus remained an inalienable part of the literary heritage in Russia, no matter what changes may have taken place in her politics, in her taste, or in her general outlook upon life and the world.

CHAPTER SIX

Lermontov

I.

The romantic movement, for various reasons, affected Russia less many-sidedly than was the case with other European countries. The influence of Byronism itself was limited only to some of its aspects, and even those were partly conditioned by a regime under the pressure of which the few liberties still left seemed to be going from bad to worse. In Pushkin's day there was at least the atmosphere of the *pléiade,* the members of which firmly believed in literary culture and were able to stimulate one another. The growing vigilance of the Nicholas' police made fellowships on such a scale impossible even in matters of culture, let alone politics. As there was no outlet for any independent initiative and ambition of one's own, a number of gifted young men were bound to turn into "superfluous" Childe Harolds of the peculiar Russian brand, so conspicuous in the literature of that country. But the danger of maladjustment loomed large from another quarter also. There were signs that the patriarchal-feudal system, based on serfdom, would have to yield, before long, to the advent of a capitalist era, demanding an economic as well as psychological change which could not be achieved overnight. A feeling of vacillation and general uncertainty was in the air, and no gendarmes, no political straitjackets were able to eliminate the bewilderment arising in the public mind.

In this respect, too, there was a difference between the generation of Pushkin and that to which his immediate successor, the poet Mikhail Lermontov, belonged. In spite of all personal adversities, Pushkin was still rooted in his age, in his class and in the culture of which the members of the advanced gentry-elite were rightly proud. Even the "Decembrists" who rebelled in 1825, did so because they believed in certain values which they, as the most progressive representatives of their own class, were called upon to uphold. Yet the social and mental atmosphere of the next generation was no longer the same. The leadership on the part of a gentry-elite became impossible, because such an elite as a compact group or body no longer existed. The best representatives of that class suddenly found themselves in a vacuum. Others were absorbed by the bureaucratic system, or else went to seed in their provincial backwaters. Even the slowly emerging intelligentsia—an amalgam of the gentry intellectuals and the educated "commoners"—was of no use to many of those who were unable or else unwilling to adapt themselves to the spirit of the age. And Lermontov, for all his genius, was the least adaptable of men.

This fact alone determined the basic character of his work. If Pushkin introduced the "superfluous man" on a romantic or quasi-romantic plane, Lermontov added two salient features to this phenomenon. First, he deepened the *inner* isolation of such an uprooted individual until he touched upon that metaphysical region which, later on, was disturbingly tackled by Dostoevsky. And secondly, he gave a psychological analysis of a tragic Russian descendant of Childe Harold (via Pushkin's Onegin) so brilliantly as to affect thereby, romantic though he

was, quite a few facets of Russian realism. He is still regarded
as being the greatest and also the most Byronic romanticist in
Russian literature; yet his Byronism was not an imitation but
had certain definite traits of its own. He himself said in one
of his early poems:

> No, I'm not Byron, I'm different,
>   I'm still unknown, a man apart,
> Like Byron by the world rejected,
>   Only I have a Russian heart.*

In spite of this "Russian heart" on which he insists, or perhaps because of it, Lermontov's *mal du siècle,* with all its ingredients, sprang not only from social but from what might
be termed spiritual causes. His nostalgia resembled that of a
fallen denizen of a different timeless realm, who still vaguely
remembers its enchantment and therefore finds it impossible to
fit into any conditions of the actual world, least of all into
those of Russia under Nicholas I. When Lermontov was only
seventeen, he wrote the following poem, called *The Angel,*
which may provide a clue to the undercurrents of his romanticism:

> An angel was flying through night's deep blue
>   And softly he sang as he flew.
> Moon, stars and clouds in a wondering throng
>   Listened rapt by that heavenly song.
>
> He sang of the blest, who live without stain
>   In God's garden, a shining train.
> He hymned the Lord's might, and his voice rang clear,
>   For he sang without guile and fear.
>
> He bore in his arms a young soul to its birth
>   On the dark and sinful earth,

* This and the next poem are translated by V. de Sola Pinto.

> And the Angel's song remained in the soul
>   Without words yet unblemished and whole.
>
> Long after on earth when the soul would tire,
>   It felt a strange, aching desire
> For the music of heaven which it sought for in vain
>   In earth's songs of sorrow and pain.

The poem could serve as an epigraph to the whole of Lermontov's work. It goes a long way to explain his difference from Byron, the character of his pessimism, and of his protest against the realities he saw around. This again was intertwined with a number of less "transcendental" elements, the nature of which will become clearer if we approach Lermontov through some of his biographical data. For in contrast to Pushkin, Lermontov was the first great poet in Russian literature who deliberately turned his entire work into an inner biography; that is into a personal confession of a poignant and often glowingly passionate kind.

2.

Born in 1814, Lermontov had some Scottish blood in his veins. One of the Learmonths entered the Russian service at the beginning of the 17th century, settled in his adopted country and altered his ancestral name to make it sound Russian. (In some of his early poems, especially in *The Wish,* Lermontov alludes to Scotland as his distant homeland.) His father was an impoverished landowner who had married the daughter of a rich, capricious, and over-bearing woman and was always treated by his mother-in-law, Mme. Arsenyeva, as a "poor relation." As his wife died after a few years of marriage, Mme. Arsenyeva took her little grandson to her own estate where he was brought up until the age of twelve. Puzzled by the family quarrels, spoiled

by his grandmother's adulation, and at the same time deprived
of congenial companions, the boy must have felt lonely even
in those formative years. Gradually he developed into a self-
centered dreamer, anxious to conceal his passionate nature
under the mask of aloofness, and his innate idealism behind the
pose of callous flippancy. His poetic gift, which remained his
only outlet for self-expression, began to develop rather early
and was fostered by two circumstances: his visit to the Caucasus
at the age of eleven, and his education in a Moscow boarding
school (from 1827 onwards) which was not devoid of literary
interests. Under the guidance of such teachers as Merzlyakov
and Raitch, young Lermontov was initiated into the principal
works of Russian literature, as well as into those of Byron,
Moore, Goethe, Schiller, and Scott. He was much impressed
by Thomas Moore's biography of Byron (he read it in 1830)
and, in his early years, his own translations from Byron helped
him to work himself into Byronic moods. At the same time he
cultivated his own aloofness to such a degree that even on
entering, in 1830, Moscow University, he showed but little
inclination to mix with his fellow-students and paid hardly any
attention to the fact that after the *débâcle* of the "Decembrists"
the University of Moscow, with its debating circles, became the
actual focus of Russian culture. The Stankevich circle, with the
subsequent critic Vissarion Belinsky as one of its members,
was exploring all sorts of literary and philosophic problems. The youths gathering round Herzen and the poet
Ogaryov showed, however, a keener interest in the social questions of the day, the liberal "Decembrist" spirit still hovering
over their debates.

German philosophy, notably the ideas of Schelling and
Hegel, happened to be one of the strong influences among
the intellectuals of that period. Another stimulus came from

the French Utopian socialists. Their theories were later combined by quite a few firebrands (Belinsky included) with
"left" Hegelianism, and the two together helped to shape the
radical and revolutionary thought of Russia.

Lermontov did not belong to any of these groups. Besides,
in 1832 he suddenly left the University and went to Petersburg
where he entered a military school and, after two years of
detestable training, obtained a commission in the Guards. In
1837 he was transferred (or, rather, exiled) to a Caucasian
regiment on account of his aggressive invective, *The Death of
a Poet,* written on the day of Pushkin's death (January 29th).
The poem could not be printed,* but as it was read in countless
written copies, it made Lermontov's name known from one end
of Russia to the other. In the Caucasus, which was fated to be
strangely connected with his life, his work, and even with his
death, he met another poet, the banished "Decembrist" Alexander Odoevsky—one of the few people he really befriended.
Owing to his grandmother's influence, Lermontov was allowed
to return at the end of the same year to his old Hussar regiment,
and he made a considerable impression in St. Petersburg. By
this time he was already regarded as one of the great hopes of
Russian poetry and a successor to Pushkin. He was admired,
lionized, but in spite of his numerous conquests among the
society ladies, he remained as bored and lonely as ever. Mixing
a life of dissipation with intensive poetic activities, he did not
care to make himself popular either in society or among his
own comrades. As for literary men, he knew very few and
seemed to avoid them on purpose. After a duel he had in
February 1840 with the son of the French ambassador, M. de
Barrante, he was arrested and again sent to the Caucasus. He

---

* It first appeared in print in 1856, in Herzen's *Polar Star,* published in London. Two
years later the poem was printed also in Russia.

took part in some dangerous expeditions against the moun-
taineers, in which he displayed reckless courage. One of such
engagements—the battle on the river Valerik (on July 11th,
1840)—he described in a most beautiful poem. In the spring
of 1841 he made a flying visit to Petersburg in the hope of being
allowed to remain there, but without success. On his return
to the Caucasus he stopped for a longer period at his favorite
spa Pyatigorsk. The place was full of summer guests. Among
them there were ubiquitous society people, including some
of his old acquaintances. One of them, a certain Major Martynov, whom he tactlessly ridiculed in the presence of a lady,
challenged him to a duel. The duel took place outside Pyatigorsk on July 27th, 1841, and the poet was killed on the spot.
He died at the age of twenty-seven, i.e. ten years younger than
Pushkin.

3.

The best of Lermontov's work is second only to Pushkin's,
but with reservations. Pushkin showed even in his early
verse great technical skill and finish. In the case of Lermontov, however, it is only the mature work—roughly from
1836 onwards—that really counts. His youthful writings,
whether poems or plays, compare with his later products chiefly
as a series of experiments. He was perfectly aware of this and
even kept returning to some of his themes again and again in
order to perfect them during his later and more mature phase,
until they received an adequate form. Yet however much he
differed from Pushkin in his outlook and temperament, he
could not do without Pushkin's influence. Even Byron was at
first approached by him mainly through Pushkin. His two immature tales in verse, *The Circassian* and *The Prisoner of the*

Caucasus (both written at the age of fifteen) were imitations of Pushkin's Byronic tales with the Caucasus as the exotic "Eastern" background. After a more thorough acquaintance with Byron's work Lermontov wrote his longer Caucasian tales *Ismail Bey* (1832) and *Hadji Abrek,* the latter having been his first longer poem to be printed in a periodical in 1835.

In the meantime Lermontov tried his hand also at plays. They are pretentiously romantic, redolent of Schiller's "storm and stress" period but much more juvenile and with an obvious tendency towards self-dramatization. *Men and Passions* (to which, for some reason, he gave a German title, *Menschen und Leidenschaften,* 1830) and *A Queer Fellow* (1831) must have been written under the impact of the family quarrels between his grandmother and his father. His later drama, *The Masquerade* (1835), over-stated though it be, is more impressive in its combination of blind jealousy (the influence of *Othello*) on the one hand, and of a conflict between the self-centered individual and society on the other. Whereas Pushkin the poet could and did rise to that affirmative attitude which made him look sympathetically upon life at large, Lermontov was too often inclined to reduce the whole of life to the moods and demands of his own frustrated ego and to treat it accordingly. He also preferred to Pushkin's visual imagery the more visionary symbols often originating in the realm of the spirit (like his *Angel*). The language of many an early poem of his seems rather blurred. At his best, however, he soon developed a matchless pictorial gift. Lermontov the romantic has certain features in common with the other-worldly romanticism of Zhukovsky; yet instead of sharing Zhukovsky's passivity and quietism, he remained a "Byronic" rebel to the end. Like Byron, too, he broke morally with his own class, even if he was unable to do so socially. And as in the case of Byron again (or for

that matter of Gogol), the virulence of his romantic indictment
taught him to watch and to expose life also by realistic methods.
These he kept perfecting with such success as to emulate, in
his mature stage, the disciplined realism of Pushkin himself.

Lermontov's unfinished realistic tale *Sashka* (1836) is an offspring mainly of Byron's *Don Juan* and, to some extent, of the
first chapter of Pushkin's *Onegin*. It is a scathing and at times
obscene satire against the provincial gentry in its process of
moral decomposition. The realism of another tale in verse, *A
Treasurer's Wife* (1837), written in the *Onegin* stanza, is modelled on Pushkin's *Count Nulin* and, through the latter, on
Byron's *Beppo*. It gives a humorously caustic picture of provincial officials, one of whom gambles away his pretty wife
to an army officer. At times Lermontov the realist actually
reaches Pushkin's simplicity and detachment. In *Borodino*
(1837), for example, he renders to perfection the tone, the
manner and also the grumbling humor of an old veteran who
talks to his grandson about Napoleon's first defeat during his
invasion of Russia in 1812. And if the realism in some of his
poems (such as his famous *Cossack Cradle Song*) can be
poignantly touching, it acquires a dynamic matter-of-factness
in the already mentioned picture of the battle on the Caucasian
river Valerik—an anticipation of Tolstoy's battle scenes in *War
and Peace*. The pathos of his *Testament* again is due to the discrepancy between the tragic situation of a soldier dying of
wounds and the almost jokingly casual tone in which he tells
his last wishes to a comrade due to go home on leave.

> But if somebody questions you
>   About me as they may:
> Just say that a certain bullet flew—
>   My chest was in the way;
> Say I died bravely for the Tsar,

MIKHAIL YUREVICH LERMONTOV (1814-1841)

> And say what fools our doctors are,
>> Tell them I send my duty
>> To Russia, home and beauty.
>
> Mother and Dad—surely they still
>> Alive can scarce remain.
> At any rate I'd hate to fill
>> Those old folks' days with pain.
> But, if one of them lingers yet,
> Just tell that there's no use to fret:
>> They've sent us to the fighting,
>> And I'm no hand at writing.*

The height of poetic detachment was reached, however, by Lermontov in a great work of a different order: *The Song about Tsar Ivan Vasilyevich, the Young Body-Guard and the Brave Merchant Kalashnikov*. This poem is the finest literary emulation of the historical folk-songs (similar to, and formally like the *byliny*). Here Lermontov came at least as close to the spirit of the people and to folk genius as Pushkin did in his poetic transposition of fairy tales. But this is Lermontov at his best rather than his most typical. Essentially subjective, he succeeded only during the last period of his life in turning his personal moods and attitudes into great poetry, notably so when face to face with nature. This poem, the whole of which consists of one single sentence, can serve as a proof:

> When o'er the yellowing corn a fleeting shadow rushes,
> And fragrant forest glades re-echo in the breeze,
> And in the garden's depths the ripe plum hides its blushes
> Within the luscious shade of brightly verdant trees;
>
> When bathed in scented dew, the silver lily,
> At golden morn or evening shot with red,

---

* Translated by V. de Sola Pinto.

From out behind a leafy bush peeps shyly,
And nods with friendly mien its dainty head;

When down the shady glen the bubbling streamlet dances,
And, lulling thought to sleep with its incessant song,
Lisps me the secrets, with a thousand glances,
Of that still corner where it speeds along;

Then does my troubled soul find solace for a while,
Then vanish for a time the furrows from my brow,
And happiness is mine a moment here below,
And in the skies I see God smile.*

Pushkin would not have used so many adjectives and "purple patches" as Lermontov was wont to do, yet this does not mean that all his poems are full of them. Nor is he often as conciliatory as in the quoted lyric. His awareness of the difference between the world to which he was chained, and the timeless realm of the spirit was too painful to make him accept his fate. Besides, like so many romantics, he derived his poetic power principally from protest, rebellion, and that proud isolation which repudiates anything tainted with the stigma of the "human-all-too-human."

Oh gloomy and dreary! and no one to stretch out a hand
    In hours when the soul nears disaster . . .
Desire! but what use is an empty desire without end?
    And the years, the best years, but fly faster.

To love! yes, but whom? It is nothing in time's little space.
    No love has an endless to-morrow!
Just look at yourself: what is past does not leave any trace.
    They are nothing—both pleasure and sorrow.

* This poem, translated by Walter Morison, and the following, translated by C. M. Bowra, are taken from *A Book of Russian Verse*, Macmillan.

What is passion? That sickness so sweet, either early or late,
   Will vanish at reason's protesting;
And life, if you ever, attentive and cool, contemplate,
   Is but empty and meaningless jesting.

So the mood of *The Angel* keeps recurring in Lermontov's poetry like a permanent refrain to his own life. And since both his pessimism and his rebellion were due to metaphysical nostalgia, they often gave him that well-nigh elemental force of negation and challenge which came out in his two principal works, *The Novice* (1840) and *The Demon* (1841).

4.

These two tales in verse represent the climax of Lermontov's romanticism and poetic genius in one. *The Novice,* in particular, is the most glowing assertion of freedom that ever came from the pen of a Russian poet. Full of unsurpassed pictures of nature, it has nothing of the slow despondent rhythm of his famous *Meditation,* beginning with the line, "Sadly do I look upon our generation." The very pace of *The Novice* (he calls it in Georgian—*Mtsyri*) is so manly and bracing that there are no feminine endings in its four-footed iambics.* The theme itself goes back to Lermontov's early period. He began to work upon it in 1830. Five years later he embodied it as one of the motifs in his somewhat confused romantic tale in verse, *The Boyar Orsha,* and completed its final draft in the last year of his life. The tale is in the form of a confession on the part of a young Caucasian mountaineer who as a child had been captured by the Russians and was then left in a Georgian mon-

---

* Zhukovsky's excellent translation of Byron's *Prisoner of Chillon* was done (in 1821) in the same meter.

astery where he became a novice. But the monastery walls did
not obliterate the memories of his childhood and his yearning
for freedom. Determined to see his native place and to taste of
a free life once again, he escapes, wanders amidst the gorgeous
Caucasian scenery, but in the end is found dying of exhaustion
and starvation not far from the spot where his adventure had
started. Having thus completed the vicious circle, he is brought
back to the monastery. He knows that his hours are numbered,
but his spirit refuses to surrender. In words burning with passion he confesses to an old monk the reasons why he escaped
and perseveres in his defiance to the end.

Tragic, but in a different sense, is Lermontov's "Eastern tale,"
The Demon. He had started working at it as far back as 1829
and 1830, took it up again in 1833, then during his stay in the
Caucasus in 1837, and completed it (after several previous
drafts) in 1841. The demon of this tale is Lermontov's own
double, projected into the realm of the spirit. He is a rebellious
exiled angel who still remembers his one-time bliss (*The Angel*
motif again), but is doomed to be imprisoned in his own isolation till the end of time. The theme bears traces of Byron's
influence—especially of his *Heaven and Earth,* of Thomas
Moore's *The Love of Angels,* of *Eloa* by Alfred de Vigny, but
in spite of this it remains Lermontov's most typical and personal
creation. For it combines, in an intensified symbolic manner,
all the features of his own nature: his feeling of loneliness, his
rebellious pride, his secret wish as well as his inability to come
to terms with life.

> Unhappy Demon, spirit of exile,
> Soared high above the sinful world,
> And memories of the days of erstwhile
> Before him brooding vision whirled,
> Of days when in the light of grace

A cherub bright and pure he shone,
When in the swift, unending race
The comet turned its smiling face
To greet him as they fastened on;
When through the everlasting gloaming,
Athirst of knowledge he pursued
The caravans of planets roaming
Through endless space without a goal,
When faith and love imbued his soul,
The happy first-born of creation,
Unknown to fear or pride's inflation,
Nor came to haunt his limpid mind
The threat of endless years of pain . . .
And much, so much he strove to find
Deep in his memory, but in vain.*

And since this is an "Eastern tale," the Caucasus—the Russian romantic East—is introduced as the only adequate background for a spirit of such stature. It is the Caucasus Lermontov had known and admired since his boyhood.

Then o'er the high Caucasian maze
The banished angel slowly rose,
Kazbek with glinting lights ablaze,
Stood clad in everlasting snows.
And deep below, an inky track
Like a dark serpent's hiding-crack,
The winding Darial met his gaze.
The Terek like a lion bounding
With shaggy mane upon the peak
Set all the hollow vales resounding;
And beasts upon the mountain bleak
And birds aloft in heaven's light

* All the passages are taken from Gerard Shelley's translation of *The Demon*, The Richards Press.

> Both harkened to its thundered word;
> And golden clouds in endless flight
> Sped with it northward undeterred.

The beauty of Gruzia or Georgia, embedded in that scenery, is

> Spread out in glittering, gorgeous views,
> Ablaze with morning's rosy dews,
> With lofty ruins ivy-decked
> And purling brooks that flow unchecked
> O'er beds of multi-colored stones.

It is amidst the most beautiful views in the world that the Demon suddenly beholds Tamara—the most beautiful of mortals, and falls in love with her. But Tamara, already betrothed, is expecting the arrival of her bridegroom who, accompanied by a whole caravan, hurries to the wedding. Tamara and her girl-friends while away the time with innocent pleasures.

> And on the roof in rich array
> The bride sits with her maiden throng,
> Filling the hours with play and song
> Till o'er the distant hills the day
> Warns them that night will not be long.
> Their palms in gentle measure clapping,
> They sing, and then the young bride takes
> Her tambourine, which, gently tapping
> Above her head, she gaily shakes
> With a lily hand that faintly quakes.
> Now lighter than a bird she dashes,
> Then, pausing, she will fix her gaze
> While two moist eyes are seen to blaze
> Beneath their jealous tapering lashes;
> Now she will raise her brows with pride,

Now suddenly ner form incline,
Then o'er the patterned floor will glide
Her foot so lovely, so divine!
And oft her face will sweetly smile
With gentle mirth devoid of guile.
A beam of moonlight faintly trembling
Upon the ruffled water's face,
Though much her wreathed smile resembling,
Can scarce compare for light or grace.

The Demon sees to it that the caravan of the wedding guests is dispersed, while the bridegroom himself is killed. In despair, Tamara retires to a convent, but here the Demon begins to tempt her in her dreams. He does this with no evil intentions, for Tamara's beauty has made such a profound change in him that he actually hopes his love for her might save him at last from isolation and even reconcile him to God and His world. Invisible, he whispers to her:

The gentle prayer of love unending
I bring to thee with heart aglow,
On earth my spirit's first unbending,
The first tears from my eyes to flow.
O let them not unheeded go!
Heaven knows that one word of thine
Can make my simple soul surrender,
And clad in thy love's light divine
In Paradise again I'd shine
Like a new angel in new splendor.

But this is not granted to him. When, finally, he embraces Tamara, she dies from the kiss of an immortal. Her soul is taken away by a messenger of God, while the Demon is left in the same cosmic loneliness as ever.

Again he roamed in desolation,
The haughty exile of creation,
On whom no hope or love shall gleam.

In spite of its somewhat operatic theme and setting, this poem remains one of the masterpieces of Russian literature. Lermontov expressed in it symbolically the depth of his own uprootedness as only a romantic of his brand could have done. Yet the plane of such poetry was too vague, too far removed from the actualities of the day and the conditions of an entire generation lost as it were in the desert of Russian life under Nicholas I. So he decided to tackle the problem from a different angle and in prose; which he did in his novel, *A Hero of Our Time* (1840).

5.

Although Lermontov himself warns us, in the preface to the second edition of this work, not to confuse Pechorin—the hero of the novel—with the personality of the author, we cannot but think that he analyzed in it above all his own negative features. But in portraying himself, he portrayed also the generation to which he belonged. In this manner he wrote his own counterpart to Alfred de Musset's *La Confession d'un enfant du siècle,* a book he must have been hardly less familiar with than he was with *Adolphe* by Benjamin Constant. Like the two works mentioned, *A Hero of Our Time* is a psychological novel, and its importance is further enhanced by the fact that it is written in a prose as perfect and lucid as the prose of Pushkin, but at the same time even more flexible.

Pechorin himself is a literary descendant of Pushkin's Onegin. But he is an Onegin of the 'thirties: intensified, psychologically dissected and presented to the reader as the new up-to-date variety of the "superfluous" man. A preliminary portrait of Pechorin can be found in Lermontov's unfinished early novel, *Princess Ligovskaya* (1836), where he combines self-analysis with a picture of the rather callous Petersburg society. But what was here only a sketch and a promise, became in *A Hero of Our Time* a fulfilment. Consisting of five parts, all of which can be read independently, this masterpiece shows in the first two narratives (*Bela, Maxim Maximych*) Pechorin as he is seen by others, and in the subsequent three parts (*Taman, Princess Mary, The Fatalist*) as he sees and describes himself in his own diary. The background is for the most part the Caucasus again; only the incidents of *Taman* (one of the best stories in Russian) is set in the Crimea.

The final impression Pechorin makes upon the reader is one of a tragic failure. He has all the marks of a strong and superior nature, but can never apply his strength to anything worth his while, since in the Russia of that period no creative outlet was provided or even possible for people of his caliber. All his potential strength thus turns against itself and becomes vindictively destructive. The more so because he is a hidden idealist by nature, whereas by conviction he is a skeptic unable to believe in any ideals. Devoid of an adequate creative task or mission, he is doomed to remain negative in whatever he does. "I have never been able to discover my mission," he confesses, "so I have succumbed to the temptation of futile and ungrateful passions. Out of their furnace I have issued hard and cold as steel, but I have hopelessly failed to pluck the most beautiful flower of life—the fire of noble impulses. How often have I been no more than an axe in the hands of fate. Like a death-dealing instrument, I fell upon the heads of the predestined victims, often without angry feelings, but always without regret."

Pechorin is in other ways, too, a rather split, "modern" per-

sonality. He is full of the will to live, to enjoy, while, at the
same time, his skeptical reason continually watches, analyzes
and undermines his best impulses. Such self-division makes
him increasingly inhibited until the only real feeling still
accessible to him is that of his power, which he duly exercises
as an end in itself. Other people, especially women (Bela, Vera,
Princess Mary) whom he fascinates, become deplorable victims of the power he has over them. He himself is aware of
this, painfully aware at times, and the only thing in his favor
is that he is at least candid enough to acknowledge it. "I see
the sufferings and the joys of others only in relation to myself;
I regard them as food to nourish my spiritual strength," he
says further in his diary. "It has become impossible for me to
do foolish deeds under the influence of passion. In me, ambition
has been crushed by circumstances, to assume another form.
For ambition is nothing but the thirst for power, and my chief
delight is to impose my will upon all with whom I come in
contact. To inspire fear, what is it but the first sign and the
greatest triumph of power? To be for some one a cause of
suffering or joy, without the least right—can pride know
sweeter food than this?" No wonder Pechorin himself comes
to the conclusion: "Substantially I was a cripple." *

6.

Frustrated strength, doomed to turn against itself or else to
degenerate into the nihilistic "will to power"—such was the
inner tragedy of Lermontov's own personality. Through his
masterly analysis of this tragedy Lermontov deepened the problem of the "superfluous man" and thus became the creator of
the psychological novel in Russian literature. He was among

* Translated by Eden and Cedar Paul, Allen & Unwin.

the first to tackle some of those aspects of individual frustration which afterwards were further developed in Dostoevsky's writings.

Even the "demoniac" pride and self-assertiveness of Dostoevsky's complex heroes, such as Raskolnikov and Stavrogin, have some of their roots in Lermontov. Whereas one aspect of Dostoevsky's work goes back to Gogol, the other points to Lermontov, and via Lermontov to Byron—however distant the affinities may be at times.

As a painter of the "superfluous man" Lermontov forms a link between Pushkin on the one hand, and Turgenev and Goncharov on the other. As a psychologist, however, he leads to Dostoevsky. By his frankness and his refusal to indulge in any shams or rosy spectacles, he introduced into Russian literature that psychological and moral honesty which often verged on recklessness. Both as poet and novelist, Lermontov inaugurated the vertical direction in Russian literature. It was he who made it *conscious* of depth (which is something different from the unconscious depth) at a time when the more horizontal "natural school" was already branching off into a number of those aspects which formed the basis of the subsequent Russian realism.

CHAPTER SEVEN

Fyodor Tyutchev

I.

Among the leading figures in Russian literature, the poet Fyodor Tyutchev (1803-73) is still hardly a name in Western Europe. But this is not surprising—even in Russia it took two or three generations before his work was appreciated at its true value. As his early poems coincided with the Pushkin period, he is often mentioned rightly or wrongly among the members of the Pushkin *pléiade*. Some of his best verses actually appeared in Pushkin's periodical *The Contemporary* (*Sovremennik*) in 1836, i.e. while Pushkin was still alive. Apart from this, however, Tyutchev had no close contacts with that group. Besides, on leaving Moscow University at the age of nineteen, he was attached, almost at once, to the Russian Legation in Munich and later to that in Turin. His stay abroad lasted some twenty-two years. During that time his genius reached its maturity away from his native land and largely under foreign influences.

The city which for several reasons he liked and enjoyed most was Munich. King Ludwig I, himself a poet, had succeeded in turning the Bavarian capital into a lively meeting-ground for writers, artists and cultural workers in general. So Tyutchev felt thoroughly at home in its atmosphere and made good use of it. Nor did he neglect stimulating personal contacts. In 1828 he was in touch with Heinrich Heine who in a letter refers to him as his "best Munich friend." In the same year he often saw Schelling whose philosophy of nature, together with Goethe's pantheism, exercised a strong influence upon his own poetry. As Tyutchev's second wife had lived in Weimar where she had known Goethe, it is possible that Tyutchev, too, had met him personally, but this is only a conjecture. Anyway, when in 1832 Goethe died, his Russian admirer dedicated to him a poem worthy of its subject.

Tyutchev was moderately prolific. The total number of poems to his credit is somewhere between 450 and 500. Considering the fact that he reached the age of seventy, this is not a great deal. He felt, moreover, rather indifferent to his literary career. It is significant that on his return to Petersburg, in 1844, he soon became famous as a brilliant society wit and causeur, whereas his poems were known only to the initiated few. Refusing to curry favor either with the critics or the readers, he had to wait until 1850 for the first competent appreciation (by the poet Nekrasov) of his work. But even after that he showed so little interest in the promise of a belated literary fame that he took no part in the first printed collection of his poems in 1854 and left it entirely to the discretion of his friend, the novelist I. S. Turgenev. The truth is that he wrote only under inner compulsion, i.e. when he could not help it, and even then with apparent reluctance. For he realized the inadequacy of the spoken or written words and felt skeptical about them. In one of his finest poems, *Silentium,* he explains the reason for his own meager output in these lines, known to every lover of Russian poetry:

> Heart knows not to speak with heart.
> Song and speech can ne'er impart
> Faith by which we live and die.

> A thought once spoken is a lie.
> Unbroken, undefiled, unstirred
> Thy fountain: drink and say no word.*

Fortunately, Tyutchev did not always adhere to this rule. There were moments when he could not abstain from singing, whether he wanted or not. His intimate contact with Nature in particular was responsible for a number of those moments. So was his emotionalized thought, aroused by his intense and distressingly visionary cosmic feeling. The spell of a tragic love which swayed him in his old age was responsible for a last and final crop of his excellent lyrics. And since he sang only when he had to, he put into his verses all the artistic and human integrity of which he was capable. Turgenev once said that Tyutchev's poems are not redolent of anything labored, but seem to have been written, as Goethe wrote, on the spur of certain moments: instead of having been made, they have grown of their own accord "like the fruits on a tree."

2.

To the average poetry-reader in Russia Tyutchev is known mainly on account of his nature lyrics. These are less ethereal but more direct and incisive in their laconic impressionism than the lyrics of his younger contemporary, Afanasy Fet. They are also imbued with frequent philosophic contemplation spontaneously arising out of his moods rather than imposed upon them. He may sing about plains and mountains, spring floods, sea-waves, seasons, mornings and evenings—the array of motifs used by thousands of poets before him; yet he does it in his own manner, and his voice can be recognized without mistake. As a rule, he selects a few details only which he arranges in

* Translated by R. M. Hewitt in *A Book of Russian Verse*, Macmillan.

such a way as to suggest the whole picture in its most striking
aspects by a minimum of means. Even such an obvious nature
poem as his *Spring Storm,* known from textbooks to every
Russian schoolboy, can serve as an example. It begins with the
simplest lines imaginable:

> I like a storm at May's beginning,
> When Spring's first thunder with wild cries
> As though in frolic gaily spinning
> Rumbles all round the pale blue skies.

The elements of the storm are then compressed into eight
lines only, but sufficient to show it in its fullness, with the
"jargon of the forests, brawl of the mountains—all gaily echoing the thunder's roar." A mental picture with an appropriate
simile is added as a final touch and conclusion:

> Hebe, you'd say, had seized a brimming
> Cup from Jove's eagle in wild mirth,
> And with laughter had dashed the swimming
> Nectar from heaven across the earth.*

But Tyutchev's lyrics are not always as cheerful as in the
poem above. His impressionism often assumes a disquieting
meditative character, tinged with a symbolic meaning. The
symbolist and the impressionist methods generally tend to converge in him and to strengthen each other—containing now
and then a summing-up comment as they do at the end of
these lines:

> The light of autumn evening seems a screen,
> Some mystery with tender glamor muffling. . . .
> The trees in motley, cloaked and eerie sheen,
> The scarlet leaves that languid airs are ruffling,
> The still and misty azure, vaguely far,

* Translated by V. de Sola Pinto.

Above the earth that waits her orphan sorrow,
And bitter winds in gusty fragrance are
Forerunners of a bleak, storm-driven morrow.
The woods are waning; withered is the sun;
Earth shows the smile of passing, meekly tender
As the grave shyness of the suffering one,
In noble reticence of sad surrender.†

The last three lines stress the symbolic kernel of the picture. The symbolism of the following motif—a willow leaning over the running water—is, however, transparent enough to explain itself without any comment:

Why, O willow, to the river
Leans thy head so low, and why
Dost thou with long leaves that tremble
And that thirsty lips resemble
Catch the ripples dancing by?
Though thy leaflets faint and quiver,
Mirrored in the fleeting stream,
Yet the current speeds and splashes,
In caressing sunshine flashes,
And but mocks thy empty dream.*

In Pushkin's poetry the phenomena of nature exist as a rule in their own right, i.e. objectively, and are described as such. Tyutchev, on the other hand, prefers to approach them either as vehicles of his own moods and thoughts, or else to look upon them as a cover of what is clandestinely working behind and beyond it all. He did not neglect nature poems pure and simple. Yet his most original contributions to Russian literature are

† Translated by Babette Deutsch and Avrahm Yarmolinsky in *Russian Poetry*, Lawrence.
* Translated by Walter Morison in *A Book of Russian Verse*, Macmillan.

FYODOR TYUTCHEV (1803-1873)

those verses in which nature itself is interpreted as a veil hiding
from man's eyes the deeper cosmic processes active at the root
of all being.

It was here in particular that certain influences of German
thought left their mark in Tyutchev's work. Under the impact
of Goethe's pantheism and even more of Schelling's philosophy
of the identity between Spirit and the Universe, he came to
consider Nature as a living organism—with a soul, a mind and
a language of its own. These are accessible, however, only when
the clarity of the day is replaced by the irrational element of
the night. During the day we see the surface of Nature in all
her alluring and deceptive beauty. But when the day is gone
man's consciousness can be attuned to the darker mysteries
coming from the depth of being. He is then able to partake of
universal life, provided he surrenders to it to the point of forgetting or even obliterating his own *moi haïssable*. Such pan-
theistic moods at the hour of approaching night are well rendered in Tyutchev's *Twilight*:

> Dove-blue shades have met and mingled,
> Colors fade and sound is sleeping—
> Life and movement all dissolve in
> Trembling twilight, far-off weeping.
> Moths upon their unseen journeys
> Murmuring through the darkness fall . . .
> Moment this of wordless yearning!
> All within me, I in all. . . .
>
> Gentle twilight, sleepy twilight,
> Penetrate my inmost soul,
> Tranquil, languid, full of odors,
> All suffusing, lulling all!
> In a mist of self-oblivion

> Every feeling softly fold!
> Let me taste annihilation,
> Merge me with the sleeping world.*

Night and twilight, imbued with this quasi-mystical flavor, became Tyutchev's favorite motifs. Appealing to his cosmic sense rather than to his sense of nature, they affected him accordingly. What during the day appeared as harmony and beauty, was bound to dissolve at night into the foreboding of chaos as the lurking primeval core of the universe. If the beauty of nature gave him moments of ecstasy, the magic of night, charged with the bigger mystery of the cosmos, filled him with *angoisse* and metaphysical horror. His pantheism thus assumed the dualistic aspect of Day and Night, the symbolic meaning of which he expresses in this key-poem:

> Across the spirits' secret world,
> Hiding the chaos and the void,
> The great gods, lest we be destroyed,
> A golden curtain have unfurled.
> This radiant veil we call the Day,
> The lustrous Day, whose golden weave
> Gleams nimbus-like on all who grieve,
> And jewels with his joys the gay.

> But Day wanes: Night shrouded in dusk,
> Stalks forward, and with gestures gruff
> Crumbles and rends the precious stuff,
> And casts it down like any husk.
> Then the abyss is bared to sight,
> Its terrors grim, its shadows vast;
> We shrink back, desperate, aghast.
> Hence men, beholding fear the Night.*

* Translated by Walter Morison.
* Translated by Babette Deutsch and Avrahm Yarmolinsky. Op. cit.

3.

Around the hackneyed antithesis of day and night Tyutchev
wove some of his boldest imagery, but always with the emphasis on the night. The poetry of night was in vogue among
the romantics, especially in Germany where it had such devotees
as Novalis, Tieck, Eichendorff and others. Its votary in Russia
was above all the tender lyrical poet Vasily Zhukovsky. Yet
it would be hard to find a poet who knew how to render this
"shrinking back aghast" with such force as Tyutchev. If one
can speak of "nocturnal" metaphysics at all, we find it in his
verses. Moreover, it was not terror alone but also the fascination
of the Night that drew him irresistibly with its mystery and
magic.

> As ocean's stream girdles the ball of earth,
> From circling seas of dream man's life emerges,
> And as night moves in silence up the firth
> The secret tide around our mainland surges.
>
> The voice of urgent waters softly sounds;
> The magic skiff uplifts white wings of wonder.
> The tide swells swiftly and the white sail rounds,
> Where the blind waves in shoreless darkness thunder.
>
> And the wide heavens, starred and luminous,
> Out of the deep in mystery aspire.
> The strange abyss is burning under us;
> And we sail onwards, and our wake is fire.*

Tyutchev's awe of the waves thundering in the "shoreless
darkness" instead of abating as time went on, only grew
stronger. He felt lost and forlorn like an orphan in the face of

* Translated by Babette Deutsch and Avrahm Yarmolinsky. Op. cit.

it, and while singing of man's "fateful heritage," often obliterated the dividing line between things visual and things visionary. His impressionism passed into strangely realistic symbols.

> The night was dark with indignation;
> With cloud the sky was shrouded deep;
> It was not threat nor meditation,
> But drugged uncomfortable sleep.
>
> Only the lightning's summer revels
> Flashed alternating, out and in,
> As if a horde of deaf-mute devils
> Were holding conference of sin.
>
> As if a sign agreed were given,
> Broad conflagration fired the sky,
> And momently from the dark heaven
> Woods and far forests met the eye.
>
> Then disappeared again the vision;
> In visible darkness all was pent
> As if some great and dire decision
> Were taken in the firmament.*

"A horde of deaf-mute devils holding conference of sin" is
one of those pregnant phrases (Tyutchev's poetry is full of
them) which, once read, cannot be forgotten. Yet as an emana-
tion of his *angoisse,* it also points to realities within his own
mind by which he was haunted. For he found there the same
conflicting tendencies as in the cosmic life at large, only more
personal, more painful—with the chaotic "nocturnal" element
frequently on top.

> Oh, thou, my wizard soul, oh, heart
> That whelming agony immerses,

* Translated by Anon. in *A Book of Russian Verse,* Macmillan.

> The threshold of two universes
> In cleaving these, tears thee apart.†

Self-division of this kind anticipated certain traits of the *fin de siècle*. The "agony" alluded to was rendered even more unbearable because of the threat of skepticism to which he was no stranger. As far back as in 1851, he described to perfection (in eight lines) the inner vacuum resulting from that disposition which was doomed to undermine the generation of the "moderns."

> No sickness of the flesh is ours to-day
> Whose time is spent in grieving and despairing;
> Who pray all night that night will pass away—
> Who greet the dawn rebelliously uncaring.
>
> Withered and parched by unbelief, the soul
> Impossible, unbearable things is bearing.
> We are lost men, and ruin is our goal,
> Athirst for faith, to beg for faith not daring.*

Tyutchev, too, was in danger of being inwardly paralyzed by such a state of mind, and he knew it. In fact, during the decade preceding the above verses he wrote surprisingly little. He might have become silent altogether, had not chance provided him with a new source of inspiration. What happened was that in 1850 Tyutchev, a married middle-aged man holding a high post in the department of censorship, fell passionately in love with a certain Mlle. Denisyeva—a niece of the headmistress of the exclusive Smolny Institute, where his daughters were educated. Far from being a mere Platonic affair, this love lasted some fourteen years (until Mlle. Denisyeva's death in 1864) and had a profound effect on Tyutchev's life and work.

† Translated by Babette Deutsch and Avraham Yarmolinsky. Op. cit.
* Translated by R. Christie in *A Book of Russian Verse*, Macmillan.

4.

There have been many poets of first love, but Tyutchev is not one of them. He sings of his last love instead. And his melancholy is not one of joy but of the nostalgic sadness of a parting day, the very beauty of which is tragic, as we can easily gather from his poem, *Last Love:*

> As our years sink away, how tender it grows,
> Our love, and how filled with fateful boding . . .
> Shine on us, shine, thou farewell glow
> Of love's last ray, of the twilight's brooding.
>
> Shades have reft half the sky away:
> Westward alone the light still lingers.
> Bide with us, charm of the dying day;
> Withdraw not, enchantment, thy magic fingers!
>
> Let the coursing blood grow thin as gall,
> If the heart but keep its tender burning . . .
> O last and latest love of all,
> Thou art bliss unending, and hopeless yearning.*

Tragic in its own way was also the love of Mlle. Denisyeva. The ambiguous position of a pretty young woman who gave birth to three illegitimate children while her lover's German wife was still alive, by no means made things easy for her. The gossip, slander, social ostracism she had to endure, can be imagined. Nor was Tyutchev himself always as tender as he says. There were times when his moods and temper became unbearable. Besides, neither of the two lovers seemed to be able to separate love from torment and subsequent self-torment. A lyric in which he gives a condensed history of his last passion

* Translated by Walter Morison.

begins with the frank exclamation, "Oh, how killingly we love;
how in the reckless blindness of passions we are sure to ruin
all that is dear to our heart!" The "immortal vulgarity of men,"
having chosen Mlle. Denisyeva for its target, did the rest. And
the result? Two wrecked lives, and a series of the most poignant
love-lyrics in Russian literature. These are written in a realistic
vein, with a frequent colloquial inflection. In some of them
Tyutchev castigates himself by putting into the mouth of his
beloved grave accusations, as though the verses had been written not by him but by her—in order to indict him.

> That, as before, he loves me, tell me never,
> Nor that he treasures me as in the days gone by . . .
> Oh no! My life's thin thread, he, ruthless seeks to sever,
> For all I see the blade his fingers ply.
>
> Now raging, now in tears, with grief and anger seething,
> Swept madly on, my soul plucked bare and raw,
> I ache, nor am alive . . . in him alone know breathing;
> And needle-sharp is every breath I draw.
>
> He measures me the air more grudgingly and sparsely
> Than one would mete it out to one's most hated foe.
> I still can breathe; though painfully and harshly,
> I still draw breath—but life no longer know.*

The contrition after each fit of harshness may have increased
the depth and the sincerity of his more tender feelings, but the
continuous ups and downs of this kind were costly for both
—emotionally and physically. After some fourteen years of such
love, it was the woman who had to pay the price. A glimpse
of her agony can be obtained from this poem:

> All day unconscious she was lying there,
> And evening shadows came and wrapt her round;

* Translated by Walter Morison.

Warm summer rain fell soft upon the leaves
In steady flow and made a cheerful sound.

And slowly she returned into herself,
And trained her sense the pleasant sound to hear,
And listened long, her mind absorbed in thought
That carried her away, yet left her near.

Then, as one speaking to herself, alone,
Now conscious of the sound and all beside
(I watched her, yet alive, though death was near)
"How dearly have I loved all this!" she sighed.

Oh how thou loved'st it! And to love like thee
Has to no other in the world been given!
My God! and can I then my death survive
And my poor heart in fragments not be riven?*

Her death was an irreparable blow to Tyutchev. "Only in her
presence was I a personality, only in her love, her boundless love
for me, was I aware of myself," he owned to one of his friends
in October 1864. "Now I am a meaningless, painfully living
nonentity." Before long his poetic gift, too, began to decline.
But while his lyrical vein seemed to be in abeyance, there was
a sudden increase in the output of his political and civic verses
—the last group of his poetry still to be considered.

5.

With very few exceptions, Tyutchev's political poems cannot
be compared either in depth or in technique with his lyrics.
They are primarily a register of the ideological attitudes typical
of Tyutchev the Russian and the aristocrat. His earliest political
poem—an answer to Pushkin's *Ode to Liberty*—goes back to

* Translated by P. E. Matheson in *Holy Russia and Other Poems*, Oxford University
   Press.

1820. Tyutchev wrote it in the liberal spirit prevalent among the advanced aristocratic youths of that generation. Later, however, he changed his opinions and after the Paris rebellion in 1830, definitely sided with reaction and with the ideas of the Holy Alliance. He also became an ardent Russian patriot (while still continuing to use in private conversation and correspondence French in preference to his native tongue). In 1841 he, moreover, paid a visit to Prague, whence he returned a convinced pan-Slavist of the Russian brand.

Russia was considered by him, from now on, the only guarantee for the old order, since the West seemed to be in a constant fermentation which reached its climax in the revolutions of 1848. As a scion of the old serf-owning nobility, he was so frightened of the revolutionary trend and movements in Europe that he wrote four essays (in French) in order to enlighten the world at large. The most important of these essays is *La Russie et la Revolution* (1849), and the gist of it was summed up by him in one of his best political poems, *The Rock and the Sea,* in which Tsarist Russia is likened to a cliff surrounded by the waves of the revolution vainly dashing against its "gigantic heel."

In spite of his one-time friendship with Heine, Tyutchev now turned his back on everything men of Heine's stamp were fighting for. Having identified Europe with the revolution, he prophesied in verse and in prose the "decline of the West" and propped up his imperialistic pan-Slavism with a rather sophisticated philosohy of history. Russia would, in his opinion, eventually become the leader of all the Slavs, and the universal monarchy she was destined to found would extend as far as Nile and Ganges, with Constantinople as its capital. A *pax russica* would then stem for ever the fury of the revolution, fomented by the "godless" masses of the West. In his poem, *Sunrise,* he gives an allegorical utterance to the adage, *ex oriente lux*—quite in the spirit of militant Slavophilism. Little did he suspect that about a hundred years later the irony of history would make Russia a communist country, whereas the European West would desperately try to save what still could be saved of the old order. It was for patriotic rather than religious reasons that Tyutchev now stressed also his allegiance to the Russian Orthodox Church. In one of his poems he mentions Christ wandering in a slave's garb all over Russia and bestowing blessings upon her—a symbol of that Messianism which was so dear to the older Slavophils.

The setbacks of the Russian army during the Crimean Campaign had a sobering effect upon Tyutchev. The morass into which the corrupt bureaucracy had plunged the country was something of a revelation to him, and when Nicholas I died (during the campaign) Tyutchev frankly said in a poem what he thought of the defunct sovereign. For whatever his prejudices, Tyutchev was not a timeserver. Even his patriotism was sincere. But as he viewed the destinies of his country through his semifeudal and imperialist spectacles, he was bound to see everything in a wrong perspective. One more proof that good poets are rarely good politicians.

6.

Tyutchev's place among the greatest Russian poets is no longer contested. Dostoevsky once called him the first poet-philosopher in Russian literature, and Tolstoy, who otherwise cared little for poetry, rated Tyutchev higher than Pushkin. Touching with one end of his development the classical eighteenth century of Derzhavin, he anticipated with the other end the Russian school of symbolism. He was a "modern" before his time. This may have been one of the reasons why he had to wait so long for recognition. For in spite of the high tribute paid to him by such contemporaries as Nekrasov, Turgenev, Apollon Grigoryev, and even the ultra-radical critic Dobrolyubov, Tyutchev's work came into its own only towards the end of the last century.

The pioneering article by the philosopher and poet Vladimir Solovyov (in 1895) was followed by a crop of essays in which some of the leading Russian symbolists proclaimed Tyutchev one of their predecessors. The peak of his vogue was reached, however, in 1913, when a complete edition of his works, prefaced by one of the leading modernists, Valery Bryusov, was launched as a supplement to the most widely spread monthly, *Niva* (The Cornfield). Nor did it suffer an eclipse after the Revolution of 1917. In spite of his political views, he is relished as a poet also by Soviet readers. Among the more recent editions of his works there is a large one even for Soviet children— surely a sign of popularity which is almost reaching danger point.

CHAPTER EIGHT

Ivan Turgenev

I.

Ivan Turgenev was the first Russian author to become generally known and admired beyond the boundaries of his own country. It was through him that Russian fiction began to penetrate into Europe as one of the major literary influences. And for good reason, since he always knew how to combine his "Russianness" with impeccable literary manners and with a technique perfect enough to challenge comparison with any great prose-writer of the West. He loses only if compared with such cyclopic geniuses as Dostoevsky and Tolstoy who can afford to be a law unto themselves. Similarly in the world of music, Mozart seems to lose if compared with Beethoven, for example: but while Beethoven may be a greater genius, Mozart remains a greater artist.

Turgenev belongs to what might be called the well-ordered Mozartian—or, for that matter, Pushkinian—type of creators. Whatever subject he took on, he handled it first of all as a perfect artist. External reality, including its most topical aspects and problems, was for him but raw material which he distilled into works of beauty. Keenly interested in the political, social and cultural struggles of the day, he had his own definite convictions, sympathies, antipathies; yet he never let them interfere with the aesthetic side of his writings. This did not exclude, of course, that unconscious interference which determines before-hand as it were one's choice of certain themes and characters in preference to others. In this respect Turgenev remained a descendant of the old "nests of gentlefolk" at the very height of the intelligentsia period of Russian culture and literature. Although himself a member of the intelligentsia and a sincere liberal with a Western outlook, he yet remained a Russian nobleman with the ancestral country-house not only in his memory but in his very blood. In contrast to the more radical intellectuals who came from the "commoners" and looked only towards the future, Turgenev the artist could not help being rooted in the past even when fighting it in the light of the vital problems of the day. The company of the impetuous "commoners," so conspicuous in the ranks of the intelligentsia during the 'sixties, hardly made him feel quite at ease. At any rate, when at the beginning of that momentous decade a split between the "gentlemen" and the "commoners" took place within the precincts of *The Contemporary* itself (the principal organ of the advanced intelligentsia), Turgenev was one of those who walked out of the editorial premises.

After that split, the "commoners"—under the leadership of Dobrolyubov and Chernyshevsky—practically monopolized the journalistic and pamphleteering activities, whereas the "gentle-men" concentrated more on literature proper. With the excep-tion of Dostoevsky and Leskov, both of whom were of mixed origin, the principal authors of the 'fifties, 'sixties and 'seventies, dealt mostly with the country-house and the village. This applies above all to Turgenev, whose work can perhaps be defined as the swan-song of a class which had a past but could no longer look forward with confidence to a future. It is against the background of this class, with its prevalent moods, that we can best see Turgenev's life and work in their right perspective.

2.

Turgenev was born in 1818 in the district of Orel. Having lost his father while still a boy, he was at the mercy of a tyrannical mother. It was probably Turgenev's hatred for his mother that made him loathe, since boyhood, that system in which such irresponsible autocrats were still possible. After his education at home he studied at the University of Moscow, then in St. Petersburg, and finally in Berlin (1838-41), where he came into contact with Western culture and was so favorably impressed by it as to remain a convinced "Westerner" to the end of his days. On his return from abroad he started writing poetry and achieved considerable success with his tale in verse *Parasha* (1843), influenced by both Pushkin and Lermontov. He seemed to waver, for a while, between poetry, drama and fiction. His plays, such as the now famous *A Month in the Country* (1850) and *A Provincial Lady* (1851), are not devoid of originality, especially the first which, in its own way, anticipated the dramatic technique of Chekhov. But an even more startling new note was brought by Turgenev into prose by those stories and jottings of his which began to appear in 1847 and were issued in book form in 1852 under the title, *A Sportsman's Sketches*.

The title looked innocent and reassuring enough: just a collection of impressions recorded by a roaming sportsman. Yet in the process of reading one becomes aware of the actual theme of the book—the serf and the squire. For the first time we meet here the serf in his everyday surroundings and in his normal everyday contacts with the serf-owner. As the liberation of the serfs was then generally expected, such a theme was topical at the time and had already been introduced in a sentimental-humanitarian manner (quite in the spirit of the "natural school") by Grigorovich. But in contrast to Grigorovich's *Village* or *Anton Goremyka,* Turgenev followed only his own artistic instinct even when dealing with such a vital theme as serfdom. Without distorting either the truth of life or that of art by any sentimental considerations, he depicted a great variety of serfs and peasants simply as human beings in their own right, with their own ways of thinking, and with their own individual defects and virtues on a par with everybody else. The same balanced objectivity comes out in his portraits of the landowners, and it was not Turgenev's fault if many of these appeared to be humanly less valuable than their serfs. The whole of it expands into a mosaic of Russian rural life, and some of his pictures—the exquisitely drawn children in *Bezhin Meadow,* or the story called *The Singers,* for example—are unforgettable. So are Turgenev's landscapes. He knows how to be impressive through reserve and never takes liberties with Nature. Hence his preference for the nuance and for that discreet lyrical intimacy with the rural scenery in which the mellowness of color and of verbal music serves as an evocative accompaniment to the atmosphere demanded by the situation. Turgenev's scenery is no longer a mere background for the characters—it merges with them as a part of the action itself. The Russian countryside has thus found in him its best "impressionistic" interpreter. With regard to his characters, too, Turgenev is above all an observer with an incredibly sharp eye for those significant trifles through which he can describe a person or a whole crowd of people by a few dexterous touches. Here is (in Mrs. Garnett's version) one of his quick portraits: "His face, plump and round as a ball, expressed bashfulness, good-natured and humble meekness: his nose, also plump and round and streaked with blue veins, betokened a sensualist. On the front of his head there

was not a single hair left, some thin brown tufts stuck out
behind; there was an ingratiating twinkle in his little eyes, set
in long slits, and a sweet smile on his red, juicy lips. He had
on a coat with a stand-up collar and brass buttons, very worn
but clean; his cloth trousers were hitched up high, his fat
calves were visible above the yellow tops of his boots."

As his descriptions are never dissociated from experience, we
see his characters as living realities and seem to know them
intimately—as though we had lived with them for years.
With the same balanced sensibility he tackles social and political problems without preaching, i.e. without making any
compromises with his artistic conscience. Paradoxically enough,
it was this trait in particular that enhanced the social and moral
appeal of *A Sportsman's Sketches*. By exposing the iniquity and
the cruelties of the serfdom system only as an artist and not as
a preacher, he made the implied but sublimated social-humani-
tarian "purpose" all the more tangible by the magic of his art.
Anyway, when the sketches appeared in book-form, they made
such a strong impression on the Tsarevich himself (the pro-
spective Tsar Alexander II) as to increase his determination
to abolish serfdom—a conspicuous example of the influence of
art upon history.

3.

Turgenev's vision, like that of Pushkin, is always concrete.
He remains an observer even when he is introspective: in his
Diary of a Superfluous Man, for instance, or in *Smoke.* As
Henry James put it in one of his notes, he "has no recognition
of unembodied ideas; an idea, with him, is such and such
a nose and chin, such and such a hat and waistcoat, bearing the
same relation to it as the look of the printed word does to its

IVAN TURGENEV (1818-1883)

meaning." And Turgenev himself said in a paper that he "had never attempted to create a type without having, not an idea, but a living person, in whom the various elements were harmonized together, to work from." In contrast to Dostoevsky, who saw all characters mainly from within; or to Tolstoy, who knew how to combine his incredible plastic power with an acute analysis, Turgenev confined himself to the surface, but without ever being superficial. His characters are as much alive as any of those created by Tolstoy and Dostoevsky, although their range may be smaller and less ambitious. Unlike many Russian authors, Turgenev was endowed with quite a rare sense of construction, proportion, and of a carefully worked out—if never very complicated—plot. All these things he perfected by learning from Pushkin and Lermontov rather than from Gogol. The first two stories he wrote, *Andrey Kolosov* (1844) and *A Reckless Fellow* (1847), bear the stamp of Pechorin in Lermontov's *A Hero of Our Time*. In another and considerably later story, *Knock, Knock, Knock* (1870), he gave a parody of the same character. Even in *A Sportsman's Sketches,* several of which are just carefully worked out "slices" of life, one cannot but admire that architectonic sense of his which achieved veritable triumphs in his later and bigger stories, and especially in his novels: *Rudin* (1855), *A Nest of Gentlefolk* (1858), *On the Eve* (1860), *Fathers and Children* (1861), *Smoke* (1867) and *Virgin Soil* (1876).

In Turgenev's novels one encounters again and again the effete gentry people, unable to cope with the task of adjusting themselves to the conditions and the age in which they live. The Childe Harold-Onegin-Pechorin tradition of the "superfluous man" therefore plays in them a conspicuous part. As early as 1851 Turgenev wrote his excellent *Diary of a Superfluous Man,* and from that time on this unheroic hero remained one of his ever-recurring figures. Rudin, his first full-size portrait in the novel bearing the same name, is actually one of Turgenev's amazing feats of characterization.* We are introduced to Rudin in the drawing-room of an "up-to-date" country-house, where he impresses everybody by his intelligence and idealism (in the style of the period). Then, to our surprise we learn that this brilliant talker is a parasite and a sponger. Soon we are compelled to revise this opinion also. After a number of contradictory features quickly following one another, he is subjected to a crucial test—in his love for the hostess's daughter Natasha. But here he shows his lack of backbone and even of ordinary courage. The author makes us alternately waver between spite, pity and affection, and each new feature of Rudin perplexes us as if it could not belong to the man we know already. Yet after a while all the contradictions adjust themselves, and we have before us an intensely real character whom, for all his strangeness, we seem to like. Full of the best impulses and intentions, but as helpless in practice as a child, this uprooted *déclassé* is unable to find an active contact with life. He does not belong anywhere. So he is doomed to remain a victim of his own dreams, and his brilliant intelligence remains sterile, however good the material out of which he is made.

If Rudin is a restless descendant of Onegin gone to seed, Natasha has affinities with Pushkin's Tatyana. Like Tatyana, she too is much stronger than the man she loves, and after her initial disappointment, finds her place in life. The whole existence of Rudin, however, is only one long series of escapes—from life as well as from himself. He embodies the woolly rootless idealism which was so often to be found among

---

* Rudin is supposed to be a portrait of the famous revolutionary Michael Bakunin, whom Turgenev had known well during his student years in Berlin.

the gentry intellectuals of the 'forties, and it is almost with a kind of relief that we learn of his death on the barricades in Paris, during the Revolution of 1848.

The note of frustration is no less strong in Turgenev's next novel, *A Nest of Gentlefolk*. Here, too, we have a picture of gentry life against the background of which the Rudin-Natasha (i.e. Onegin-Tatyana) motif assumes, in the love between Lavretsky and Liza, a rather tragic turn. Lavretsky, a disillusioned married man whose lewd wife is enjoying herself on the French Riviera, is in essence as "superfluous" as Rudin but more purposeful. During his wife's absence he falls in love with Liza—a woman after his own heart and, in spite of their mutual reticence, knows that his feelings are reciprocated. Suddenly Lavretsky reads in a newspaper that his wife has died. The situation is changed at once. The two lovers joyfully realize that now they can become man and wife. But here Mme. Lavretsky unexpectedly turns up, the rumor of her death in France having been false. She actually comes back with the diplomatic intention of obtaining her husband's forgiveness. Unable to disentangle himself from the grip of his depraved wife, Lavretsky surrenders to his fate without a struggle, while Liza buries her own life in a convent. Here, after a considerable lapse of time, the two once happy lovers meet again in a scene which might have become melodramatic but for Turgenev's supreme artistic tact and restraint. For not a single word is exchanged, and the two pass each other by like two pathetic ghosts.

Delicate on account of its pitfalls, the subject-matter is worked out in a symphonic manner—with numerous secondary motifs, episodes, and characters held together by the basic theme. The contrasted and mutually complementary characters; the background, the "atmosphere," and the plot itself are so well blended that here the truth of life is not only distilled but also deepened and intensified by the truth of art. Even Turgenev's mood of gentle fatalism, which pervades the book, is so well sublimated as to cease to be personal: it becomes part and parcel of the "atmosphere" itself. And so does his admiration for Liza. She may be idealized, but this does not prevent her from being alive and real—a thing which can be said, perhaps, with less emphasis of Helena, the heroine of *On the Eve*.

In this novel Turgenev portrayed the generation of the 'fifties, that is of the years which saw the Crimean Campaign, the death of Nicholas I, and anticipated the great reforms that were to come during the next decade—the years of expectations. But were the Russian intellectuals equal to the tasks ahead? Turgenev's answer was in the negative; at least with regard to men if not to women. The heroine of this novel is represented (on the very eve of the Crimean Campaign) as the new active woman, capable of a heroic task without any heroic pose or self-admiration. Surrounded by charming and intelligently talkative Rudins, she falls in love not with a member of her own class or even of her own nation, but with the rather angular Insarov, a Bulgarian fanatically devoted to the idea of freeing his country from the Turkish yoke. But if Helena remains convincing, Insarov is overdrawn, too much of a one-track mind, to be entirely alive. One admires his firmness rather than his personality, but in the end it is his one-sided firmness which makes one feel somewhat dismayed. It is worth noting that even this novel, in which Turgenev was so anxious to portray a strong man, has an unhappy ending: Insarov dies in Venice, while on his way to foment a rising in his own country.

It was only in his next and greatest novel, *Fathers and Chil-*

dren, that Turgenev succeeded in giving a convincing portrait of the strong new man—this time a Russian—the age was clamoring for. And since he was doubtful of the members of his own class, he had to look for him among the "commoners." He found him in the person of the nihilist Bazarov, whose prototype was a Russian doctor Turgenev had actually met in 1860, in Germany. It was not without malice that he transferred Bazarov to a "nest of gentlefolk," confronting him with the rather fossilized representatives of the 'forties. Devoid of any respect for traditions, canonized ideas or class-distinctions, Bazarov is frankness itself: always matter-of-fact, inconsiderate, even aggressive, but at the same time hard-working and full of guts. One can well imagine that the rôle he plays in the genteel "Victorian" country-house of his hosts is none too pleasant for either party. Various conflicts, hidden and open arise almost at once. They are caused not so much by the differences in opinions as by those imponderable unconscious attitudes towards certain things in life which are often a much more formidable class-barrier than rank or wealth. Turgenev surpasses himself in the fineness of touch and delicate humor when dealing with such imponderables. On the other hand, he may admire Bazarov, but does not really like him and feels more at home with the "gentlefolk." Yet he realizes that the future is with Bazarov and not with Bazarov's hosts, whom the "nihilist" * cannot quite stomach. Bazarov was in fact the "commoner" who emerged among the leading figures in the intelligentsia of the 'sixties, and with whom the "gentlemen" had to put up whether they liked him or not. A "gentleman" himself, Turgenev gave in Bazarov one of the great portraits in the nineteenth century literature.

From a purely formal standpoint, *Fathers and Children* is as

---

* It was Turgenev who introduced the word "nihilist" into literature.

perfect as *A Nest of Gentlefolk,* but its texture is richer, while
the interplay of the characters is considerably deeper. The
"tame" Arkady (with whom Turgenev himself must have
had quite a lot in common), Arkady's father and immaculate
uncle, Bazarov's pathetically simple parents, the shy Fenitchka,
the self-possessed (and undersexed) Mme Odintsova, her gentle
sister Katya—they all fit perfectly into the pattern devised by
the author and are alive even in their most casual words and
movements. The finale is again a tragic one. Yet the scene of
Bazarov's death is one of the most powerful ever described by
an author; powerful precisely on account of its reserve. The
contrast between Bazarov's manly stoicism and the frantic
state of his parents—so anxious to conceal their despair from
their dying son—is one of those marvels of art which are
more real than reality itself. Although the novel is full of the
atmosphere of the early 'sixties, it is easy to perceive behind
it the eternal tragi-comedy of human relations in general:
those between parents and their grown-up children; between
men and women; aristocrats and "commoners"; dreamers and
realists; leaders and followers. It is again a case of the truth
of life being deepened and enriched by the truth of art.

4.

The impatient younger generation of the 'sixties repudiated
Fathers and Children. The storm raised by the novel brought
so much disgust to its author that, for a while, he intended
to give up literature altogether, as one can gather from his
autobiographic sketch, *Enough* (1864).* Turgenev's irritation
at the Russian life of the period came out with a great deal

---

* This sketch was cruelly parodied by Dostoevsky (under the title, *Merci, Merci,
Merci*) in *The Possessed.*

of bitterness in his next novel, *Smoke*. As if feeling that he himself was now becoming more and more "superfluous," he preferred to live abroad where he counted among his friends and admirers some of the foremost literary figures of the day: George Sand, Gautier, Sainte-Beuve, Flaubert, Renan, the brothers Goncourt, Taine, Daudet, Zola, and Maupassant. Yet life seemed to have lost its flavor, its contents and intensity— even its *negative* intensity—as far as he was concerned. "The most terrible thing is that there is nothing terrible in life; that life's very essence is meanly-uninteresting and beggarly-flat." This brief saying of his (so much like Gogol's complaint about the great Tedium) sums up his weariness and pessimism, both of which may have been a partial outcome of his infatuation for the famous singer Mme. Viardot-Garcia. Turgenev had met her in his twenties, while at Petersburg, and that virile and in her own way brilliant woman remained his life-long love. Although, for some curious reason, their relationship seems to have been purely platonic,† the enamored author followed her all over Europe and spent also his last years near her.

Because of these wanderings he must have felt the more sadly uprooted at times. Still, he was less out of touch with what was going on in Russia than many of his critics thought. Turgenev the artist may have been above parties, but as a citizen he was keenly interested in the political and social life of his country. Even after his differences with the "commoners" in *The Contemporary,* his outlook remained that of a liberal Westerner, for which the patriotic Slavophil Dostoevsky lampooned him (so mercilessly) in the figure of the author Karmazinov in *The Possessed*. The controversy between the two factions found an echo in *Smoke*—a novel in which biting

† One is inclined to suspect that Turgenev embodied some of Mme. Garcia's features in the portrait of Mme. Odintsova in *Fathers and Children*.

personal indignation and political satire, directed against all
the factions of Russian life, often loom large even at the expense
of the finely worked out romance, or the unsuccessful renewal
of an old romance, between Litvinov (another "superfluous
man") and Irina. On the other hand, Turgenev the portrait
painter achieves here one of his greatest triumphs with Irina—
a more sparkling, more complex and subtly evasive personality
than any of his previous heroines. Mr. Edward Garnett is right
in defining her in his study of Turgenev as a woman with
"that exact balance between good and evil which makes good
women seem insipid beside her and bad women unnatural. She
ardently desires to become nobler, to possess all that the ideal of
love means for the heart of a woman; but she has only the
power given to her of enervating the man she loves. She is
born to corrupt, yet never to be corrupted. She rises mistress of
herself after the first measure of fatal delight. And, never giving
her heart absolutely to her lover, she nevertheless remains ever
to be desired. Further her wit, her scorn, her beauty, preserve
her from all the influences of evil she does not deliberately
employ. Such a woman is as old and as rare a type as Helen of
Troy."

With all its occasional flaws, *Smoke* is one of Turgenev's
masterpieces. His last novel, *Virgin Soil,* on the other hand,
can more aptly be called a brilliant failure. Here the author
obviously wanted to prove that, in spite of his stay abroad, he
was able to understand and to interpret the aspirations of the
advanced currents in his native country. In this case he tackled
the current prevalent in the 'seventies—the "populism" which
aimed at bridging the gap between the intelligentsia and the
people and caused a number of enthusiastic youths and girls
to sacrifice everything in order to help the masses and prepare
them for the hoped-for revolution. In *Virgin Soil* we can follow

the activities of a whole group of such enthusiasts up to their complete disappointment. Anxious to blend the social-political theme with the artistic side of the novel, the author nearly succeeded—nearly but not entirely. His weakness comes out first of all in the portrait of the principal character: the "strong man" Solomin. For instead of producing a new counterpart of Bazarov, Turgenev gave here something like an abstraction of a sober, reliable, practical idealist. Solomin is too much of a "perfect" dummy to be credible as a human being. The other characters of the novels are, however, convincing and alive: the actively generous Marianna (almost a twin-sister of Helena in *On the Eve*), for example; the "superfluous" revolutionary Hamlet—Nezhdanov; or the pompous opportunist (this time of a "liberal" brand) Sipyagin. The love between Nezhdanov and Marianna is, of course, a new variation of the Rudin-Natasha motif. The general tenor of the book is rather pessimistic about the populist movement, and Turgenev's own conclusions seem to tally with the allegorical poem by one of his heroes, *A Dream,* which contains the following not exactly flattering lines:

"The Peasants sleep like the dead; they reap and plough asleep, they thresh
And yet they sleep. Father, mother, all the family, all sleep.
He who strikes sleeps, and he who receives the blow!
Only the tavern is wakeful—and never closes its eyes;
And clasping a whisky-pot with a firm grip,
Her forehead at the Pole and her feet in the Caucasus,
Sleeps a never-ending sleep our country, our holy Russia."

Turgenev described the various aspects of Russian life at a time when the sleeper, rubbing his eyes, was preparing to have his own say at last. What that say would be like remained a puzzle even for Turgenev. Russia's riddle and destiny were much too intricate for him to find an adequate formula, let alone a solution.

5.

In spite of all the changes in literary fashions, Turgenev still remains one of the great artists in Russian as well as European fiction. Apart from his mellow style, his polish, his delicate irony, and his sense of construction, one admires in him that indefinable intimacy with which he impresses his characters upon us even before we are aware of it. However strange they may appear at first, we soon move among them as among personal friends whose misfortunes often agitate us as much as our own. He excels in particular as psychologist and poet of love. And whatever theme or plot he may choose, he always knows how to treat it in perspective as something deeper and more permanent than the passing show of a period. The variety of his characters, too, is surprisingly big. This is true also of his women portraits, despite his predilection for the Tatyana-type. Take the hysterically exalted girl in *A Strange Story;* his gallery of old maids; his worldly cocottes (Mme. Lavretsky in *A Nest of Gentlefolk,* or Mme. Polozova in the largely autobiographic *Spring Torrents*); his blue-stockings; his enchantingly sensuous Irina in *Smoke.* Turgenev's weakness for Mme. Viardot-Garcia may have been responsible for the large number of weak men in his novels and stories; yet his weaklings are more interesting, more complex, and certainly more successfully worked out than his strong men. The futility of his own love is further reflected in his "atmosphere," reminiscent of a melancholy autumn afternoon, with gentle fatalism permeating the air.

The same kind of mood can be felt in his stories which are

deservedly among the best in European literature. A master of impressionism in *A Sportsman's Sketches,* and a superb story-teller in such narratives as *First Love, Asya, A King Lear of the Steppes, The Spring Torrents,* and many others, he can stand comparison with any famous artist of the word. Most of his stories resemble well-organized reminiscences, told in the first person (his favorite device is that of setting a story within a story) and vibrating with that vague nostalgia for the past which was typical of Turgenev himself. As a "superfluous" member of an already "superfluous" class, he felt so homeless in the rapidly changing world that the atmosphere of doom eventually seemed to emanate from his very personality. Mme. Herzen once compared him with an uninhabited room: "Its walls are damp, and their dampness gets into your bones; you are afraid to sit down, afraid to touch anything, and you only wish to get out of it as quickly as possible."

Disillusioned and tired as he was, he even had a few lapses from his high artistic level when, in *The Song of Triumphant Love* (1881) and *Clara Milich* (1882), he began to dabble in dilettantish spiritism and occultism. His exquisite *Poems in Prose* (known as *Senilia*) on the other hand reflect the weariness and the resignation of an old man who has nothing more to wait for than death. Turgenev the man died in 1883. But Turgenev the author continues to live as a world classic, belonging not to one, but to all ages and countries.

CHAPTER NINE

Nekrasov

I.

Nekrasov's poetic activities coincided with a time when the Pushkin tradition was already in the hands of epigones rather than original creators. Unwilling as well as unable to be an epigone, he eventually struck a new path of his own, the novelty of which can perhaps best be explained through his personality on the one hand, and the character of the age in which he lived on the other. Born in 1821, Nikolai Nekrasov matured with the generation of the 1840's—the period of the rise of the intelligentsia. The "Decembrist" spirit was not yet dead, and there was a regular cult of the political martyrs still toiling in the mines of Siberia. Typical products of that spirit, grafted upon Hegel's philosophy, were such members of the gentry class as Herzen and Bakunin, both of whom contributed to the revolutionary thought of Russia and indeed of Europe. It was in the 1860's that the share of the "commoners" in the literary, cultural and political activities rapidly increased. But whereas the "gentlemen," relying on their estates, had enough leisure to write without worrying about their daily bread, most of the "commoners" lived from hand to mouth as journalists and pamphleteers. At times they were compelled to be purveyors of vaudevilles, hastily written *feuilletons,* topical doggerel, and other commercialized genres.

Nekrasov, who belonged to both generations, had to do his literary apprenticeship towards the end of the 'thirties and in the early 'forties. It was a hard school and full of bitter experiences. The more so because his father, an officer and a landowner of the old brutal type, had left him without any support at the age of seventeen. He sent his boy from Yaroslavl on the Volga to Petersburg with the intention of making him an officer, but as the future poet refused to have anything to do with the Cadet Corps, he was at once deprived by his parent of financial help and left to his own devices. Starving and freezing in the streets of Petersburg, Nekrasov lived for a while the life of a down-and-out. Things were often so bad that he had to be sheltered by compassionate beggars in doss-houses. He never forgot the lessons learned during these trials, but he managed to get out of it comparatively soon. His first step towards something better consisted of journalistic hackwork. Prolific as he was in both verse and prose, he acquired already at this time a certain cheap facility and disregard for good taste—a feature which stuck to him to the end even during his best period. The ambition to succeed as a poet made him write a volume of "serious" verse, *Dreams and Sounds,* which he published in 1840. It was a collection of immature and derivative poems (with traces of Zhukovsky's influence), and the critic Belinsky attacked it so violently that the book had neither literary nor financial success. Undaunted, Nekrasov looked for a more remunerative outlet as editor and publisher. He was introduced to Belinsky, and before long the two men were friends and fellow workers. At the beginning of 1846 he edited *Petersburg Miscellany,* with Turgenev's *Three Portraits* and Dostoevsky's first novel, *Poor Folk,* as its *pièces de résistance.* The success was enormous. In the same year he was able to acquire (together with Panayev) *The Contemporary*

which he turned from a rather tame organ into a periodical
of the revolutionary democracy in Russia. In addition to the
best authors of the day, he succeeded in having among his
contributors such radical "commoners" as Chernyshevsky
and Dobrolyubov—the leading pamphleteers and critics during the 'sixties.

That decade had begun with the liberation of the serfs and
other far-reaching reforms, but the unfortunate Polish rising
of 1863-64 marred a number of hopes. The suppression of the
Poles by Muravyov, nicknamed the "Hangman," was so brutal
indeed that the Tsar himself, who was still under the influence
of liberal advisers, felt disgusted and made no bones about it.
Yet after the attempt on the Tsar's life (on April 4th, 1866) by
Karakozov, the previously sacked "Hangman" came into power
once again, and this created considerable panic among the
radicals. Nekrasov, known by then all over Russia as a poet
and also as the editor of the most liberal periodical in the
country, hoped to bribe Muravyov by writing some verses in
his honor (which he himself recited at a banquet), but even
such a shameful trick failed to work—*The Contemporary* was
suspended forthwith. It was only two years later (1868) that
Nekrasov managed to get hold of another important periodical,
The Fatherland's Annals, which he edited with the help of
Saltykov-Shchedrin (the author of *The Golovlyov Family* and
the greatest Russian satirist of that period) and the sociologist
Mikhailovsky. Under their joint guidance the periodical became the leading organ of the "populist" trend of thought. The
strange thing, however, was that Nekrasov managed to combine
his editorial and literary energy with all sorts of excesses which
also required money. He gambled, hunted, entertained on a
lavish scale, kept expensive cooks and even more expensive
mistresses. In the end he became involved (together with his

mistress Mme. Panayeva) in a shabby financial transaction which concerned the entire fortune belonging to the feeble-minded wife of the expatriated poet Ogaryov—all this, while he was writing sincere, deeply felt poems about the people's woe and injustice. But he was already afflicted with an incurable disease in his throat, which started in 1853 and lingered on until, on January 8th, 1878, he died. He was accompanied to his grave by the "populist" generation of the 'seventies which saw in Nekrasov, whatever his private character, their inspiring mouthpiece and a truly great poet.

2.

After his lack of success in 1840, Nekrasov found his own poetic voice rather late—towards the end of the 'fifties and in the first half of the 'sixties. As for the general trend of that poetry, it had a number of causes, some of them fairly complicated and going back to his experiences at home and in St. Petersburg. In boyhood he witnessed the cruel treatment meted out to the serfs, as well as to his own mother (a Polish woman of some education and refinement), by his rough father. In Petersburg again he saw the very depths of misery bred by a modern city. His opposition to everything that was connected with serfdom and autocracy made him write civic poetry, whereas his sympathy with the oppressed serfs drove him towards the people and was responsible for the voice of a "repentant nobleman" in his work. To this the realism of his big city poems, dealing with the Petersburg he had learned to know, should be added. In one of them, beginning with the line, "When I drive at night in a darkened street," he describes, with haunting directness, a starving couple whose baby has died. Both of them have been reduced to such straits in their garret as to be unable to buy a coffin in which to bury their child. In the end the young and still pretty mother is compelled to go on the streets whence, after a while, she returns—her eyes full of despair and shame—with the money for the coffin. The extremes of such misery appealed to Nekrasov as much as they did to Dostoevsky, and he was among the first to add the big city motifs to Russian poetry. His *Street Scenes* and pictures of Petersburg outcasts were further enlarged by social satires, by caustic scenes from bureaucracy and high life. These border, however, on his civic poems proper. The bulk of his civic and political poetry can be dismissed as rhymed pamphleteering. If we want to find Nekrasov at his best and most original, we must look for him in the poems he wrote about the people and often also in the manner of the people.

Had Nekrasov relied upon a solid literary and poetic culture, he might perhaps have become a follower of the Pushkinian tradition at a time when the polished "Parnassian" school of Alexey Tolstoy, Apollon Maikov, Polonsky, and Fet was in the ascendant. But he either had no wish or no time to acquire such culture. So he trusted entirely his innate poetic feeling which came not from literary poetry but from the rhythmic and melodic patterns of the folksong. All that is great in Nekrasov the poet came from this source. It was on this ground, too, that his sympathy and affinity with the people served him in good stead. Whatever one may think of his political, civic, and didactic verses, there can be no doubt of the power and the melody he extracted (in the case of his best poems) from the folksong. He is one of the few instances of great individual poetry created as it were on the plane of the collective folk-genius. Elements of such creative *rapprochement* with the people can be found before him—in Pushkin,

NIKOLAI ALEXEYEVICK NEKRASOV (1821-1878)

Lermontov, and especially in Koltsov, but none of them went as far in this direction as Nekrasov. It may have been partly for this reason that the "populist" Chernyshevsky put Nekrasov higher than Pushkin and Lermontov.

Nekrasov's flair for the melody of the folksong (with its peculiar rhythms and verbal instrumentations) was certainly stronger than in any of the previous poets. It was he, moreover, who introduced and cultivated on a large scale the dactylic endings* typical of the *byliny* and of the Russian folksong in general. He came so near the genius of the people that some of his poems have been included in the folksongs and are now sung by the Russian masses from one end of the country to the other. Through his peculiar assimilation of the folk-style (especially his blend of anapaests and iambics with dactylic endings) he enlarged the scope and the area of Russian poetry, while building up a bridge between literature and the people. Having turned, on so many occasions, against the accepted canons, he made the next step and tried to de-poetise literary poetry by introducing all sorts of unpoetic "peasanty" words.† It is the genuine folk-flavor that makes a number of his poems (including *The Pedlars, The Green Rustle,* and the whole of his epic *Who Can Be Happy and Free in Russia?*) untranslatable. For even the best rendering of the contents does not do justice to the poems unless one catches all the peculiarities of Nekrasov's rhythm and melody, and these are inseparable from the Russian language. So much for Nekrasov's technique. Another strong point of his work is its village realism which also deserves to be dwelt upon.

---

* They were used before him by Lermontov and Koltsov.
† This process of de-poetization was equally strongly marked in his civic verses (addressed mostly to the "populist" intelligentsia) and abounding in words taken from ordinary journalism.

3.

Nekrasov's big city realism has already been mentioned. It was partly connected with his civic poetry, and owed a great deal to the "natural school," sponsored by Belinsky. The same holds good of his poems directed against his own class—the poems of a "repentant nobleman" who, for moral as well as humanitarian reasons, became a defender of the peasant and the village; his best political verses can however be linked to those of the executed "Decembrist" Ryleyev.* In some of his poems, such as *Meditation at a Porch, Song to Eré-mushka, A Knight for an Hour, The Railway,* all these motifs converge, imbued as they are with Nekrasov's own gloomy and aggressive moods. One of the typical examples is his *Home.* It makes one think of Lermontov's indictments and of Pushkin's *In the Country,* with the difference that the "repentant nobleman" Nekrasov openly accuses himself, his own ancestors and particularly his own father. This is how it begins:

> Behold it once again, the old familiar place,
> Wherein my fathers passed their barren vacant days!
> In muddy revels ran their lives, in witless bragging;
> The swarm of shivering serfs in their oppression found
> An enviable thing the master's meanest hound;
> And here to see the light of heaven I was fated,
> And here I learned to hate, and bear the thing I hated;
> But all my hate I hid within my soul for shame,
> And I at seasons too a yokel squire became;

* His unfinished series *Russian Women* (1872) was originally called *The Decembrist Wives.* The two sections completed deal with Princess Trubetskaya and Princess Volkonskaya, both of whom joined their husbands. The series is by no means among his best products.

And here it was my soul, untimely spoilt and tainted,
With blessed rest and peace too soon was disacquainted;
Unchildish trouble then, and premature desires,
Lay heavy on my heart, and scorched it with their fires.
Nay, from those younger years of harshness and rebelling
No recollection brings one comfortable ray.

Vividly remembering the sad lot of the serfs, he was never able to dissociate it from the sufferings of his own bullied mother, for whom he conceived—at least after her death—a regular cult, as one can conclude from the following lines in the same poem:

Here is the dark, dark close. See where the branches thicken,
What figure glimpses down the pathway, sad and stricken?
Too well the cause I know, my mother, of thy tears;
Too well I know who marred and wasted all thy years.
For ever doomed to serve a sullen churl untender,
Unto no hopeless hope thy spirit would surrender;
To no rebellious dream thy timorous heart was stirred;
Thy lot, like any serf's, was borne without a word.*

In the end Nekrasov—a descendant of serf-owners—experiences something like moral satisfaction when seeing his ancestral home well-nigh ruined. On the whole, the virulence of his indictment was always in direct ratio with his own repentance. Repentance, or rather a mood of ever-recurring moral masochism and self-castigation, may well have been needed by him even as a creative stimulus. This alone would be enough to throw some light on the duality of his behavior during the years of his prosperity: on the one hand the sumptuous living typical of a former squire, and on the other his constant and sincere self-reproaches, turned into poetry. And the more he hated the remnants of the squire in him, the more

* Translated by Oliver Elton in *A Book of Russian Verse*, Macmillan.

acutely he felt also the people's tragedy and the people's cause, with which he was anxious to identify himself as a poet.

No other Russian intellectual has ever succeeded in coming so close to the simple folk and the village as Nekrasov did during his "populist" moments. His realism of the countryside is often similar to that of George Crabbe, although he does not entirely concentrate on the negative and tragic side of village life. There are bright verses in it, too, especially those depicting the village urchins. What could be more delightful than the realism of his poem, *Peasant Children,* in which he describes a bevy of village boys, clandestinely looking at him through a cranny and making comments! Here is its beginning:

> Again in the country! A life full of pleasure,
>   I shoot; I write verses in solitude deep;
> And yesterday, searching the moorland for treasure,
>   I came to a cowshed, turned in, fell asleep.
> I woke. Through a crack in the wall had come prying
>   The sun's joyous rays, in profusion of gold,
> A pigeon is cooing; some young rooks are flying
>   Just over the roof, in a chorus they scold.
> Another bird raises an outcry uncanny,
>   I think by its shadow a crow it must be,
> But hark! There's a whisper! And lo, through the cranny
>   A row of bright eyes gaze intently at me.
> Yes, grey, black and blue eyes in earnest reflection
>   Are mingled together like flowers in a field.*

Equally delightful are his poems—humorous, descriptive, didactic—dedicated to Russian children: *Uncle Jack,* for instance; or *General Toptygin,* in which the frightened peasants mistake a run-away bear for an angry General; or *Grandad*

* Translated by Juliet Hoskice in *Poems by Nekrasov,* O.U.P.

Mazay, who during a spring flood rescues a boatful of hares and would not touch the bewildered creatures, but releases them instead, though with a warning:

> God speed you! Hurry
> Straight to shelter.
> But look, my friends,
> Though now I free you,
> When summer ends
> Don't let me see you:
> I raise my gun—
> Your day is done! *

Few of his poems about the peasants and the village are written in this vein. In the majority of them the sad and gloomy disposition prevails. Nekrasov's verses about the people's woe always strike the right note and are particularly moving when he sings of the hard lot of the Russian peasant woman. The account in *Orina—a Soldier's Mother* of how an old woman's only son, a healthy young giant, had been forcibly conscripted and after a few years returned home a complete wreck only in order to die of tuberculosis, is heart-rending in its tone and simplicity. Then there are the suffering toilers on the Volga and elsewhere, whom the poet asks at the end of his famous *Meditation at a Porch,* whether the only thing they have given to the world is their "song resembling a groan," after which they are perhaps doomed to disappear. Nekrasov himself wavers in his answer, but not very long. For behind the tragedy of his people he feels also their strength, as well as that broad, generous goodness which only comes from strength. And his admiration for them is testified by a number of his best poems, such as *The Green Rustle, The Pedlars, Vlas,*

* Translated by Juliet Hoskice. Op. cit.

The Red-Nosed Frost, and *Who Can Be Happy and Free in Russia?*

4.

The first of these is a lyrical drama in miniature. The bracing rhythm of the opening verses (in which the dactylic endings prevail) is itself sufficient to suggest the arrival of spring. The manner, the accent and the imagery are those of the peasants. Even the blossoming trees sway as white as if someone had "poured milk over them." And then we listen to a peasant who, on his return home from Petersburg (where he had been working), learned that his wife had been unfaithful to him. All through the winter he had brooded resentfully, until in the end he sharpened a knife with which he intended to kill her. Suddenly the spring arrived and drove all evil thoughts out of his mind. As though spell-bound, his heart could not resist the wave of generosity and forgiveness brought along by so much beauty. The final note of the poem is a conciliatory one:

> Love as long as you can,
> Suffer as long as you can,
> Forgive as long as you can,
> And God be your judge!

The Pedlars is a series of poems about two enterprising Yaro-slav peasants, peddling their wares in the country-side:

> Making profit with each mile;
> Everything they chance to meet with
> Serves the journey to beguile.

In this series Nekrasov came so near to the accent and the spirit of the people that its opening poem has actually become a folksong:

> Oy! How full, how full my basket!
> Calicoes, brocades, a stack,

> Come, my sweeting, make it lighter,
> Ease the doughty fellow's back.
> Steal into the rye-fields yonder,
> There till night-fall I'll delay,
> When I see thy black eyes shining
> All my treasures I'll display.*

There follow the pedlars' jokes, arguments and adventures with the village folk. As a contrast to their carefree gaiety the *Song of a Poor Pilgrim* is interpolated, the wailing words and rhythm of which can hardly be rendered in a translation.

> I pass through the meadows—the wind in the meadows is moaning:
>   "Cold I am, pilgrim, cold I am.
>   Cold I am, dear one, cold I am."
> I pass through the forest—the beasts in the forest are howling:
>   "We are hungry, oh, pilgrim, we're hungry!
>   Hungry, oh dear one, hungry!"

The whole of the unhappy, neglected and exploited peasant Russia is thus reviewed, and each line ends with the refrain of either "cold" or "hungry," the slow repetition of which in Russian (*hólodno, gólodno*) suggests the moaning of the wind or the howling of the hungry beasts. The motif of desolation in this poem also prepares the reader for the tragic end of the cycle. For the two pedlars are murdered by a woodman who robs them of all their money and is, in his turn, arrested the same evening, while carousing in a village inn.

The poem *Vlas,* which was much admired by Dostoevsky (he wrote about it in *The Diary of an Author*), portrays a thoroughly Russian figure: a repentant sinner after the people's heart. He is a former village *kulak* who used to exploit without mercy friend and foe alike—

---

* Translated by Juliet Hoskice. Op. cit. The same applies to all quotations from Nekrasov, except the last one (at the end of 5).

> Snatched the bread from needy neighbors
> While, in famine's hideous reign,
> Not a coin would leave his pocket
> Unrepaid by threefold gain.

But during a heavy illness he had a vision of hell, horrifying enough to make him repent of all his evil deeds and to become a new man. With the same firmness of purpose with which he formerly robbed his fellow-beings, he now gave up his earthly possessions and became an ascetic—

> All his wealth in gifts bestowing,
> Destitute did Vlas remain.
> Wandered barefoot, homeless, begging
> Money for God's church to gain.

Red-Nosed Frost (1863) is a gem of Nekrasov's poetry. Although written in conventional metres, it is a perfect blending of realism, peasant-mentality and folklore. The theme is simple. Prokel, the husband of young Darya, has died and, in severe wintry weather, is buried with all the peasant rites and customs. After the burial Darya returns to her cold cottage, and in order to make it warm for her tiny children, she drives her horse Savraska to the neighboring wood. While she gathers logs, King Frost spies her, swoops down, and makes her fall asleep. Freezing to death amidst the gorgeous scenery of the wintry forest, she dreams of all the best moments connected with her married life, her fields, her two children Grishouka (Gregory) and Masha (Mary). The following section of the poem is typical of Nekrasov's realism, applied to the more idyllic side of a peasant's life and work:

> In sparkling white hoarfrost encrusted
> To cold overpowering she yields,
> She's dreaming of radiant summer:
> Some rye is still left in the fields—

It's cut though; relieved they are feeling,
The peasants are piling it high,
And she, in another allotment,
Is digging potatoes close by.

The grandmother too is there working,
And on a full sack at their feet
The pretty rogue Masha is sitting,
And clasping a carrot to eat.

The big, creaking wagon approaches,
Savraska is turning her head,
And close to the bright, golden burden
Comes Prokel with ponderous tread.

"God keep you! And where is Grishouka?"
The father inquires, passing by,
"Among the sweet peas," say the women,
"Grishouka, Grishouka!" they cry.

He looks at the heavens. "I'm thirsty,"
He says, "and it's late too, I think."
And Daryushka rises and hands him
Some kvass in a pitcher to drink.

And meanwhile Grishouka comes running.
With garlands of peas he is bound,
A living green bush one might fancy
Is skimming along o'er the ground.

He runs! Eh! . . . As swift as an arrow!
He's burning the grass in his flight!
Grishouka is black as a raven,
His little head only is white.

He's shrieking with joy. There's a circlet
Of peas round his neck, like a wheel.
He gives some to mother and granny,
And sister. He twists like an eel!

From mother the mite gets caresses,
From father a sly little pinch,
And meanwhile Savraska's not idle:
She's stretching her neck, inch by inch.

She's reached them, the peas, sweet and juicy!
She's chewing and licking her lips
And raising her mouth, soft and loving,
The ear of Grishouka she nips.

5.

There still remains Nekrasov's central work, *Who Can be Happy and Free in Russia?* (1873-76)—an epic, quite unique of its kind and occupying in his writings a position similar to that of *Evgeny Onegin* in the work of Pushkin. If *Onegin* combines and completes as it were all the ingredients of Pushkin's poetry, *Who Can be Happy and Free in Russia?* shows all the principal features of Nekrasov the poet. The epic aims at giving a picture of the whole of Russia after the abolition of serfdom in 1861 and is written throughout in the people's style and language. The loom on which it is woven is that of a folk tale, but this only gives the poet a pretext for displaying all the realism, indictment, satire, boisterous humor, and also didactic "purpose," of which he is capable. Seven poor peasants meet on a high road and begin to argue as to who is happy and free in Russia. They go on arguing until they come to blows. Then a little peewit is captured by them. The mother-bird, seeing this, offers them as ransom a magical napkin which, at their bidding, will produce in a moment all the food they ask for. They agree to it. Provided with such an unexpected gift,

The peasants unloosen
　　Their waist belts and gather
Around the white napkin
　　To hold a great banquet.
In joy, they embrace
　　One another and promise
That never again
　　Will they beat one another
Without sound reflection,
　　But settle their quarrels
In reason and honor
　　As God has commanded;
That nought shall persuade them
　　To turn their steps homewards
To kiss wives and children,
　　To see the old people,
Until they have settled
　　For once and forever
The subject of discord:
　　Till they have discovered
The man who, in Russia,
　　Is happy and free.

Their Odyssey begins. In the course of it they encounter
all sorts of people, take part in a rowdy village fair, get ac-
quainted with such remarkable and truly strong characters as
Klim the Elder and the peasant woman Matryona—a worthy
counterpart of Darya in *Red-Nosed Frost*. Uneven as a whole,
the epic contains wonderful descriptive and lyrical passages,
including fine paraphrases of folk songs—*The Song about the
Two Infamous Sinners,* for example. The scenes at the village
fair are grotesquely amusing. Both humor and satire are provided by the figure of the doddering, crazy landowner Obolt-
Obolduyev who refuses to accept the reforms of 1861. His

heirs, afraid of making him angry and thus forfeiting the
expected fortune, have—through bribery—persuaded the peasants to behave, until his rapidly approaching death, as though
they were still serfs, which they do with much amusement.
The panorama of Russia passes before us in a variety of scenes,
and whatever her trials, she has enough vigor and vitality to
overcome them all. So the epic, although unfinished, ends in
a note of faith. A spirited youth, Grisha from among the
"commoners," sees in his poetic dreams what is in store for
his country and his people—dreams which are enough to chase
away despondence and pessimism from the reader's mind.

> Then Grisha tried vainly
> To sleep; but half dreaming
>   New songs he composed,
> They grew brighter and stronger . . .
>   Our peasants would soon
> Have been home from their travels
>   If they could have known
> What was happening to Grisha.
>   With what exaltation
> His bosom was burning;
>   What beautiful strains
> In his ears began chiming;
>   How blissfully sang he
> The wonderful anthem
>   Which tells of the freedom
> And peace of the people.

Such was the apotheosis of Nekrasov's own "populism" in
poetry at a time when this trend prevailed in the intelligentsia.
Finally, some mention should also be made of his purely personal lyrics. The best of them can be divided into two parts:
one dealing with the continuous wrangles he had with his mis-

tress Mme. Panayeva (the wife of his fellow-editor of *The Contemporary*), and the other consisting of the poignant and tragic poems he wrote during the last period of his illness. Nekrasov was not a pleasant person to live with. Moody and sullen, he often would not say a word for days; and as for loyalty, he was no more addicted to it than the flighty Mme. Panayeva. The years during which they lived together were certainly not years of harmony. But Nekrasov tried to make up for it at the end of it all by addressing to his mistress these lines:

> Goodbye! Forget the days of wane,
> Dejection, bitterness and pain,
> Forget the storms, forget the tears,
> Forget the threats of jealous fears.
> But the days when the sun of love
> Uprising kissed us from above,
> And bravely we went on our way—
> Bless and forget not one such day.*

As for Nekrasov's poems referring to the last phase or phases of his illness, it is enough to say that they are among those deservedly famous lyrics, in which his "Muse of grief and vengeance" received a final touch.

6.

And what about Nekrasov's place in literature? Turgenev once said that the Muse of poetry had never spent a night in Nekrasov's verse. With all respect to Turgenev's aesthetic sense, such a verdict no longer holds good. By turning against the accepted canons, Nekrasov opened up new possibilities with regard to both technique and contents. Through his nearness to folk-poetry and folk-genius he actually helped to bridge

* Translated by M. Baring in *A Book of Russian Verse*, Macmillan.

the gap between the people and literature. By introducing a number of "unpoetic" themes in a purposely depoetized language, he divested his verses of all solemnity on the one hand and of the danger of "prettiness" on the other. As a result, his directness made him accessible to the wider circles of readers. Even his journalistic verses (which are not of a high quality) performed a useful task in so far as they awakened and kept alive the interest in poetry among those readers who otherwise had little mental equipment for literature.

This was the reason why Nekrasov found so many ardent admirers among the "commoners" whose cultural background was considerably smaller than that of the "gentlemen" in the Russian intelligentsia. One of his recent critics, K. Chukovsky, is therefore justified in saying that Nekrasov wrote for a new type of political and social *consciousness*. Anyway, his work served as an important literary link between the intelligentsia and the masses.

Nekrasov failed to create a school of his own. Nevertheless, his attitude towards the village, the people and the folk-poetry acted as an inspiration for several poets who came from the people (the greatest of them being Sergey Esenin). His attempt at marrying civic poetry to topical journalism may not have been a happy union, but it has had a strong following in Soviet Russia, where Mayakovsky and his group had made —after 1917—a series of further brave experiments of this kind. Also the technical devices of Nekrasov's work have drawn much attention of late. This proves that Nekrasov is again coming into his own. In fact, the interest in him has increased of late almost out of all proportion. We may no longer think (as some of his contemporaries did) that he is "greater than Pushkin." Still, with all his faults and virtues, he occupies one of the very high places in the Russian Parnassus.

CHAPTER TEN

Goncharov

I.

Ivan Alexandrovich Goncharov (1812-91) is known outside Russia mainly by his novel *Oblomov* which now belongs to the world classics. At home, however, he is regarded as one of the pillars of Russian realism, almost on a par with the great trio of Tolstoy, Dostoevsky, and Turgenev. He was born in the remote Volga town of Simbirsk (now Ulyanovsk) into a merchant family living in the comfortable gentry style. The practical and sober bourgeois-merchant strain in him on the one hand and the more indolent gentry-tradition on the other were largely responsible for his personal outlook upon life and even for the character of his writings. His secondary and University education took place in Moscow, but most of his subsequent life was spent in Petersburg. He started his career as a punctillious civil servant who secretly trained himself as a writer. As if diffident of his talent, he was reluctant to publish anything until he was thirty-five; but once he felt ready for it he made it worth while. In 1846 he met the critic Belinsky whose theory of the "natural school," that literature should be a reflection and interpretation of life, affected his own type of realism. Yet he did not seem to be on good terms with Belinsky and his circle of radicals. Years later, when looking back to that period, he candidly confessed: "From a literary standpoint I merged with the circle, but in much, especially in its extreme negations, I did not agree with its members. The differences in our religious views, as well as in some other ideas and attitudes, prevented me from being more intimate with them. Most of all did I sympathize with Belinsky's sound views on literature, love of art, and finally with the honesty and severity of his character."

When in 1847 Goncharov's first novel, *A Common Story,* appeared, it was Belinsky who welcomed it at once and indeed proclaimed it the best work of fiction since Gogol's *Dead Souls.* The sudden success did not turn Goncharov's head. Slowly and as if methodically he kept writing his next novel, *Oblomov,* which was published only twelve years later. Meanwhile in the autumn of 1852 he started on the Russian frigate "Pallas" a hazardous sea-journey to Japan which lasted over two years and took him practically round the world. The expedition, with some five hundred men aboard had the task of concluding a trade agreement with Japan. Goncharov, who travelled in an official capacity, recorded what he saw in a number of letters, sketches, and diaries all of which appeared in various periodicals and were later, in 1858, published in two big volumes under the title of *Frigate Pallas*—an interesting but almost deliberately "pedestrian" account of his adventures. As though defying his own hidden romantic propensities, Goncharov avoids here any "purple patches" or effusions. The scenery of the East hardly moved him at all. And as for the majesty of the sea-storms on the Pacific, he saw in them only disorder and chaos. He had a good eye, though, for the ordinary daily life of the countries and races he visited. There is much humor in his descriptions of the frigate's stay at Nagasaki. His impressions of Japan and the Japanese certainly form the most amusing section of the book.

I. A. GONCHAROV (1812-1891)

About a year later Goncharov's *Oblomov* appeared and se-
cured him a place in the front ranks among the Russian authors.
The critic Dobrolyubov wrote in *The Contemporary* a whole
essay about it which is still considered a classic of interpre-
tative criticism. There followed scores of other articles, reviews
and polemics, but Goncharov was in no hurry to exploit his
fame by further writings. It was only after a lapse of another
ten years that he brought out his third and last novel, *The
Ravine* (1869). This work was a great success with readers but
not with the critics. The radicals in particular were fuming at
him on account of a portrait which was supposed to be a skit
on the younger generation.

Goncharov, who had by then retired from the civil service,
defended himself but it did not help. As if feeling that he had
given what he could, he was now retiring also from literature.
Henceforth he wrote mainly various kinds of reminiscences and
one or two pieces of criticism. Nor was he prone to cultivate
literary connections on a big scale, especially after some previous
misunderstandings with Turgenev. In the end he became a
recluse, tormented by persecution mania. Half-blind and paralyzed, he died on September 15th, 1891.

2.

Goncharov's main contribution to Russian literature consists
of his three novels. He himself said once that, in spite of their
differences, all three were actually one single novel the subject
of which was Russia during her transition years between 1840
and the end of the 1860's, when a number of changes and social-
economic reforms took place. The greatest of them all—the
abolition of serfdom in 1861—had actually become unavoidable
after the Crimean War. Besides, Russia was bound to adjust

herself sooner or later to a more modern system of life based on money. The slow infiltration of this system had actually been going on long before serfdom was relegated to the past.

The theme of Goncharov's first novel, *A Common Story,* was precisely the urgent need of such an adjustment, or rather of a switch-over from the old "patriarchality" to something new and more in tune with the spirit of the age. The very structure of the novel is built upon the contrast between the old and the new as experienced by the generation of the 1840's. The narrative opens with the setting of a typical old "nest of gentlefolk" on the Volga. Prosperity and affection at home, magnificent scenery around, a pleasant carefree existence—all this is in store for young Alexander Aduyev. Yet in spite of his dreamy and romantic nature, Alexander finds his idyllic home much too remote and devoid of any real prospects. Spurred on by vague ambitions, he has decided to leave for Petersburg. Preparations for his departure are in full swing, and they offer Goncharov an opportunity for drawing excellent portraits of both masters and house-serfs he had observed in the neighboring estates of the Simbirsk district.

Then we are transferred to Petersburg where the newcomer is confronted by his uncle Peter Aduyev—a man of substance and a great success not only in the civil service but also in industrial enterprise. A sober realist through and through, Aduyev senior is the opposite of his dreamy provincial nephew whom he scrutinizes with a hardly concealed mixture of pity and contempt. But he gives him a chance. In a couple of years time Alexander has adapted himself (at least externally) to the metropolitan style of life, although he makes no headway either in the civil service or in his private love-affairs. As a result, both he and his uncle come to the conclusion that he is a failure who ought to go back to his country estate and be content with it.

And this is what he does. At first he finds it pleasant to be at home once again. Yet as time goes on he becomes a prey to restlessness and boredom. There is no other alternative for him except a new flight to Petersburg. Only this time he returns to the capital with a firm resolve to follow in his uncle's footsteps and to take life just as it is. The metamorphosis becomes clear in the Epilogue where we see him (a few years later) strutting about puffed up with success and on the eve of contracting a most profitable *mariage d'argent*. Ironically enough, he displays his bourgeois pomposity and self-importance at the very time when his uncle, too, has undergone a change—in the opposite direction. Under the influence of his sensitive wife Aduyev senior begins to wonder whether his own wealth and position are really worth all the sacrifices they have cost him in the past. At the end of it all he feels distressed and unhappy like a man whose life has been wasted. The author thus concludes his novel with a secret chuckle, as if guessing what the future holds in store for Aduyev's smart nephew.

The plot of *A Common Story* is simple and unexciting, but it is told in a vivid colloquial language. Admired by critics and readers alike, this novel gave Goncharov a name to be reckoned with. Expectations aroused by it were great, and they were more than justified by his next work, *Oblomov*.

3.

Oblomov can be approached from three angles: the artistic, the psychological, and the social. As a work of art it is above all a great character study in slow motion as it were, and its background is all of a piece with the dramatis personae. The novel is based on the same motif as *A Common Story,* i.e. on the struggle between the old and the new; only here the chief character, Ilya Ilyich Oblomov, does not triumph over the "old"—he is engulfed by it instead. The process of his going to seed is the actual subject-matter of the narrative.

Like Alexander Aduyev in Goncharov's previous work, Oblomov was a product of the comfortable though parasitic existence based on serfdom. His ancestral Volga estate was a "series of picturesque, bright, and smiling landscapes" for some ten or fifteen miles around. All the needs of its owners were provided by some three hundred toiling serfs. The only snag was that after generations of such existence Oblomov's stamina and will power became utterly paralyzed. He, too, like the younger Aduyev, went to Petersburg in order to make the usual career befitting a nobleman, but he soon gave up all his ambitions and, instead of facing the demands of life, began to drift in his own placid way year in year out. With his sloppy and eternally grumbling valet Zakhar—also a product of the serfdom system but from the other end—he continued to vegetate in the Russian capital with that absolute passivity which cannot but lead to one's doom.

The very opening of the novel shows us Oblomov's predicament when, at eight in the morning, he woke up and suddenly remembered that a disturbing letter, received from his steward, had to be answered. But he postponed the answer, as he had been doing on so many previous occasions. Then he "made up his mind to get up and wash, and, after drinking tea, to think matters over, taking various things into consideration and writing them down, and altogether to go into the subject thoroughly. He lay for half an hour tormented by his decision; but afterwards he reflected that he would have time to think

after breakfast, which he would have in bed as usual, especially
since one can think just as well lying down. This was what he
did. After his morning tea he sat up and very nearly got out
of bed; looking at his slippers, he began lowering one foot
down towards them, but at once drew it back again. It struck
half-past nine."

Yet Oblomov, who was so afraid of work and indeed of the
slightest effort, drifted with a good conscience. In his opinion
it was perfectly right that, in spite of his indolence, he should
receive a regular income provided by his serfs. This privileged
parasitism, moreover, raised him in his own eyes to the status
of a superior human being. When on one occasion his valet
Zakhar likened him to other people, Oblomov was touched to
the quick and flared up with moral indignation.

"Comparing me to other people! Why, do I rush about or
work? Don't I eat enough? Do I look thin and wretched? Do
I go short of things? I should hope I have someone to wait
on me and do things for me. Thank Heaven, I've never in my
life put on my stockings myself! As though I would trouble!
Why should I? And to whom am I saying this? Haven't you
waited on me since I was a child? You know all this; you
know that I have been brought up tenderly, have never suffered
from cold or hunger or poverty, have never earned my living
or done any dirty work. So how could you bring yourself to
compare me with other people?" *

The strange thing was that Zakhar entirely agreed with his
master—agreed not only from a sense of duty but from his
innermost conviction. Such was the effect the serfdom system
had on the lower orders. What its effect on Oblomov himself
was like, is illustrated by the whole of this novel. Yet the ma-

* Quotations are taken from *Oblomov*, translated by Natalie Duddington. Every-
man's, 1932.

terial of which he was made was essentially good, as anyone
who came into contact with him was bound to feel. This was
why such a woman of character as Olga Ilyinskaya fell in love
with him and did all she could to drag him out of his sloth.
But her high demands upon him only made him the more
painfully aware of his own weakness which he was both unable and unwilling to overcome. Hence the pathos of the last
meeting between the two.

'"Why has all been wrecked?" Olga asked suddenly raising
her head. "Who laid a curse on you, Ilya? What have you
done? You are kind, intelligent, affectionate, noble . . . and
. . . you are doomed. What has ruined you? There is no name
for that evil."

'"Yes, there is," he whispered almost inaudibly.

'She looked at him questioningly, with her eyes full of tears.

'"Oblomovism," he whispered.'

And that was that. The disease which he had inherited
from his ancestors became incurable in him. Even the loyal
efforts of his enterprising friend Andrey Stolz proved as futile
as Olga's love had been before. The half-German Stolz, who
subsequently married Olga, was an efficient bourgeois counterpart of Alexander's uncle in *A Common Story*. He did his
uttermost to save his friend from "oblomovism," yet it was in
vain. Besides, when he appeared on the stage, Oblomov had
already found a new shelter under the wing of the plump lower-
middle-class widow Agafya Pshenitsyna in whose suburban
house he had taken rooms. There he felt as safe as a child in a
nursery. The more so because Agafya was unable to resist either
the spell of the child or of the gentleman in Oblomov. He
soon became her lover, had a child by her, married her eventually, but the "great thing was that all went on peacefully:
he had no lump at his heart, he never once wondered anxiously

whether he would see his landlady or not, or worried as to what she would think, what he would say to her, how he would answer her question, how she would look at him—there was nothing of the kind. He had no yearnings, no sleepless nights, no sweet or bitter tears. He sat smoking and looked at her sewing, sometimes he said something and sometimes he said nothing, and all the time he felt at peace, not needing anything, not wanting to go anywhere, as though all he needed were here. . . . It was as though some unseen hand had placed him as a precious plant in a spot where he was sheltered from the heat and the rain, and nurtured him tenderly."

In this vegetative paradise Oblomov drifted also to eternal sleep as peacefully as any mortal could wish. And with him died a whole era of Russian history, the era of serfdom, even if the aftermath it left behind proved to be of a complex and disturbing nature.

Oblomov himself is an unsurpassed portrait of the "super-fluous man" produced by the serfdom system. But he becomes also something more than that if we look upon him as a symbol of man's inherent tendency towards escapism, arrested develop-ment and the line of least resistance. On the other hand, Gon-charov asserted through the active yet somewhat abstract Stolz his faith in progress without the ironic implications one feels at the end of *A Common Story*. Some ten years later he was compelled, though, to check a great deal of his optimism, or at least to modify its perspective. This he did in his next novel *The Ravine*.

4.

The theme of this novel, too, is based on the struggle between the old and the new, between "fathers" and "children," but

with a difference. Unfortunately, there is a certain confusion
of the periods in this novel: its general background is that of
the 1840's, whereas some characters, conversations and incidents
are typical of the 1860's. Although Raisky, the main character
of *The Ravine,* is first presented to us in Petersburg, the action
of the novel takes place entirely on Raisky's Volga estate Malinovka, ruled over by one of his relations—a remarkable old
woman, commonly referred to as "granny." His two pretty
nieces, Vera and Marfinka, live there under her wing, but they
differ in character as much as did Mary and Martha of the
Gospels. As Malinovka is in the vicinity of a Volga town (Goncharov's Simbirsk), the author parades before us quite a few
of its inhabitants: officials, old-world gallants, schoolmasters,
"emancipated" women, and even an exiled revolutionary—a
certain Mark Volokhov who is under police supervision.

The central figure is at first Raisky. He is an aesthetic dilet-
tante with an abundance of talents which he is yet unable to
organize and use in a creative way. Vacillating all the time
between literature, music, painting, and even sculpture, he is
another variety of the "superfluous man" who never achieves
anything worth while. The emptiness of his life in Petersburg
makes him leave for Malinovka whose quiet and idyllic charm
is a revelation to him at first. He is equally impressed by the
"granny," as well as by the beauty of his two nieces with whom
he falls, consecutively, in love.

"Granny," with her poise and wisdom, is one of Goncharov's great creations: a positive character whom he has made
fully convincing and alive. In some respects she is a symbol of
all that was solid, good, and honest in the traditions of the old,
patriarchal Russia without being in the least unreal or stilted.
As for the two nieces entrusted to her care, Marfinka is like
"granny"—active, uninhibited, dominated by traditions, and

all of a piece with her background. Her elder sister Vera, on the other hand, wishes to go beyond the narrow if pleasant sphere of Malinovka and join the stream of the new progressive forces of the age without even suspecting the price she would have to pay for such a step.

As it happened, Vera thought she had found a representative of those new forces in the "nihilist" Volokhov. In spite of his defects, she became deeply attached to him at the very time when Raisky, too, was—rather unsuccessfully—in love with her. During these peripeties the center of gravity is transferred to Vera whose surrender to Volokhov and her violent reaction to it forms the climax of the novel. Having discovered, to her horror, that she had been in love not with a man but with a fake, she had a complete moral and physical collapse after her "fall." She began to recuperate only when she made an attempt to adjust her inner self to those values of life which were embodied in "granny." To make her recovery more certain, Goncharov even sent her another admirer in the person of Tushin: a new but not very convincing edition of Stolz—this time of pure Russian extraction. Determined to develop the progressive bourgeois-capitalist forces on what was good and solid in the old Russian traditions, Tushin thus corrected as it were the one-sided tendency to ape the West blindly and uncritically. The proper thing was to blend the best qualities of the two and thus produce something that would be Russian and European in one.

Such, approximately, was the *arrière pensée* of Goncharov himself, although here too he was concerned with characters and human relationships rather than with ideas. Needless to say, the denouement of the novel is more or less happy for all except Raisky. Feeling more "superfluous" than ever, he leaves Malinovka a sadder but hardly a much wiser man.

5.

The Ravine is colorful and richer in incident than Goncharov's other novels. But it is long, often rambling, and now and then marred by the author's outbursts against the followers of Western radicalism and materialism. He charged them with the crime of having "degraded man to a mere physical being and rejected all that was not animal-like in him." Volokhov was commonly interpreted as a malicious caricature of the radical-democratic youths of the 1860's, and this put the novel among the reactionary works of the period.

Goncharov tried to "explain" Volokhov away in his autobiographic *Better Late than Never* (written in 1870), which had, however, little effect on those who were determined to think otherwise. As if tired of the present he now preferred to look back to the past. The changes that were going on in so many branches of life were either too sudden or much too rapid for him to be followed or properly assimilated. In spite of his violent hatred of serfdom, for example, he yet felt much more at home in the Russia he had known before 1861. *My University Reminiscences* (1870), *Notes about Belinsky's Personality* (1874), *At Home* (1887), as well as his *Old-Time Servants* (1888) are all based on his recollections of the past. His critical essay, *A Million Torments* (1872) is a brilliant analysis of Griboyedov's comedy *Woe from Wit,* whereas in *A Literary Evening* (1877) he uses a narrative frame in order to air his own opinions about literary trends and theories. Finally, Goncharov's posthumous autobiographic *An Uncommon Story,* written in the second half of the 1870's and printed only in 1924, contains a savage attack on Turgenev whom he accuses of having repeatedly plagarized *The Ravine*. While writing it Goncharov evidently suffered from fits of persecution mania.

All said and done, the bulk of Goncharov's art differs from that of his contemporaries by its quiet sobriety, its common sense, and also its good-natured (almost English) sense of humor. In contrast to Dostoevsky who revelled in the irrational or the abnormal, Goncharov had a flair for what was settled and normal. A keen observer and an analyst in one, he was at his best when dealing with human characters and human relations on the one hand, and with genre pictures on the other. In his style again he combined the simplicity inherited from Pushkin with Gogol's attention to detail. The *diapason* of his creations may not be very broad, yet his work, such as it is, entitles him to a place of honor in Russian literature, while *Oblomov* links his name with the literature of the world.

CHAPTER ELEVEN

Ostrovsky

I.

There is a current opinion that in spite of her first-rate theatres, actors, and producers, Russia has failed to give a first-rate playwright to the world. A contention of this kind can be challenged, though, by the name of Alexander Ostrovsky (1823-86) who is commonly regarded by the Russians as their greatest and most typical dramatist even if he is hardly more than a name abroad. Paradoxically enough, his very "Russianness" has been so far the chief obstacle to his international reputation. His fifty odd plays, with all their colorfulness, are too remote for non-Russian audiences who would probably miss in them some of the very points Ostrovsky's own countrymen enjoy most.

This is true of Ostrovsky's early works in particular. Born and bred in the old merchant quarter in Moscow, where his father was a lawyer, he served for a number of years (from 1843 to 1851) as a clerk in the "Conscience Court" * and then in the Commercial Court of Justice. The milieu he thus moved in was one of close-fisted patriarchal tradesmen who formed a social caste, indeed a peculiar world of their own. It was here

---

* This court in which Ostrovsky worked for some two years had been established by Catherine II, and its special task was to settle all sorts of disputes between parents and their grown-up children.

above all that Ostrovsky found plenty of material—most of it untapped—for his plays.

This strange world (now a matter of the past) has been, and still is, of great interest to the Russians, but uninitiated foreign audiences might find it baffling at first. This applies even to some of those realistic plays in which Ostrovsky expanded his area so as to present the entire Russia, say, between 1840 and 1880 in terms of drama. Then there is the language. Many of his dialogues are so idiomatic and racy that even in the best of translations they cannot help losing much of their flavor. Nor should we overlook Ostrovsky's peculiar dramatic method which requires a certain adjustment on the part of a Western spectator. To begin with, Ostrovsky never cared for a closely knit, elaborate, or artificial plot. Nor was he keen on too much external action on the stage. In this respect his art was the opposite pole of what Shaw understood by "Sardoudledom." It would be equally futile to look in his works for any cheap stunts, family triangles, or bedroom scenes full of that gloating exploitation of sex and adultery which is rampant in the commercialized theatres all over the world. Like the great prose-writers of his country, Ostrovsky avoided any spectacular sensationalism for its own sake. He preferred to concentrate on a faithful but creative presentation of the *byt* (mores) and of the characters instead.

Furthermore, having come out of Belinsky's "natural school," he was unable to look upon the theatre as a mere place of amusement. The element of civilized relaxation and amusement was, of course, taken by him for granted. But he also demanded that the stage and its repertory should be one of the most important social-cultural institutions in the life of a nation, while the plays should be first of all good art. To quote his own words, each play ought to have a "strong dramatic vein, a great deal

of comicality, ardent and sincere feelings, and characters who
are strongly alive." Such was the principle he himself adhered
to. So instead of indulging in stock-in-trade artifices, he relied
on the living material at his disposal. This he organized in such
a way as to get out of it not only a maximum of contents but
also a maximum of art.

2.

Ostrovsky made his debut in 1847 when two scenes of his subsequent comedy, *It's a Family Affair* (its original title was *The
Bankrupt*), appeared in a Moscow newspaper. In this satirical
comedy Ostrovsky followed in the footsteps of Fonvizin, Griboyedov, and Gogol. Gogol's *Marriage* in particular left a mark
on it. So did the tradition of indictment.

The *byt* or setting is that of a God-fearing patriarchal merchant family with a marriageable daughter who is as stupid
as the heroine of Gogol's comedy but more mean and vulgar.
Bolshov, the head of the family and owner of a number of
prosperous shops, is rather busy. For he has just devised a
scheme of how to arrange a would-be bankruptcy and thus get
hold, with one stroke, of a big sum of money by simply not
paying his creditors for the extant supply of goods. In all this
he is helped by his equally fraudulent clerk Lazar Podkhalyuzin who has an eye on his boss's daughter Lipa. The gist of the
scheme is as follows.

Bolshov. Now is the proper time; we have a great deal of
ready cash, and all the notes have fallen due. What's the use
of waiting? You'll wait if you please, until some merchant just
like yourself, the dirty cur, will strip you bare, and then you'll
see, he'll make an agreement at ten kopeks on the ruble, and
he'll wallow in his millions, and won't think you're worth

spitting at. But you, an honorable tradesman, must just watch him, and suffer—keep on staring. Here's what I think, Lazar: to offer the creditors such a proposition as this—will they accept from me twenty-five kopeks on the ruble? What do you think?

Podkhalyuzin. Why, according to my notion, if you are going to pay at the rate of twenty-five kopeks, it would be more decent not to pay at all.

Bolshov. Why, really, that's so. You won't scare anybody by bluff; but it's better to settle the affair on the quiet. Then wait for the Lord to judge you at the second Coming. . . . Why the devil should I scratch around for pennies. I'll make one swoop, and that's an end to it! Only God give us the nerve! *

He did make the swoop. Despite his cunning he was naïve enough to trust his clerk (who, as a reward for collaboration, obtained Lipa's hand) and to settle fictitiously all his property on him. But once on horseback, the clerk forgot their amicable agreement—their "family affair" as he styled it, and even refused to save his dear father-in-law from the debtors prison.

When *It's a Family Affair* was published, in 1850, its invective against the practices of the merchant class was a pretext for the censor to ban the comedy from the stage—its first performance took place only in 1861. The author was dismissed from the civil service and put under police surveillance. Meanwhile he achieved one stage success after the other, beginning with his comedy, *A Poor Bride* (1852), into which he introduced the background of petty officials and matchmakers, a "substantial" aged wooer, and the triumph of money over affection—to crown it all. A great success was scored also by his *Poverty is no Crime* (1853). In this weaker and melodramatic comedy the merchant *byt* is displayed once more to the full. Its invective is balanced, though, by a sudden conversion of the chief char-

* *Plays by Alexander Ostrovsky,* tr. by George Rapall Noyes, Scribner, 1917.

acter, the bully Gordey Tortsov who at the end of the play becomes quite human. In another comedy, *A Lucrative Post* (1856), we are again in the world of officials, whereas in *A Protégée* (1859) Ostrovsky gives us a picture of the landed gentry with their appalling self-will and lust for tyranny. To the same period belongs his amusing trilogy of comedies about the foppish minor clerk Balzaminov and his silly mother, with a typical lower middle-class atmosphere.

It would be wrong, though, to look in Ostrovsky of that period only for indictments. For one thing, he was associated from the outset with the Slavophil sympathizers grouped round Pogodin's periodical *The Muscovite* (in which Ostrovsky's early plays were printed). The members of that group were prone, almost as a matter of duty, to idealize everything "Russian." Their mouthpiece Apollon Grigoryev was a preacher of organic rootedness in the soil and the spirit of the nation, and Ostrovsky himself found that doctrine much to his taste. True enough, his comedies, especially those dealing with the "dark kingdom" of the commercial bourgeoisie are rather gloomy. "We find in it no light, no warmth, no space," commented his critic Dobrolyubov; "the dark, narrow prison reeks of dampness and putrefaction." In spite of that, Ostrovsky's indictments were not imbued with scorn, like those of Gogol. Even when attacking, he did so because he believed in the compensatory qualities as well. In *Poverty is no Crime,* for instance, the drunkard and wastrel Lyubim Tortsov displays a wealth of inner nobility and kindness almost in the style of the proverbial *âme russe,* supported of course by an excess of folkloristic and ethnographic elements (folksongs, ritual songs, etc.). Ostrovsky, like Apollon Grigoryev, actually stood somewhere half-way between the Slavophils and the *narodniki* or

Sovfoto

ALEXANDER NIKOLAEVICH OSTROVSKY (1823-1886)

the "populists." * But he was and remained too much of an artist to sacrifice his plays to any ideology. What he cared for above all was life expressed in terms of the stage. And whenever he had to choose between the truth of life and the conventions of dramatic plots, he sided with the former. In his plays, as in life, it is often baseness, vulgarity, and rascality that triumph even at the expense of "poetic justice": in *It's a Family Affair, A Poor Bride,* or *A Protégée,* to name only a few.

Here, too, the realism which he took over from the "natural school" served him in good stead. Anyway, whatever he touches is transformed into life. He can get away even with farcical or melodramatic scenes, or with the queerest and craziest of types. In fact he is fond of people who are comic buffoons by nature (especially if there is a tragic undertone in them). And however sad the subject matter, he likes to relieve it, wherever possible, with comicality. Life, *byt,* and character—such are the three pillars of his art. They are reflected in his very language which differs not only according to the individuals but also according to the social categories they belong to. And as for dramatic contrasts, he is particularly fond of confronting the old-fashioned *samodurs* (bullies) of both sexes with tender, weak, or fatalistic characters, as he did in one of his best plays, *The Storm.*

3.

This work appeared in 1860 and marked Ostrovsky's temporary passage from comedy to drama whose realism is here charged

---

* The group gathered round Grigoryev, who in the early 1860's was connected with Dostoevsky's successive periodicals, *Vremya* ("Time") and *Epokha* ("The Epoch"), called themselves *pochvenniki,* i.e., the "rooted ones," from the noun *pochva* (the soil).

with a strong poetic and tragic atmosphere of its own. The scene of action is a merchant family in a God-forsaken Volga town, the most respected (and feared) citizen of which, the trader Dikoy, knows only one law of life: "If I choose I spare you; if I choose I trample you under foot." Not less of a tyrant is old Kabanova whose sensitive and lovely daughter-in-law Katerina is the heroine of this drama. The general cultural level is aptly summed up by the artisan Kuligin: "They are a coarse lot, sir, in our town, a coarse lot! Among the working people, sir, you'll find nothing but brutality and squalid poverty. And we've no chance, sir, of ever finding our way out of it. For by honest labor we can never earn more than a crust of bread. And everyone with money, sir, tries all he can to get a poor man under his thumb, so as to make more money again out of his working for nothing." *

Katerina, a repressed, deeply religious, and morally inhibited young beauty, has been compulsorily married to Mme. Kabanova's son whose personality is entirely squashed by his bullying mother. Suffocating in the atmosphere of that "dark kingdom," Katerina is in revolt against it, yet she is too much under the spell of her inherited taboos to take an independent step. Her husband's kindness towards her only makes things worse, especially when she has fallen in love with Dikoy's charming but spineless nephew Boris. While her husband is away, she surrenders to Boris, but the sense of guilt which gets hold of her after her husband's return is heavy enough to crush her. Pursued by her mother-in-law, by her own mental and moral spooks, even by the stormy heaven, she vainly tries to escape and in the end she drowns herself in the Volga.

Out of this simple plot Ostrovsky extracted a great deal of poetic and dramatic power. The play excels also in the beauty

* *The Storm,* translated by Constance Garnett, Duckwords, 1898.

of the language which—in Katerina's case—has the flavor of the people's language at its best. The high quality of this drama was recognized at once. No one gave it a greater praise than the critic Dobrolyubov. And in 1898 Edward Garnett summed up his impressions of the play in his preface to its first English edition in these words: *"The Storm* will repay a minute examination by all who recognize that in England to-day we have a stage without art, truth to life, or national significance. There is not a superfluous line in the play: all is drama, natural, simple, deep. There is no falsity, no forced situations, no sensational effects, none of the shallow or flashy caricatures of daily life that our heterogeneous public demands. All the reproach that lives before us in the word *theatrical* is worlds removed from *The Storm*. The people who like 'farcical comedy,' and social melodrama, and 'musical sketches' will find *The Storm* deep, forbidding, and gloomy. The critic will find it an abiding analysis of a people's temperament. The reader will find it literature."

4.

The Storm was partly connected with the "literary expedition" sent in 1856 by one of the Ministries to the Volga region in order to collect linguistic and ethnographic material. Ostrovsky, who worked mainly on the upper Volga, found the journey stimulating. He himself asserted that the "best school for any artistic talent is the study of one's own people whose recreation in terms of art is the finest emporium for one's activities." Following up this principle, he cultivated his affinity with the people and made ample use of their idioms, sayings and proverbs in his writings, or in the very titles of his plays: *Poverty is no Crime, Don't Sit Down in Somebody Else's Sledge, Every*

Wise Man Can Be a Fool, Sin and Sorrow are Common to All,
etc. No wonder Apollon Grigoryev claimed him to be a
pochvennik, a man of the soil.

A further outcome of Ostrovsky's journey on the Volga was
a cycle of historical dramas in verse. Most of them are about
the "troubled period" (1595-1613) and with the Volga setting,
but their pathos often reminds one of the cheap patriotic plays
by Kukolnik—a contemporary of Gogol.* None of these
"Chronicles" was as successful on the stage as was his dramatized fairy tale in verse, *The Snow Maiden* (1873). Inspired
by the folklore (and to some extent by Shakespeare's *Mid-
summer Night's Dream*), it is a kind of Rousseauesque-Slav-
ophil idealization of the people. Rimsky-Korsakov used it later
for his famous opera under the same title.

In spite of these digressions, Ostrovsky never forgot that his
proper medium was the satirical comedy of manners, or just
"scenes of life." His favorite themes remained those about the
merchant *byt,* yet his attacks on the decaying landed gentry
continued and became most conspicuous in his *Forest* (1871)
and *Wolves and Sheep* (1875)—the two comedies which have
fully inherited the spirit of Fonvizin's *The Young Hopeful.*
It is significant that the principal character in each of them is
an autocratic woman bullying a meek and helplessly bewildered
human "sheep" as a matter of course. "Wolves" and "sheep"
actually became one of Ostrovsky's favorite dramatic contrasts.
His "sheep" may be snatched, now and then, from disaster in
the nick of time, but only after they have been thoroughly
mauled and mangled by the "wolves."

After the great reforms of 1861, the Russian merchant caste
was being gradually replaced by industrialists, speculators, or

---

* Ostrovsky also provided the librettos for two operas on historical themes: one by
Tchaikovsky and the other by Serov.

simply by reckless financial gamblers of a more up-to-date type. These, too, figure in Ostrovsky's plays: in *Easy Money* (1870) for example, in *Late Love* (1874), *Dowerless* (1879), etc. Peasants qua peasants, however, are hardly noticeable in his works, although he wrote two comedies about the people's *byt: Do not Live as You Want to* (1854) and *A Lively Spot* (1865). Nor does he portray any memorable representatives of the intelligentsia proper. On the other hand, he wrote a few plays about actors, two of whom emerge—very much apropos—in *The Forest*. The comedy, *Talents and Adorers* (1882), and the somewhat melodramatic "Volkstück," *Guilty without Guilt* (1884), are about the strolling actors in the provinces.

Towards the end of his life Ostrovsky's dramatic vein began to decline.* As if aware of this, he increased his practical work on behalf of the theatre instead. One of his cherished dreams was to establish in Moscow a People's Theatre, accessible to the masses yet at the same time preserving a very high artistic level. After having been rather shabbily treated by the government for years, he became, in 1885, director of the Moscow State Theatres and of the School of Dramatic Art. It was an appointment according to his heart's desire. But just when he was beginning to develop his new activities, he died on June 2nd, 1886.

5.

The first thing which is likely to strike any student of Ostrovsky's plays is that practically all of them, with the exception of his "Chronicles" and *The Snow Maiden,* can be classed as a combination of the comedy of manners with critical realism.

* A mention should also be made of Ostrovsky's translations which ranged from Plautus to Shakespeare (*Antony and Cleopatra, The Taming of the Shrew*), and from Cervantes to Goldoni.

His satire, though, was not an aim in itself (as it was in Gogol's *Revizor*), but rather a by-product of the *byt* which was his main concern. For him *byt* was more important than either the plot or any psychological disquisitions. It was within its frame that he tackled—Russian fashion—all sorts of moral and social values. And however much he criticized at times, he still preserved his broad common sense and, together with it, also his faith in man and life.

Last but not least, Ostrovsky is the only significant Russian author who gave the whole of his life to the stage. His manner and technique put him somewhere half-way between Gogol and Chekhov. Like Chekhov he often replaced the plot just by a sequence of scenes or pictures taken straight from life: "scenes of merchant life," "scenes of Moscow life," "scenes of village life." The first dramatic sketch he ever wrote was called *A Picture of Family Happiness* (1847). Like Chekhov again he preferred the dialogue and the "atmosphere" to purely external action. Yet despite his technical innovations, he preserved such an old-fashioned expedient as the monologue. His practice of making the names of his dramatis personae suggestive of their inner defects or virtues is also a remnant which goes back (via Gogol) to Fonvizin and the 18th century drama.

Always attracted by life in terms of the stage, Ostrovsky is fond of simple characters (even when these are a bit "crazy") and of simple situations. In this respect he is worlds apart from the grotesque complications typical of another famous Russian dramatist of that period, Alexander Sukhovo-Kobylin (1817-1903) whose drama *The Process (Delo)* is one of the cruellest indictments of bureaucracy ever written for the stage.

The novelty of Ostrovsky's plays demanded of course a new technique of acting—a technique based entirely on truth to life. This style soon found a galaxy of fine interpreters, such as Sadovsky, Martynov, Lensky, Ermolova, Varlamov—right down to the members of Stanislavsky's Moscow Arts Theatre. In the same way Ostrovsky left his imprint on a number of dramatists who came after him: Chekhov, Naidyonov, Gorky, and others. As for his own plays, they have been and still are the mainstay of Russian theatres big and small. It is only fair to say that in present-day Russia there are two great playwrights whose popularity remains—for different reasons, though—unchallenged. One is Shakespeare, and the other Ostrovsky.

CHAPTER TWELVE

Dostoevsky and Tolstoy

I.

When in the 1860's and 1870's Russian fiction reached its peak, it became clear that even apart from a considerable novelty of material, it differed, or tended to differ, from European fiction as a whole. What must have astonished many a Western reader was the spaciousness, the depth, the frankness, as well as the moral earnest, with which the Russian authors tackled the problems of man and life. From Gogol onwards, Russian literature showed what might be called an instinctive tendency to go beyond mere entertainment or even beyond "mere art." Besides, in a country where literature was the only realm in which it was still possible to express—at least by using the "Aesop language"—that freedom of mind and spirit which was banned from the ordinary walks of life, the writers were being looked upon not only as artists of the word, but also as guides and teachers in a deeper sense. They were supposed to know and to understand life better than ordinary mortals; so it was their duty to impart this knowledge to others in an appropriate shape and form. No wonder that many a Russian novel showed a propensity to combine fiction with moral, social, and political ideas not necessarily at the expense of art but as one of the vital ingredients of art itself.

It is at this point, however, that a philosophic novel can easily become a mere philosophizing novel of a didactic kind. For, in spite of their resemblance on the surface, the two are poles apart. In a didactic-philosophizing novel the characters have no existence apart from, and independently of, the author. They serve above all as pegs upon which the author hangs his own attitudes and ideas—usually with foregone conclusions. Instead of being embodied in the characters, the ideas are only stuck on them. The characters themselves thus resemble cleverly manipulated puppets which may look very lively at times without being really alive.

Quite a few "philosophic" tales—so popular in the eighteenth century—can serve as illustrations. A brilliant modern equivalent of the same didactic kind is Bernard Shaw's *The Black Girl in Search of God,* the pedigree of which goes at least as far back as Voltaire's *Candide.* In a true philosophic novel, however, ideas are embodied in the characters organically, i.e. as part and parcel of their inner lives and destinies, no matter whether the author himself agrees with them or not. But no sooner has be begun pulling the strings than the game is up. The same applies, and even more obviously, to dramatic works. There is a world of difference between a lively dramatization of a public lecture and a drama of thoughts and ideas clashing with each other on equal terms and, as it were, outside the author's own sympathies and antipathies. All this is not new. Yet it may be worth mentioning in order to point out the difference between Shaw and Ibsen, for example; or to take a more complicated case, between Tolstoy and Dostoevsky.

A comparison between these two greatest representatives of Russian fiction has become somewhat trite since D. Merezhkovsky's pioneering study,* published in 1901. Others, notably the philosopher Lev Shestov and the novelist V. Veresayev, have

* *Tolstoy and Dostoevsky.*

explored some further aspects along similar lines. Still, the fact remains that the very differences between Tolstoy and Dostoevsky are so complementary that it is almost impossible to talk of one without mentioning the other. Even as artists, supreme as each of them may be in his own sphere, they seem to stand at two opposite poles. Yet whereas Dostoevsky succeeded in creating the type of a modern philosophic novel at its best, Tolstoy, despite his literary genius, failed in this particular genre at least in his later works, since he was either unwilling or unable to detach his main characters (the mouthpieces of his ideas) from himself. In this respect his narratives and novels, however interesting in their own right, are often didactic and philosophizing as distinct from the philosophic novels of Dostoevsky.

2.

One of the principal reasons may be the fact that in Tolstoy there was a gap between the great artist and the not so great moralist and thinker, whereas in Dostoevsky thought and art were never quite severed or differentiated. Nor were art and psychology. It was above all as the greatest psychological novelist of our times that he became read all the world over. And for good reason. For, long before Freud, he had not only explored but illustrated (in a creative manner) man's unconscious mind and shown the irrational roots even of our rational behavior. What he was mainly interested in as artist was the riddle of human personality and its place in the scheme of the universe. He was not in the least concerned with the psychology of textbooks. His realm was that borderline where the normal and the abnormal elements of man's psyche meet and where their interactions may lead to most unexpected contrasts, conflicts, and crises in the face of which one's rational self may be utterly helpless. But this was not the whole of his task. To quote from a work of mine:*

"Dostoevsky introduced new themes and vistas into litera-ture. He also replaced the leisurely broadness of the manor novelists Goncharov, Turgenev, and Tolstoy by a quickened pace and by a dramatic tension hardly paralleled in modern letters. An epileptic, an unstable and unbalanced city dweller himself, he was anxious to unravel the chaotic urbanized man of our age—the man whose most secret inner problems and contradictions he tried to explore to the end. With all this he combined a lack of restraint; a metaphysical attitude towards evil as one of the most mysterious and disturbing problems of existence; and a spiritual thirst directed towards 'the city of God' for which he fought all the more desperately the more his profoundly religious temperament was being undermined by his own skepticism or even latent nihilism. It was the clash be-tween the two opposite tendencies that drove him all the more to his own daring psychological experiments during which he obliterated the line between the rational and the irrational, between the normal and the abnormal. Deliberately, he placed his heroes into the most unusual situations and conditions in order to see how they would react and how much doubt and travail their spirit could endure. He thus hoped to extract the secret of man and life from the exceptional and the abnormal rather than from the normal. The French author, Melchior de Voguë, called him the 'Shakespeare of the lunatic asylum.' But such a statement is too sweeping to be applied to Dostoev-sky literally. The kernel of his writings is and remains not that of an alienist but of a philosophic seeker in the deeply tragic sense of this word."

* *Dostoevsky*, Macmillan, 1946.

3.

It is hardly necessary to enumerate all those circumstances which contributed to the formation of Dostoevsky's type of mind. They are known to every student of literature. One ought to point out however at least three facts of his early life which may shed some light on the complexities of his work and character.

As a boy he seems to have conceived an instinctive loathing for his father—a hospital doctor and a miser who was murdered by his own serfs. Dostoevsky's chronic "guilt complex" may have arisen from his involuntary satisfaction at his father's death. Owing to his own extravagant nature, the young Dostoevsky—an engineer by training—must have passed through penury and all sorts of personal difficulties and humiliations even before his first novels *Poor Folk* (1846) and *The Double* (1847), both of them influenced by Gogol, made his name generally known. Those were the years when he stood close to the circle of Belinsky and also became a member of the frankly revolutionary group of young atheists and followers of Fourier, organized by a certain Petrashevsky. Denounced by an *ageant provocateur,* the members of the group were arrested. After months of imprisonment and investigation they were sentenced to death. In December 1849 they all marched to the place of execution, but at the last moment they were reprieved and sent to Siberia instead. Here Dostoevsky spent over eight years: four among the most hardened criminals in the penal settlement at Omsk, and four in a line-battalion at Semipalatinsk on the Mongolian border. In 1859 he was allowed to return to European Russia where, after an interval of some ten years, he resumed his literary activities on a big scale.

The strange thing was that the first two narratives he wrote when freed again, *The Village Stepanchikovo* and *The Uncle's Dream* (in 1859), do not provide a single hint of the terrible experiences the author must have gone through in Siberia. They are both boisterously funny and their grotesque character makes one think of Gogol and Dickens. The influence of Dickens—this time the humanitarian Dickens—is felt also in his first long novel, *The Insulted and the Injured,* which appeared (1861) in the short-lived periodical *Time* ("Vremya") edited by Dostoevsky and his brother Michael. The novel contains some remarkable psychological passages—his analysis of the "injured" child Nelly, of the cynic Valkovsky, or of the self-divided Alyosha; but the narrative as a whole only proves that Dostoevsky was still groping for the right kind of creative self-expression. A greater work was his *Notes from the House of the Dead* (1862), describing his life at the penal settlement. His remarks about the criminal mind, which he knew from personal observations, are invaluable. And the conclusion he arrived at was new indeed for that period, namely that great criminals are often endowed with unusual will-power and talents both of which have gone wrong. "For I must speak my thoughts as to this: the hapless fellows there were perhaps the strongest and, in one way or another, the most gifted of our people. There was all that strength of body and mind lost. Whose fault is that?"

He found his true direction at last in his *Notes from the Underworld,* published in 1864. This work can serve as a key not only to his mentality but to his work as a whole. It is decidedly a philosophic-polemical narrative directed against the positivist utilitarians of the 1860's (Chernyshevsky, Dobrolyubov, etc.). But the ideas expressed in it are first of all the outburst of a frustrated individual—of a nobody who has been rejected by life and by society and whose only compensation is his jeering criticism of all and sundry. For in jeering at them, he has at least a temporary illusion of his own superiority over those whom he ridicules in so scathing a manner.

The thing which Dostoevsky pointed out in this work was the irreconcilable contrast between the man of the statistics and the same man as a living human being. For statistics, even for utilitarian statistics aiming at the "greatest happiness of the greatest number," each individual is interchangeable with other individuals in the same manner as standardized articles are interchangeable with each other. In reality, however, each living individual is unique, and his personal fate and suffering cannot be interchanged with anybody else. Still less can they serve as a means, as mere manure for the happiness and harmony of some future generations—harmony and happiness which he himself will never share. The very idea of such a standardized and compulsory Millennium, established by science and reason, whether on communist or any other lines, is hateful to Dostoevsky's man from the underworld.

"Does not reason err in estimating what is advantageous? May it not be that man occasionally loves something besides prosperity? May it not be that he loves *adversity*? Certainly there are times when man *does* love adversity, and love it passionately. Man is a frivolous creature, and like a chess-player, cares more for the process of attaining his goal than for the goal itself. Besides, who knows (for it never does to be sure) that the aim which man strives for upon earth may not be contained in this ceaseless continuation of the process of attainment—that is to say, in the process which is comprised in the living of life rather than in the aim itself, which, of course, is contained in the formula that twice two make four? Yet, gentlemen, this formula is not life at all: it is only the beginning of death! At all events, men have always been afraid to think that twice two make four, and I am afraid of it too! . . . I should not be surprised if amidst all this order and regularity of the future, there should arise suddenly, from some quarter or another, some gentleman of low-born—or, rather, of retrograde and cynical demeanor, who, setting his arms akimbo, should say to you all: 'How now, gentlemen? Would it not be a good thing if, with one consent, we were to kick all this solemn wisdom to the four winds, to send those logarithms to the devil, and to begin to live our lives again according to our stupid whims? 'Yet this woud be nothing: the really shameful part of the business would be that this gentleman would find a goodly number of adherents. Such is man's way. . . . Whence do the savants have it that man needs a normal, a virtuous will? What, in particular, has made these pundits imagine that what man needs is a will which is acutely alive to man's interests? Why, what man most needs is an *independent* will—no matter what the cost of such independence of volition, nor what it may lead to!" *

The whole of Nietzsche's subsequent philosophy of Will to Power could be derived from such a premise. But Dostoevsky did not stop at this stage of mere individual self-assertion. He saw only too well that such a stage by itself is also a blind-alley and a most destructive one when it does not take man beyond himself. The starting point made here by Dostoevsky thus invariably led to further questions: *What* is that individual self which insists so passionately on its own "independent volition"? How and in the name of what values could this self go beyond

---

* All quotations in this chapter are taken from Mrs. Constance Garnett's translation of Dostoevsky's works. Heinemann.

its own narrow limits and fulfil its destiny in the truest sense? What, then, is its ultimate destiny and meaning? Or is it devoid of any meaning at all?

These were the "existentialist" problems Dostoevsky set out to tackle in his great novels, *Crime and Punishment* (1866), *The Idiot* (1868-69), *The Possessed* (1871-72), *A Raw Youth* (1875), and *The Brothers Karamazov* (1879-80). And, let it be stressed once again, he tackled them not as a mere thinker but as a great creative artist.

4.

Raskolnikov, the hero of *Crime and Punishment,* is a talented but frustrated youth—frustrated by poverty as well as by his own unadaptable character. Yet in his self-will he goes much further than the man from the "underworld." Full of spite and resentment, he divides (like Nietzsche after him) the whole of mankind into two categories: the "herd" whose business it is to obey, and a few exceptional individuals—such as Napoleon— who are clever and strong enough to be a law unto themselves. As a votary of science and reason, Raskolnikov rejects the very possibility of any absolute standard of good and evil; for such a standard could have been given only by an absolute Being, i.e. by God, in whom he does not and cannot believe. Since God does not exist, all values of good and evil are relative, man-made, and therefore fictitious. There is no such thing as either virtue or crime in itself. Nor is there any higher meaning in our existence. Man is nothing but a casual bubble produced by the blind laws of nature, and if he has become aware of this, why should he not take his destiny into his own hands, ignore the laws and live according to his own whims, or his own "will to power."

FEODOR MIKHAIOVICH DOSTOEVSKY (1821-1881)

Working from this premise, Raskolnikov yet remained something of a Hamlet. He was not quite sure whether he belonged to the exceptions or to the "herd." So he decided to prove to himself that he was strong and daring enough for an exceptional individual (who was "beyond good and evil") by deliberately breaking one of the fundamental laws, i.e. by murdering an old pawnbroker woman. He did it so cleverly that there was not the slightest evidence against him. Yet no sooner had the crime been committed than something strange began to happen. It should be remembered that his rational and logical reason, with its truth that all values of good and evil are relative and fictitious, gave him its full sanction to wipe out such a stingy "louse." It was only after the murder that his irrational self, with its own peculiar truth, reacted in such a way as to inwardly cut him off from all living beings, his mother and sister included. He had murdered the old woman physically only, but he himself was murdered spiritually by her. And he was now aware of it. It was not repentance but a complete inner vacuum—the vacuum of a corpse—that made him so frantically restless after the crime. In the end it drove him to a voluntary confession and surrender to the authorities, in spite of the fact that even after he had made such a decision, he was logically not in the least aware of being a criminal.

"Crime? What crime?" he cried in a sudden fury. "That I killed a vile, noxious insect, an old pawnbroker woman, of use to no one! Killing her was atonement for forty sins. She was sucking the life out of the poor people. Was that a crime? I am not thinking of it and am not thinking of expiating it, and why are you rubbing it in on all sides? I am further than ever from seeing that it was a crime."

Yet he gave himself up, and accepted the punishment (Siberia) as a last hope that through suffering he might perhaps alleviate the *inner* punishment his crime had inflicted upon him, and be resurrected to life like Lazarus from the tomb. In short, his rational self had one truth, and his irrational self had another. And there was no bridge between the two.

5.

It was the nature of the irrational that Dostoevsky tried to probe further into when he wrote *The Idiot*. The title of this novel is ironical in so far as from a rational angle its hero Prince Myshkin, helpless and naïve as a child, may actually resemble an idiot. But he is all the stronger on the irrational plane, where his intuitive clairvoyance abounds in what might be called flashes of genius. Or as one of the heroines (Aglaya) puts it: "Even if your surface mind be a little affected, yet your real mind is far better than all theirs put together. Such a mind as they have never dreamed of, because really, there are two minds —the kind that matters and the kind that does not matter."

Myshkin is amply provided with the second, but not with the first. He is also morally as clear as a crystal without in the least being improbable. What may diminish the value of his sexual morality is, however, the fact that according to all sorts of allusions, he is physically unable to be anything but "pure" in this respect. Otherwise he is perhaps one of the few Christ-like personalities in modern literature, although he remains much too passive, and therefore at the mercy of circumstances. Moreover, like the majority of Dostoevsky's heroes, he too is self-divided. His inability to make a definite choice between Nastasya and Aglaya becomes his undoing. After Nastasya has run away from him only to be murdered by the semi-mad Rogozhin, Myshkin is deprived of the last remnants of his rational mind and ends by becoming an idiot—this time a real one.

The Idiot gives the impression as if the author had too much to say to put it all into a single novel. It does not take long, though, before one discovers that here too he was preoccupied with Raskolnikov's dilemma. The character who links up *The Idiot* with *Crime and Punishment* is the consumptive nihilist Ippolit—an "enlightened" youth of the 1860's. Believing neither in God nor in any higher meaning of man's existence, he sees in the world but a kind of "dumb monster" which crushes human beings and makes them suffer mechanically, blindly, without even being able to take notice of it. More uncompromising than Raskolnikov, Ippolit refuses to accept life on such terms and sees in suicide the only logical and psychological answer. "If I had the power to prevent my own birth, I should certainly never have consented to accept existence under such ridiculous conditions. However, I have the power to end my existence."

We will find the same conclusion turned into practice by Kirillov in Dostoevsky's next book, *The Possessed*—one of the most gruesome and cruel novels ever written. Irreligiosity, destruction, and self-destruction meet in this novel as in a focus, and all three prove to be interdependent. One of the Russian critics (Volynsky) referred to *The Possessed* as the "book of great wrath"—directed against those ultra-radicals of the 1860's whose revolutionary activities could have been summed up as destruction for destruction's sake. But in attacking them, Dostoevsky went much further than Goncharov in *The Ravine*. He tried to unveil—whether rightly or wrongly—the metaphysical roots of the revolution as mere will to destruction originating in a nihilistic (i.e. irreligious) view of life. Both

Stravrogin and Peter Verkhovensky make out of Raskolnikov's fundamental dilemma some further practical conclusions, but on a much bigger scale. If life has no higher sense, then it should either be finished with, or else turned into a series of daring experiments upon one's own fate and that of others, no matter how much bloodshed and how many crimes such a sport should involve. It is all a part of that orgy of destruction which has become with them a demoniacal urge, an end in itself, and finally an obsession whose social consequences are incalculable.

"Listen," Peter Verkhovensky raves in front of Stravrogin, "first of all we will make an upheaval. We shall penetrate to the peasantry. . . . On all sides we see vanity puffed up out of all proportion, brutal, monstrous appetites. . . . Do you know how many we shall catch by little ready-made ideas? Oh! this generation has only to grow up. One or two generations of vice are essential now; monstrous, abject vice by which a man is transformed into a loathsome cruel reptile. That's what we need. And what's more, a little fresh blood, that we may get accustomed to it . . . We will proclaim destruction. . . . We will set fires going . . . We'll set legends going . . . There's going to be such an upset as the world has never seen before. . . . Russia will be overwhelmed by darkness, the earth will weep for its old gods. Listen, Stravrogin, to level the mountains is a fine idea, not an absurd one. Down with culture! The thirst for culture is an aristocratic thirst. . . . We will make use of drunkenness, slander, spying; we will stifle every genius in its infancy. We'll reduce all to a common denominator. Complete equality! Only the necessary is necessary: that's the motto of the whole world henceforward."

Starting with absolute license (mistaken for freedom), revolution on these terms is thus bound to end in that absolute tyranny of which Dostoevsky had warned his generation when there were as yet hardly any signs of the shape of things to come. One of the nihilists, Shigalyov, gives a complete program of such a totalitarian tyranny, while Kirillov, starting again with Raskolnikov's premise, arrives at self-destruction as the only logical conclusion. "If God exists all is His will and from His will I cannot escape! If not, it is all my will and I am bound to show self-will. . . . Because all will has become mine." The acme of his own self-will is however self-destruction as a protest against a world in which he sees only mockery and a universal "vaudeville of the devils." And the alternative? Dostoevsky explored both sides of the problem in his last and greatest novel, *Brothers Karamazov*.

6.

Before embarking upon this masterpiece, Dostoevsky wrote *A Raw Youth*—a subtle study of an adolescent's mind and at the same time a compendium of problems, some of which were of topical interest to his contemporaries. Intelligentsia and the people, Russia and Europe, culture and the elite, "fathers" and "children"—all this comes out in the conversations between the fastidious aristocrat Versilov and his illegitimate son (by a peasant woman) Arkady. The main theme of the novel is the gradual adjustment between the two. Whereas Arkady is all fermentation, Versilov is an unusually mature yet self-divided character, unable to come to terms with himself or with life. But after a series of hectic peripeties and crises it all ended in a conciliatory note. Some of the problems indicated here were carried over to *Brothers Karamazov*.

In this book we see first of all two generations facing one another: the dissolute and morally disintegrating old Karamazov, and his children. Mitya, his eldest son, has inherited his father's formidable *libido,* but in a somewhat nobler aspect, however chaotic his impulses may be. In Ivan the father's vitality has become transmuted into a powerful intellect—disturbed by an instinctive hatred for his parent, as well as by Hamlet-like broodings and doubts of all and everything. Cold and aloof, he is incapable either of Mitya's spontaneous generosity or of the equally spontaneous human sympathy typical of his youngest brother Alyosha. In Alyosha all has been sublimated into spirit, and he himself is a novice living in a near-by monastery. Then there is their illegitimate half-brother Smerdyakov—a rancorous physical and moral cripple who suffers from epilepsy and is employed as a flunkey in Karamazov's household. It should also be pointed out that Ivan and Alyosha were sons of Karamazov's second wife and therefore inherited certain tendencies different from those of Mitya—an offspring of the first marriage.

The framework of the novel, which is crowded with incident and characters, rests above all on the rivalry between Mitya and his father for the favors of the elusive *femme fatale* Grushenka: a rivalry in which hatred between father and son comes out in all its ugliness, breeding scandal in the gossipy provincial town. At an opportune moment Smerdyakov takes advantage of the clash between the two and contrives to murder the old *roué* (whose hidden money he steals) in such a way that all the circumstances point to Mitya as being the actual murderer. Mitya is arrested, tried, and sentenced to penal servitude in Siberia. While he is in jail, both he and the woman he loves undergo a profound inner change. Far from feeling rancorous about the injustice done to him, he accepts his punishment as a path towards a new life—better and cleaner than the life he has known before.

Of particular interest are, however, all sorts of inner relationships and conflicts so conspicuous in this novel. Ivan and Smerdyakov, for instance, were like the two opposite poles of humanity, yet for some curious reason they were subconsciously drawn together. Ivan sensed in the sneaking and scheming epileptic the same hatred for the old Karamazov which was one of his own secrets. He also suspected that Smerdyakov would be capable of murdering the sensuous old "reptile," if given some encouragement. So he infected Smerdyakov with the ideas of "beyond good and evil," until the flunkey grasped only too well the reason why "all things are lawful." Ivan thus indirectly helped to murder his own father. For after the crime had been committed, Ivan knew that the murderer was not Mitya but Smerdyakov. Smerdyakov actually confessed to Ivan all he had done and even handed to him the old Karamazov's money he had stolen during the murder. For he, too, was undergoing a reaction he had never expected to take place.

"I did have an idea of beginning a new life with that money in Moscow or, better still, abroad. I did dream of it, chiefly because 'all things are lawful.' That was quite right what you taught me, for you talked a lot to me about that. For if there's no everlasting God, there's no such thing as virtue, and there's no need of it. You were right there. So that's how I looked at it."

The inner reaction in Smerdyakov was so terrible that in the end he found the only escape from it by hanging himself. But Ivan, too, had his share in it. Although he had been only a theoretical accomplice, he now experienced the same kind of restlessness and punishment *from within* which Raskolnikov had felt after the murder. And, like Raskolnikov, he, too, decided to confess everything and give himself up, while yet not believing in such things as crime and virtue.

This is why his *alter ego* (the devil he sees in delirium) keeps taunting him: "You are going to perform an act of heroic virtue, and you don't believe in virtue, that's what tortures you and makes you angry, that is why you are so vindictive . . . Why do you go meddling, if your sacrifice is of no use to anyone? Because you don't know yourself why you go! Oh! you'd give a great deal to know yourself why you go! That's the riddle for you."

Self-divided as he is, Ivan is drawn (for entirely different reasons) also to Alyosha. It is to him that he pours out some of his most secret and most painful doubts and ideas about man, God, the universe, and the future of mankind. For Ivan, who is a kind of Russian Hamlet, is intelligent enough to realize that human intellect, such as it is, is incompetent either to affirm or to deny the existence of God and those ultimate values which depend on the solution of this problem. But even while admitting the possibility of God's existence, he repudiates Him and rebels against Him for moral reasons, i.e. because he feels profoundly disgusted on account of all the suffering and injustice inflicted upon the world. Having mentioned some revolting cases of cruelty inflicted upon innocent children in particular, he exclaims with that kind of moral indignation which goes far beyond mere morality.

"Without suffering, I am told man could not have existed on earth, for he could not know good and evil," Ivan complains to Alyosha. "Why should he know that diabolical good and evil when it costs so much? The whole of knowledge is not worth a child's suffering. What comfort is it to me that there are none guilty and that cause follows effect simply and directly and that I know it. I must have justice or I will destroy myself. . . . Surely I haven't suffered simply that I, my crimes and sufferings may manure the soil of the future harmony of somebody else. . . . If I must suffer for the eternal harmony, what have children to do with it? It's beyond all comprehension why they should suffer, and why they should pay for harmony. Why should they too furnish material to enrich the soil of the harmony of the future? And if it really is true that they must share responsibility for their father's crimes, such a truth is not of this world and is beyond my comprehension . . . I don't want harmony. From love of humanity I don't want it. I would rather be left with my unavenged suffering and unsatisfied indignation, *even if I were wrong*. Besides, too high a price is asked for harmony; it is beyond our means to pay so much to enter on it. And so I hasten to give back my entrance ticket, and if I am an honest man I am bound to give it back as soon as possible. And that I am doing. It is not God I don't accept, only I most respectfully return Him my ticket."

And as for Ivan's conception of mankind's future, he unfolded in his *Legend of the Grand Inquisitor* such an appalling picture of totalitarian humanity, based on a pre-fabricated ideology for the sake of man's compulsory "happiness" and "harmony," as to outdo any nightmare. Ivan's tragedy was that he had an insatiable secret thirst for faith, for religion, which he could not accept—worse: which he refused to accept because of his own intellectual honesty. Yet without religion, that is without faith in some higher transcendental values as well as a meaning of life, he could not and would not exist, since to his awakened consciousness existence, such as he saw it, seemed utterly meaningless and idiotic. So where was the outlet? Once again we see the clash between the rational and the irrational truths in man's consciousness, without any point of contact between the two. Even an intuitive acceptance of some "higher" truth may only be an escape from logic into one's own wishful thinking and by no means a guarantee that such a truth really exists. Or can the idea of God, instilled in man's consciousness as an everlasting postulate, lead one to the conclusion that there must be something behind it? Ivan does not know the answer. Nor does Dostoevsky, in spite of the religious outlet which he so forcibly imposed upon himself.

A counterpoise to Ivan Karamazov is Alyosha's spiritual guide Father Zosima. Dostoevsky put into this *pater Seraphicus* some of his own ideas about Christianity which may not tally with any official denomination under that name. Zosima's Christian religion does not preach medieval (or any other) asceticism. Its ideal is that fullness and joy of existence which can only be attained by a religious conception based on sympathy with all life. For only by recognizing a higher sense in the whole of humanity and of the cosmos can we also accept and love them. Otherwise a sensitive uncompromising consciousness is bound to repudiate life itself. To repeat Zosima's words: "God took seeds from different worlds and sowed them on this earth, and his garden grew up and everything came up that could come up only through the feeling of its contact with other mysterious worlds. If that feeling grows weak or is destroyed in you, the heavenly growth will die in you. Then you will be indifferent to life and will even grow to hate it."

This is only a very brief illustration of Dostoevsky's novels from the philosophic angle. The same applies to quite a few of his stories and short novels, although in most psychology or pathology—told with an amusing inflection—prevails: in *The Eternal Husband,* for instance, or in *The Gambler.* The surprising thing is not only that all the thoughts and ideas in Dostoevsky's novels spring from the innermost experience of the characters concerned, but that all the pros and cons are pitted in them against each other on equal terms. For Dostoevsky too, like Ivan Karamazov, was a skeptic and a clandestine

unbeliever who was passionately anxious to overcome his skepticism and to arrive at least at some certainty. But as Ivan's
nightmare devil aptly put it: "Till the secret is revealed, there
are two sorts of truth for me—one, their truth, yonder, which
I know nothing about so far, and the other my own. And there
is no knowing which will turn out the better."

7.

Dostoevsky felt at home most of all in that border region
where rational and irrational elements mingle, and where "all
contradictions exist side by side." Hence there was no gap
between Dostoevsky's thought and his art. In Tolstoy, on the
other hand, the two seemed to be curiously severed. No one in
his right senses will deny Tolstoy's great artistic genius. But,
as has already been pointed out by Merezhkovsky, his is the
clairvoyance of the body and of the emotional sphere as distinct
from Dostoevsky's clairvoyance of the spirit. More than any
other author, Tolstoy knows how to project into his characters
all that touches upon the full-blooded instinctive, physical, and
emotional side of man. Here he goes to the very root of things
with that sureness of integrity which cannot but amaze even
the most exacting of readers. It was prominent in his first effort,
Childhood (1852), in his short novel, *The Cossacks* (1861),
and reached the height of its plastic and analytical power combined in his two central works, *War and Peace* (1862-69) and
Anna Karenina (1875-77). At the same time, his propensity to
moralize, conspicuous in most of his early stories and particularly in *The Cossacks,* was always there—ready to interrupt the
artist, to warn him, or even to interfere with him in a rather
perplexing manner. However much Tolstoy the man was in
love with life, the reasoning and didactic moralist in him de-

manded a meaning of life, or rather the meaning of death of which Tolstoy was so afraid. Yet his very fear of death was only another aspect of his truly pagan love of life. He felt the physical and metaphysical horror of death to a well-nigh incredible degree. So he entrenched himself from this irrational horror in his moralizing reason which was on the look-out for a "rational" explanation and justification of the fact of death.

In Tolstoy's early works one can detect his method of showing in a parallel manner the various aspects of one and the same dilemma in such a way as to leave one in no doubt as to which of them is preferable, without exactly forcing the intended issue. His story, *Three Deaths,* is an example. It consists of three parallel pictures of death, each of them almost independent of the other, but differing in the amount of the physical and moral torment involved. In the end it is quite clear what kind of death, and on what conditions, is least painful and therefore preferable. The reader's conclusion is of course expected to coincide with that of Tolstoy, even though it may not be unduly insisted upon by the author. The short novel, *Family Happiness,* gives us a parallel analysis of a young woman's love before and after her marriage to a much older husband. And again the reader is led to decide "independently" why non-sexual motherly love is preferable to the more passionate love in the first part of the novel. In *War and Peace* there are a number of themes, developing parallel with each other, or else intertwining as in a symphony, but for our purpose a comparison between the two principal seekers in the novel, Prince Andrey and Pierre Bezukhov, is of importance. Both of them represent the two contending doubles in Tolstoy's own personality; yet he knew how to integrate, as far as possible, their quest with their total inner life and make it psychologically convincing.* He coped with the same task, though less objectively, when dealing with the torments of Levin in *Anna Karenina*. The antagonism between "ideology" and psychology which came to a head after his poignant book *My Confession* (1879), or after his so-called conversion, is here clearly anticipated. One feels that at the back of it all his moral consciousness kept watching, censoring, and shaking the rod, until at last Tolstoy was on the defensive against his own instincts of the "flesh," which he began to disparage so vehemently precisely because he was afraid of them. His moralizing was a continuous struggle with and against himself. Tolstoy the moralist thus came to loggerheads with Tolstoy the man and the artist both of whom had to yield repeatedly in order to make way for the preacher. Having reduced the meaning of life only to its *moral* meaning in the sense of the "improved" Sermon on the Mount, Tolstoy, who once had known and enjoyed the throbbing fullness of existence in all its aspects, eventually postulated in his writings that life itself—his own and everybody else's—should be sacrificed to what he himself considered the meaning of life. According to him, the variety and broadness of human existence ought to be clipped down to those five moral rules to which he had reduced the Sermon on the Mount even if all our cultural and technical achievements were doomed to perish because of it. Some of his later works are blatant examples of how destructive all abstract morality of this type can become, especially when divorced from life, history, and culture. Sooner or later it identifies culture itself with immorality and turns against it as was the case with Tolstoy's idol Jean Jacques Rousseau and even more so

* At the same time the whole of his reasoned out anti-individualistic philosophy of history is interpolated as something which could have been left out without any harm to the novel. In fact the novel would have improved.

with the converted Tolstoy. In short, once Tolstoy had "found" the truth, he ceased to be a seeker and became a preacher. It was Tolstoy the preacher that turned against Tolstoy the artist.

8.

Yet despite the victory of the preacher over Tolstoy the artist after 1879, in several works such as *The Death of Ivan Ilyich, Master and Man,* and *The Power of Darkness,* the author's genius succeeded in balancing the two antagonists—probably by means of an incredible *tour de force.* His preaching double asserted himself, however, without mistake in a number of his other writings, including the well-known *Kreutzer Sonata* and *Resurrection.* Both works are powerfully written—after all Tolstoy remained Tolstoy. Still, no one can pretend that Nekhlyudov, the "converted" hero of his last big novel *Resurrection,* is convincing either as a convert or as a preacher. However excellent the other portraits and descriptions may be, Nekhlyudov is a dummy. His "Christian" (i.e. Tolstoyan) teaching and preaching is so obviously pasted upon him by the author that in the end he bores us as he did the ex-prostitute Katyusha Maslova whose soul he was so anxious to "save"—not for her sake, of course, but in order to allay his own guilt towards her and thus regain a peaceful conscience. One is not surprised that Maslova, after her contact with the political convicts, instinctively began to seek for something like a new life in the warmer and more charitable sphere of the revolutionaries who must have seemed to her a relief from Nekhlyudov's principled, cut-and-dried morality. In this way Tolstoy the psychologist turned (as he did often before), inadvertently as it were and in spite of his own intention, against Tolstoy the preacher.

Unable to sublimate his puritanical tendencies even through

his own powerful art, Tolstoy was bound to be tossed between the two even after he had condemned all art (his own included) which could not be stated in terms of morals. His brilliantly misleading book, *What Is Art,* is a case in point. So is his scathing attack on Shakespeare. Despite all this, Tolstoy was too much of a dogmatic preacher to be a true seeker. What he wanted was inner security rather than the kind of quest in which everything—morality included—becomes unsafe and problematic. If we want to see the drama of this quest in all its intensity, we must again look for it in the novels of the less puritanical but more religious Dostoevsky whose very psychology was, among other things, also a search for the integration of his own split up personality. It needed Dostoevsky's creative genius to embody such a complicated quest in a series of novels—the most dramatic novels in European fiction. This, by the way, explains the texture of his language, his style, and his feverish pace which is so different from the leisurely tempo of Tolstoy's great epics, *War and Peace* and *Anna Karenina.* The difference between a passionate seeker and a moral preacher is perhaps best illustrated by the difference between Ivan Karamazov on the one hand, and Nekhlyudov in Tolstoy's *Resurrection* on the other. Yet as artist pure and simple, i.e. outside his preaching, Tolstoy is as great in his own sphere as Dostoevsky is in his.

9.

To draw a final comparison between Tolstoy and Dostoevsky, it might be helpful to be reminded that Tolstoy's longing was turned to an utterly static past the very essence of which was a denial of history and civilization. It was Rousseauism sifted through the Sermon on the Mount and reduced to absurdity.

He wanted to entice mankind back to a primitive communal existence where there should be no functional or any other division. What he postulated was an amorphous pre-individual mass clinging together and toiling on the land in the name of that "love" which constituted the Categorical Imperative of Tolstoyanism. Such a "Kingdom of God" on earth was offered by Tolstoy the prophet as an alternative to civilization. To put it briefly, instead of coping with and overcoming civilization he ran away from it back to a mythical past in which the very idea of history becomes unthinkable.

Dostoevsky, on the other hand, wanted to go not back, but forward—to a new kind of history and civilization to be achieved through a change in man's consciousness by means of what he regarded as creative Christianity and creative religion. Otherwise he saw nothing but ruin for a world whose scientific and technical progress had become much too rapid to be followed by an adequate moral and spiritual growth. He, moreover, foretold the possibility of civilized cannibalism: of the kind that had been practiced *en gros* by Hitler and Himmler in the death-factories of Auschwitz as a matter of daily routine and according to the last word of science.

Readers who are interested in these aspects of Dostoevsky's work should turn to his *Diary of an Author,* published in 1873, 1876-78, and resumed shortly before his death. Here we see what Dostoevsky was like apart from his novels and stories. Yet even as a journalist he could be as acute as he was stimulating. What is more, his articles—like some of his private letters —provide many a clue to his novels, as well as to his personal attitudes with regard to the problems of the day, and especially the problem of Russia and Europe. Like Alexander Herzen before him, Dostoevsky was appalled by the pettiness and Philistinism of the European bourgeoisie. Yet his attitude to-

LEO TOLSTOY (1828-1910)

wards Europe was, as we can see also from his famous Pushkin speech delivered in 1880, one of conciliation rather than of hatred. Aware of the fact that mankind must either unite or perish, he aimed at a co-operation between Russia and the West even if his own conception of the so-called "Russian Idea" was not entirely devoid either of political prejudices or of national pride.

From a literary angle one is interested above all in those ideas of his which he embodied so organically in the characters of his novels that it is almost impossible to separate the two. If Tolstoy endangered at times his artistic genius by trying to turn art into preaching, Dostoevsky knew how to turn even preaching into art. Instead of mere philosophizing novels he thus offered true philosophic novels to the world. And by this method he added as it were a new dimension to Russian and European fiction as a whole.

CHAPTER THIRTEEN

Nikolai Leskov

I.

Russian realism up to Chekhov is known abroad mainly through the works of Turgenev, Goncharov, Dostoevsky, and Tolstoy. But important though they be, these authors do not exhaust either the width or the pattern of that prodigiously creative period. One of its major representatives, Alexey Pisemsky, for instance, is hardly a name outside the boundaries of his own country, despite the fact that his novel, *A Thousand Souls* (1858), still ranks as a masterpiece in Russia. The same was the case, until quite recently, with Nikolai Leskov (1831-95) whose work is now finding, slowly but surely, due appreciation abroad, while at home his reputation stands very high indeed. No less a person than Maxim Gorky said of him (in the preface to one of Leskov's stories) that as a literary artist, Leskov can beyond any doubt be placed on a level with such masters of Russian literature as Tolstoy, Gogol, Turgenev and Goncharov. According to his verdict, Leskov's talent is in no way inferior to theirs, and what is more—in his broad variety of themes he even surpasses any of his great contemporaries. His knowledge of Russian speech is supreme; so is his gift of narrative for its own sake, not to mention his understanding of human beings. He may and does shape his characters by an artistic method different from, say, that of Tolstoy.

On the other hand, he makes them speak for themselves in such a way that in the end they are as true, as convincing and even physically tangible as the characters created by his more famous contemporaries. Gorky further refers to him as the "most truly Russian of all the Russian writers" and "entirely free from outside influence."

A younger contemporary of the great realists, Leskov occupies a place of his own in Russian fiction, which, broadly speaking, developed along two main paths: one of them followed the lucid simplicity of Pushkin, while the other preferred the somewhat overcharged style of Gogol. But Leskov's work fits into neither of these two categories. He stands by himself, and this fact can perhaps be explained partly by his origin and partly by the peculiar conditions which contributed to the development of his talent. Whereas practically all the old leaders of Russian realism came from the gentry, Leskov was of mixed origin, counting among his ancestors priests, traders, and minor officials. This may explain the wide range of his themes, his lack of any social bias, as well as his general approach to life. Socially he stood nearest to those "commoners" who came into their own in the active 'sixties. On the other hand, Leskov was much too independent, both as man and artist, to be pigeon-holed into any group or doctrine. Least of all was he inclined to indulge in the enthusiastic but often somewhat adolescent radicalism of the 'sixties, and openly defended religion at a time when "scientific" materialism was considered the hall-mark of fashion.

The same independence was shown by Leskov in his style, in his choice of subject-matter, even in his attitude towards the accepted literary language. For, not unlike Nekrasov in poetry, it was he in particular who broadened Russian prose (hitherto based on the speech of the gentry) by grafting upon it the pattern and the inflection of the people's speech at its best. No author of his period was endowed with so strong a flair for the living spoken word as he. The word as such was something more than just a means to him—it assumed a value of its own, which he learned to feel and to appreciate mainly through his contact with the simple folk. He also enlarged the area of Russian literature by introducing a great variety of new themes—some of them new enough to confound the contemporary critics and to defer his fame, making it posthumous. This had, however, a certain advantage: retarded fame is taken as a rule more seriously than that which comes too soon.

2.

Born in the town of Orel, the environs of which were made famous by Turgenev (in his *A Sportsman's Sketches*), Leskov breathed from his childhood the atmosphere of that provincial Russia which later became inseparable from his writings. While still at the Grammar School, he witnessed the loss of the family fortune—a blow which compelled him to interrupt his education and fall back upon his own resources. Full of vitality and common sense, he took his courage in both hands and went into the world. Eventually he worked in Kiev, in the 'fifties, under a Briton—a certain Mr. Scott, the manager of the vast estates belonging to the Perovsky and the Naryshkin families. In the capacity of Mr. Scott's agent, Leskov travelled all over Russia, and especially in the Volga provinces, thus widening his own experiences, his knowledge of the people and of the world. It was his British chief who, moreover, discovered in him a potential author and urged him to write. Having made his debut in 1860 (when he was nearly thirty years old), Leskov soon gave all his energies to literature and settled down in Petersburg, where he wrote for several periodicals, including Dostoevsky's *Vremya* ("Time"), the peculiar populism of which must have been after his own heart.

It should be borne in mind that the 'sixties were a period of wrangles between political groups, notably between the conservative Slavophils on the one hand, and the liberal intellectuals of the "Western" orientation on the other. But whatever the differences among them, the fact remained that the intelligentsia as a whole had hardly any real contact with, or understanding for, the peasant masses. It was above all Dostoevsky who saw, or foresaw, the deeper implications of such a state of things and never wearied of pointing out that Russian intellectuals had no roots either in the soil or in the people of their native land. Hence his call for a deeper organic rootedness in both—a call which was endorsed by the poet and critic Apollon Grigoryev in essays, by Alexander Ostrovsky in drama, and by Leskov in fiction. Incidentally, Grigoryev was one of the first critics to welcome Leskov's talent, which blossomed out in the second half of the 'sixties and continued to enrich Russian literature for a period of over thirty years. During that time Leskov wrote a vast amount of works which can be roughly divided into novels, chronicles of provincial life, stories pure and simple, semi-didactic legends, apocrypha, and lastly the so-called *skaz*—a sort of narrative connected mainly with his name and technically more important than any other facet of his work.

Leskov's two bulky novels, *The Impasse* (*Nékuda*) and *At Daggers Drawn* (*Na nozhákh*), are political and touch upon the problems which the generation of the 'sixties was called to face and to cope with. The first novel—it appeared in 1864—can be looked upon as an attempt on the part of the author to clear up his own attitude with regard to the extreme radical currents among the younger intelligentsia of the period. For this reason it is often included, though less so than *At Daggers Drawn,* in the series of novels comprising Turgenev's *Fathers and Children,* Goncharov's *The Ravine,* Pisemsky's *The Troubled Sea,* and Dostoevsky's *The Possessed.* As it happened, two years before the publication of his first novel, Leskov had written an article about a number of mysterious conflagrations in Petersburg, generally ascribed to the activities of the "nihilist" section among the students. Although written in defence of the students, the article was misinterpreted by the radical press which all at once discovered in Leskov an ideological enemy and raised a hullabaloo against him. In spite of his liberal tendencies and opinions, the author was thus willy-nilly driven into the opposite camp, and this made him adopt, in his very first novel, an aggressive attitude towards his accusers. But even *The Impasse* was a diagnosis rather than a direct attack. Leskov did not conceal in it his sympathy with the true and sincere idealists among the revolutionaries, while condemning without mercy the frauds, the fools, and the opportunistic camp-followers of radicalism. Like Dostoevsky in *The Possessed,* he saw in the extreme left section of the intelligentsia an uprooted and purely destructive element, unable to grasp either the real needs or the real tasks of Russia after the abolition of serfdom. It is a pity that he cheapened the plot by showing the revolutionaries as the dupes of Polish Jesuits in disguise, supposedly preparing the ground for the rebellion in Poland (in 1863) by fomenting internal troubles in Russia.

Although vivid and full of incident, this work does not go beyond the average novels of the period. It falls infinitely below the level of such an apocalyptic book as *The Possessed.*

So the hue and cry it caused among the radicals was quite out of proportion to its actual merit. As a result Leskov was, from now on, either ignored or else slandered by the radical press. But this only made him adopt an even more aggressive attitude towards his opponents, and he gave vent to it in his second political novel, *At Daggers Drawn* (1871), after which a reconciliation was out of the question. Still, it is worth mentioning that he never took part in any reactionary activities and was as outspoken about the excesses on the right as he was about those on the left. In a number of his narratives he attacked the bureaucracy of the State and of the Church with such virulence as to risk—in 1883 for example—an open conflict with the authorities. In 1889 one of his works was actually confiscated by the police on account of its "harmful" tendency.

Some of Leskov's earlier writings could conveniently be left out but for the fact that they point to certain questions of nineteenth century Russia—questions which transcend mere politics. The already mentioned "accursed problem" of the relationship between the intelligentsia and the people was one of them. Then there was the problem of individual adjustment during the economic and social changes after 1861; the problem of the *déclassé* from among the gentry, which made the once romantic "superfluous man" a topical character of Russian realism. Leskov himself—a rooted Russian if ever there was —broached the theme of the "superfluous man" in his short novel *The Ones Passed-by,* and, very originally, in *The Islanders,* the hero of which is a gifted but unaccountable Russian artist, shown against the background of the ultra-respectable German settlers in Petersburg, whose milieu produced uprootedness of its own (illustrated by the heroine of the novel).

Leskov would probably have continued to write in the same vein, had he not come to the conclusion that after the

hostile reception of his two political novels his literary future
lay not in the novel at all. So he was on the look-out for a
new genre, as one can gather from his next two works, *Cathedral Folk* and *The Sealed Angel*.

3.

In spite of its length, *Cathedral Folk* (1872) is not a novel in
the usual sense of this word, but a bracing chronicle of life
in a Russian cathedral town—with the clergy as the central
characters. It was through this work that Leskov introduced
the clergy into Russian literature as a new thematic element
with such competence as to have added the two principal
figures described, the archpriest Tuberozov and his helper
Akhilla, to the memorable characters in Russian fiction. The
contrast between the dignified, active idealist Tuberozov and
the impulsive Akhilla (a typical Cossack who by some mistake
joined the Church but could never quite fit into his profession)
abounds in comic as well as pathetic incident. Akhilla worships
his superior with the unquestioning admiration of a child and
behaves like a jealous woman whose love, appreciated though
it be, is studiously ignored. The amusingly colorful account
of events is obscured by Tuberozov's troubles with the Church
bureaucracy and ends in a sad note—the death of the archpriest
and, not long after him, of the turbulent Akhilla as well.

The whole of this narrative is so admirably interwoven with
the life of a provincial town and the surrounding district that
some of its passages (the storm in the forest, for example) are
among the gems of Russian prose. With the same success are
rendered the peculiarities of the archaic speech used by the
clergy. But while showing the vanishing patriarchal life in a
sympathetic light, Leskov lays bare, and most scathingly, the

NIKOLAI LESKOV (1831-1895)

dry, pedantic opportunism of the higher Church authorities. With even greater relish he caricatures the antics of the unscrupulous or frankly stupid sham-radicals and the would-be "new men" of the 'sixties.

But since *Cathedral Folk* is referred to as a chronicle and not as a novel, it is essential to stress the difference between the two, although they may overlap—in *War and Peace,* for example. Briefly, a novel is based on a plot the pattern of which is decisive for its structure. A "chronicle," on the other hand, is a sequence of incidents and happenings which occur as they do in real life. They may concern the same set of people, the same town or region, but the structure of the narrative is more loose than in a novel, and single incidents can often be added or else deleted without impairing the whole. In 1875 Leskov wrote about the "artificial and unnatural form of the novel" and pointed out the fact that in life things happen differently. "A man's life is like the unfurling of a scroll, and I am going to use the same method." He was as good as his word. He, moreover, endowed each of his characters with a voice and intonation corresponding to his profession and social position. This again led him to the *skaz*—a story usually told by a man of the people or by a lower middle-class person, with all the idioms, inflections and popular etymologies typical of the narrator himself. At the same time, Leskov took good care to render the traits of his characters not by means of analysis or by plastic descriptions, but by an accumulation of incidents and anecdotes. This method brought him, in turn, close to the picaresque story which he skilfully blended with the *skaz*.

Less than a year after *Cathedral Folk* another of Leskov's masterpieces, *The Sealed Angel,* appeared. This is one of his finest and alas! least translatable works. It combines in a striking manner his innate religious sense with the so-called *skaz* and is told by an artisan from among the dissenters or "Old-Believers" (the most patriarchal and staunchly religious portion of the Russian people) with that admirable use of the people's idioms and phrasing the flavor, or rather the stylization, of which became, at the beginning of this century, something of a test for one's verbal art. While keeping to the chronicle-pattern in some of his other works, notably in the longish narrative *A Decayed Family* (1875), Leskov preserved the *skaz* and gave full scope to its form in such bracing stories as *The Enchanted Wanderer, The Amazon (Voitelnitsa), The Steel Flea,* and *The Hare Chase.* The first of these is a picaresque tale of adventures told by an ordinary Russian who, after years of roaming, travels to a monastery and shares his reminiscences with a few pilgrims. The story is not only an illustration of the vitality and stoicism of the character concerned, but also of Leskov's skill in narratives of this kind. Some of the scenes, such as the dance of the gypsy belle whose tragedy is interwoven with the story, are described with an intensity of vision and of feeling which takes one's breath away.

The Amazon is another *skaz.* It is told by a lower middle-class match-maker who, in the broadness of her character, becomes a procuress, and yet in spite of this preserves so much warmth and generosity in her simple heart that in the end one cannot help liking her. The hero of the hilarious *Steel Flea* is a left-handed smith from Tula whose sagacity outstrips even the inventive genius of England, but as was so frequently the case in old Russia—to no constructive or practical purpose. This *skaz* (perhaps the best known specimen of its kind) also reflects what might be called the instinctive attitude of the Russian masses towards the English—an attitude of benevolence and admiration, but hardly devoid of the spirit of rivalry.

The story itself was suggested to Leskov by the popular Russian saying: "The English made a flea of steel, but our artisans of Tula shoed it." As for *The Hare Chase*, first published in 1917, it is a life-story told, in the inimitably comic mixture of Russian and Ukrainian, by an upstart who came to grief. Devoid of brains and of scruples, but full of "zeal" for the powers-that-be, he wormed his way into the position of a police officer. Eventually he lost both his career and his reason through having failed to catch a dangerous revolutionary who, during all that time, had been employed—cleverly disguised— as his coachman. *The Hare Chase* sparkles with fun and with that satirical spirit which marked Leskov's writings in the 'eighties and the 'nineties, often bringing him close to Saltykov-Shchedrin—the Russian Swift of those days.

4.

Even if Leskov was not the actual inventor of the *skaz* (the beginnings of which go back to Gogol and Pushkin), he nevertheless became its first undisputed master and brought it to such perfection as to secure for it a high place in Russian fiction. But he can be equally relied upon in the straightforward traditional story to which he added certain features of his own, such as an exciting plot and a quick and vivid action. A good example of this kind is his *Lady Macbeth of the Mtsensk District* (1865).* Taken from the *milieu* of the old-fashioned provincial merchants, it depicts a woman's blind passion—an obsession rather than a passion—and the crimes resulting from it, with brutal yet powerful directness. The colors are plain, and the inner logic of the crime and the punishment that fol-

---

* The Soviet composer Shostakovich made use of this story for his well-known opera under the same title.

lows is as inexorable as is the sway of carnal lust—the cause of it all. Needless to say, Leskov made even here splendid use of the people's language which, for all its realism, he often stylized in the manner of the chap-books of that period. It is one of Leskov's early stories, showing his ability to make characters alive exclusively in terms of incident.

This method can be studied in a number of his other narratives, especially those in which he keeps to the *skaz* type. The whole of *The Amazon,* for example, is but a string of episodes and anecdotes arranged in such a manner as to make the woman convincing and real—as real in fact as if we had known her for years. The same can be said of *The Enchanted Wanderer,* or of *An Iron Will*—with its humorously ironical portraiture of a German engineer in Russia. Leskov's experience of life was so rich indeed that quite a few of his jottings were left in the state of raw anecdotic and semi-documentary reportage. Nor did he mind using the actual names of the people, historical or otherwise, who had taken part in the happenings recorded. *Cheramour,* Leskov's lower middle-class counterpart of Turgenev's *Rudin,* is an instance. So is *The Immortal Golovan* based, like *Cheramour,* on his reminiscences of a real person, the memory of whom still lingered in Leskov's native city of Orel. To this category can be added *On the Edge of the World:* an account of the hair-raising experiences of a Russian bishop (the Bishop of Yaroslavl) whose life was saved, during one of his diocesan journeys in the Arctic wastes of Siberia, by the loyalty and devotion of a pagan, while a Christian convert of the same tribe behaved like a cad. But since the implications of this story point to another group of Leskov's work, we can pass to those of his narratives which touch upon religious and ethical problems.

5.

It is known that in the 'eighties Leskov became temporarily interested in Tolstoy and Tolstoyanism. Tolstoy, in his turn, commended the essential "Russianness" of Leskov and thus helped, as far as possible, towards his literary rehabilitation. For all that the gospel of the much-too-conscious self-perfection on the part of Tolstoy was unlikely to appeal, in the long run, to Leskov, whose Christianity (based on spontaneous warmth and goodness rather than on parading one's contrition, or the white robes of one's moral purity) was nearer to the people than that of Tolstoy. This attitude found an expression in his parables and legends—some of them paraphrased from the old Church-Slavonic *Prologue,* while others were taken from the folklore, or else from the general stock of the East-European Christian tradition. Such legends as *The Juggler Pamphalon, The Mountain, The Fair Azra,* deal with the early Christian period in Alexandria, but they lay stress on charity in Leskov's sense rather than on morality in the exacting sense of Tolstoy.

In Tolstoy the moral element was so much stronger than his religious consciousness that it actually throve at the latter's expense. Instead of integrating, it only further divided his incredibly rich personality by increasing the gap between Tolstoy the man and Tolstoy the moralist. This gap he tried to cope with by turning his reasoned-out puritanism into a new Categorical Imperative, that is, into a universally obligatory straitjacket in which there was more severity than genuine charity and love. Leskov, on the other hand, was endowed with a religious instinct spontaneous and warm enough to save him not only from lack of charity, but also from conscious or unconscious moral exhibitionism—the two pitfalls of many a frowning puritan. If Leskov's art harbors a "message" at all, to which our (or any other) period might listen with profit, it is the simple truth that the thing most needful is human warmth and sympathy—as a preliminary condition of everything that makes life worth while. Leskov himself was richly endowed with this virtue. In his attitude towards the world there was nothing reminding one either of Gogol's rancor and distrust, or of Tolstoy's severe moral book-keeping. On the contrary, he found life attractive precisely because he approached it in the spirit of broadness, tolerance and charity. This explains why he was one of the few Russian realists able to depict also good characters convincingly without any stilts, rhetorics, and sermons. One of such characters is Tuberozov in *Cathedral Folk*. But we can find plenty of them in his other works too: in *The Musk-Ox, Kotin and Platonida, Cheramour, The Immortal Golovan,* etc., which only enhances his place in literature.

6.

The range of Leskov's talent is further illustrated by the wealth of his motifs and genres. Novels, naturalistic stories, *skaz*-tales, legendary and folklore themes, anecdotic reminiscences, intensely documentary pictures of the serfdom period (*The Beast, The Make-up Artist, The Vale of Tears,* etc.)—all these contributed to the variety of his work without impairing either its artistic or its human integrity. "He narrates, and in this art he has no equal," says Gorky. Gorky who, incidentally, had learned a great deal from Leskov, also points out Leskov's profound love of Russia. Nor was it a small merit that Leskov preserved this love—together with his sense of humor and faith in life—even at the time of the general "Chekhovian" despondency in the 'eighties and early 'nineties.

Ignored or else deprecated by the critics while alive, Leskov yet succeeded in creating quite a large audience interested in his work. But he came really into his own at the beginning of this century, when he was taken up by a number of modernists. Alexey Remizov, a virtuoso of the word and of the *skaz* in Russian modernism, made Leskov (including his legendary and hagiographic motifs) the starting point for his own art. Another conspicuous follower of Leskov was Evgeny Zamyatin (he died in 1934) who excelled in the *skaz*-manner *both* before and after the revolution of 1917. Quite a few elements have been taken from Leskov by some of the best-known Soviet authors, especially during the early phase of Soviet fiction. The most popular living representative of the *skaz* is the Soviet author Michael Zoshchenko, whose shrewdly stylized sketches have been translated into all European languages. Told in the lower middle-class jargon and full of amusing pinpricks, Zoshchenko's stories reflect the life of the Soviet citizens in its everyday humdrum: they are its unofficial history. The fact that, in spite of so many literary and other changes, the influence of Leskov's work still persists, is the best proof of its vitality. And there is no reason why it should not continue.

CHAPTER FOURTEEN

The Dramatic Works
of Chekhov

I.

Chekov's fame spread in two waves—one through his stories, the other through his plays—and each of them brought something new with regard to subject-matter as well as the manner of presentation. Sincerity, simplicity and the sense of the obvious, bequeathed to Russian literature by Pushkin, reached in Chekhov's art that degree of truth and of elusive subtlety beyond which they could not possibly go. And since his impressionistic vision lent itself to pregnant brief statements rather than to carefully worked out disquisitions, Chekhov became a great master of the short story even before he was recognized as one of the pioneers of modern drama and the theatre.

As an interpreter of the "boring" eighties and early 'nineties, he depicted above all the weariness, the helpless despondency, of that period which he himself deplored as well as disliked. And if he, too, remained helpless and bewildered in the face of it all, he did so primarily because his artistic conscience would not allow him to accept, let alone preach, remedies in which he could not believe if he wanted to remain entirely honest with regard to himself and to his age.

ANTON PAVLOVICH CHEKHOV (1860-1904)

While comparing (in one of his letters to the founder and the editor of *Novoe Vremya,* A. Suvorin) himself and the authors of his time with those of the great realistic period, he said: "The best of them are realistic and paint life as it is; but because every line is permeated, as with a juice, by awareness of a purpose, you feel, besides life as it is, also life as it ought to be, and this captivates you. And we? We paint life as it is, and beyond that—no 'gee up' nor 'gee-down.' . . . Beyond that, even if you lashed us with whips, we could not go. We have neither immediate nor remote aims, and in our souls—a great emptiness. We have no politics, we do not believe in revolution, we have no God, we are not afraid of ghosts, and personally I have no fear even of death and blindness. He who desires nothing, hopes for nothing, and is afraid of nothing, cannot be an artist. Whether it is a disease or not the name does not matter; but it must be owned our situation is worse than bad. . . . I am at least clever enough not to hide my disease from myself, nor to cover up my emptiness with borrowed rags, such as the ideals of the 'sixties and so on. I shall not, like Garshin, throw myself down a flight of stairs, but neither am I going to delude myself with hopes of a better future. I am not to blame for my disease, nor am I called to cure myself, since this disease has, it must be supposed, some good purpose of its own hidden from us, and has not been sent in vain." *

The last line evidently leaves a loophole just wide enough to prevent him from falling into complete pessimism and to make him preserve a glimmer of hope which kept secretly burning in spite of all. He had little in common with the sermonizing Tolstoy or with the dissecting Dostoevsky, but felt

* From *The Life and Letters of Anton Chekhov.* Translated and edited by S. S. Koteliansky and Philip Tomlinson, Cassell.

a curious affinity with Turgenev the artist. It was above all
Turgenev's lyrical impressionism and also his dispassionate
aesthetic attitude towards life that left a mark upon Chekhov.
Like Turgenev again, he may have been interested in the
tasks and problems of the day, without however committing
himself to any of them as an artist. He was explicit about this
in another letter to Suvorin (October 1888) in which the passage in question runs as follows: "To deny that artistic creation involves problems and purposes would be to admit that
an artist creates without premeditation, without design, under
a spell. Therefore if an artist boasted to me of having written
a story without a previously settled design, but by inspiration,
I would call him a lunatic. You are right in demanding that
an artist should take a conscious attitude to his work, but you
confuse two conceptions: *the solution of a question and the
correct setting of a question.* The latter alone is obligatory for
an artist. It is for the judge to put the questions correctly; and
the jurymen must decide, each one according to his taste." *

Keeping to this dictum, Chekhov abstained (with the exception of a short spell of Tolstoyanism, reflected in his longer
story, *My Life*) from any "isms," any political and other parties, thereby preserving his artistic freedom to the end. "I am
not a liberal, nor a conservative, nor a meliorist, nor a monk,
nor an indifferentist," we read in a further letter of his (October 1889). "Pharisaism, stupidity, and arbitrariness reign not
in shopkeepers' houses and prisons alone. I detect them in
science, in literature and in the younger generation. . . . For
this reason I nurse no particular partiality for gendarmes, or
butchers, or savants, or writers, or the younger generation. I
look upon trademarks and labels as prejudices. My Holy of
Holies is the human body, health, mind, talent, inspiration,

* Op. cit.

love, and the most absolute freedom—freedom from violence
and falsehood in whatever they may be manifested. This is
the program I would follow if I were a great artist." *

2.

Having such pronouncements of his at our disposal, we can
perhaps more easily approach the spirit and the general character of Chekhov's work. The first thing likely to strike one
is the dispassionate manner in which he judged one of the
drabbest periods of Russian life—a period which coincided
with a rapid growth of capitalism all over the country. Yet
its very drabness was shown by him in a form both new and
provocatively stimulating. This applies particularly to his plays
the creation of which demanded a thorough overhaul of the
traditional theater and drama. Chekhov, incidentally, proclaimed (in one of his letters) the theater of his time a "skin
disease, a world of muddle, of stupidity and high-faluting"
which should be swept away with a broom. He himself did
not mind playing the part of such a broom in the 'eighties,
when the only conspicuous reformer in this respect was Hen-
rik Ibsen; Gerhardt Hauptmann, Maurice Maeterlinck and
others were yet to come. So Chekhov's pioneering was not
devoid of courage even if he faltered, now and then, under
the burden of his own innovations. Thus after the mixed
reception of *Ivanov,* written in 1887 and first performed in
1889, he decided to abandon the theatre altogether. He made
the same resolution after the unsuccessful production of *The
Seagull* in October 1896. Fortunately, three years later his *Uncle
Vanya* (a rewritten version of his previous and not very successful play, *The Wood Demon*) was staged by the Moscow

* Op. cit.

Arts Theatre with unheard-of success. From now on Chekhov was closely associated with that theatre, so competently run by Stanislavsky. In 1901 he wrote for it *Three Sisters,* and in 1903—roughly a year before his death at the age of forty-four—*The Cherry Orchard.* In addition, he was responsible for the one-act play, *On the High Road* (anticipating as it were Gorky's famous *Lower Depths*), and for a few short but highly amusing vaudevilles and farces, such as *The Bear, The Proposal, The Jubilee,* etc. These can be regarded as dramatized counterparts of his humorous anecdotes and sketches, the boisterous laughter of which makes one think of the early stage of Gogol.

Chekhov's technique is of course widely different from that of Gogol. Yet, like Gogol, he too became haunted by the great Tedium as something inseparable from human existence. This attitude he expressed in accents entirely his own at an age when—partly because of the increased reaction after the murder of Alexander II, and partly because of the rapidly changing social-economic pattern of Russia—the bulk of the intelligentsia was plunged into a state of aimlessness and frustration. Feeling out of gear with the age, with the entire *Zeitgeist,* the best intellectuals of that period did not know what to do either with life or with themselves. And since Chekhov happened to be one of them, he was able to render their mood of bewilderment to perfection not only in his stories but also in his plays. His characters are "superfluous" in a more acute sense than those of Turgenev, for example. Their nostalgia, too, is different and comes frequently from their dissatisfaction with the very core of life. Their state of mind is further complicated by their feeling of isolation, by a strange inner barrier separating them even from those whom they once regarded as their nearest and dearest. Such above all is Ivanov, the principal character of the play under the same title. Treplev in *The Seagull;* Voinitsky, Astrov, and Sonya in *Uncle Vanya* belong to the same category. So do Olga and Irina in *Three Sisters;* and, to some extent, even the pathetically stupid owners of the bankrupt manor in *The Cherry Orchard.*

Chekhov connects, as a rule, this kind of helpless bewilderment not so much with weakness as with a surplus of sensitiveness, of thwarted refinement, on the part of the characters themselves. According to him, a highly sensitive person, confronted by the rough and ruthless competition in modern life, is almost doomed to failure, which, morally speaking, does him credit. On the other hand, success is a prerogative of the unscrupulous, the coarse, and the vulgar. Chekhov, at any rate, looks upon it with a suspicion which only increases his sympathy and tenderness with regard to those *hommes manqués* who have been crushed because they expected or even demanded from life more than it could give. But the price they have to pay for their failure is, perhaps, not entirely in vain. Maybe they are paying the bill for the happiness of the generations to come, whose life will be less muddled and stupid than ours— a thought which does not alleviate the present trials, but confers upon them at least that possibility of a meaning which refuses to slam the door on all hope. Still, Chekhov's characters have to pay the bill. Quite a few of them know it and accept it in this spirit without any profound quest or "rebellion" à la Dostoevsky, but simply in order to avoid the temptation of utter nihilism.

"Those who will live a hundred or two hundred years after us, and who will despise us for having lived our lives so stupidly and tastelessly—they will, perhaps, find a means of being happy; but we. . . . There is only one hope for you and me. The hope that when we are asleep in our graves we may, perhaps, be visited by pleasant visions." * Such is Dr. Astrov's comment in *Uncle Vanya*. But the same non-committal faith is voiced by Vershinin in *Three Sisters;* by Trofimov in *The Cherry Orchard;* and assumes a haunting aspect in the tragic symbolism of one of Chekhov's most powerful narratives, *The Black Monk*. Chekhov himself must have looked for occasional solace in hopes of this kind, as one can judge from his letter to Serge Diaghilev (December, 1902), where he says: "Modern culture is but the beginning of a work for a great future, a work which will go on, perhaps, for ten thousand years, in order that mankind may, even in the remote future, come to know the truth of a real God—that is, not by guessing, not by seeking in Dostoevsky, but by perceiving clearly, as one perceives that twice two is four."

3.

Flashes of such faith did not redeem, however, the drabness of that present which Chekhov had to put up with and which he used, moreover, as the raw material for his stories and plays. The surprising thing is that he was able to transmute it into perfect art, the new devices of which are particularly worth studying in connection with his dramatic technique.

In the same way as Nekrasov once tried to de-poetize poetry, Chekhov did his best to de-theatralize the theatre by depriving it of everything "heroic," noisy, externally conspicuous, and artificial. Yet in doing this he increased the effect of his plays in a strangely suggestive manner. In his first long play, *Ivanov,* he still depended to some extent on tradition, but he purposely abstained from a worked-out plot and made full use of what

---

* All quotations from Chekhov's plays are taken from Mrs. Constance Garnett's translation of Chekhov's works (Chatto and Windus).

he called the "belletristic" as distinct from the dramatic method in the old sense. "Each act I finish as I do my stories," Chekhov says in a letter; "I develop it quietly and calmly, but at the end I give a slap to the spectator. All my energy is centered on a few really strong passages, but the bridges connecting these passages are insignificant, weak and old-fashioned." The main hero is of course unheroic—a "superfluous" intellectual who, suddenly and through no fault of his own, has lost his hold upon life and feels, at the age of thirty-five, an old man.

"Exhausted, overstrained, broken, with my head heavy and my soul indolent, without faith, without love, without an object in life, I lingered like a shadow among men and don't know what I am, what I am living for, what I want. . . . My brains do not obey me, nor my hands, nor my feet. My property is going to ruin, the forest is falling under the axe. My land looks at me like a deserted child. I expect nothing, I regret nothing; my soul shudders with the fear of the morrow. . . . What is the matter with me? To what depths am I making myself sink? What has brought this weakness on me?"

But there is no answer. Surrounded by fools, knaves and nonentities, he sinks deeper and deeper into his own morass and cannot help offending even his devoted consumptive wife whom he used to adore. And when, after her death, he is free to marry Sasha, who had been in love with him all that time, he (again for no apparent reason) goes and shoots himself when on the point of taking her to the altar. We watch in him the tragedy of a sensitive man doomed to disintegrate, although he himself does not know why. There is no plot in the play, and even the normal logical causation seems to be absent; yet as a picture of life turned into art—"on the wing" as it were—the piece is convincing and impressive.

In *The Seagull,* written some eight years later, Chekhov's

peculiar technique is even more noticeable than in *Ivanov*. This time, too, the plot is replaced by a string of seemingly casual incidents, cemented by that lyrical "atmosphere" which both in his plays and his stories became the principal if not the only unifying factor. Here the tragedy of frustration in Treplev (a counterpart of Ivanov) and Nina is the more poignant because of all the trivialities leading up to it. While Nina, after her mistakes and disappointments, finds a shelter in the profession of an actress, Treplev cannot fill the void of his life even with his growing success in literature. These are his parting words to Nina after she had deserted him for a man who cared for her as little as he did for a shot seagull: "You have found your path, you know which way you are going, but I am still floating in a chaos of dreams and images, not knowing what use it is to anyone. I have no faith and I don't know what my vocation is." Chekhov again made use of the "belletristic" method but was not quite sure whether to approve of it or not, and he said so in a letter to Suvorin (November 1895): "I began it *forte* and finished it *pianissimo* against all rules of dramatic art. It came out like a story. I am more dissatisfied than satisfied with it, and, reading over my newborn piece, I become once more convinced that I am not a playwright at all." One can agree with him only in so far as he was not a playwright in the traditional sense, some further proofs of which he gave in his *Uncle Vanya, Three Sisters,* and *The Cherry Orchard.*

In *Uncle Vanya* we meet the same type of gentry-intellectuals, sunk in the morass of a trivial existence, as in *Ivanov* and *The Seagull.* Plot as such is replaced by a series of "scenes of country life in four acts." The "atmosphere" is all-important, while the subject is as simple as it can be. A retired professor, suffering from conceit and gout, comes with his beautiful second wife Elena to settle down on the estate, where his brother-in-law, Voinitsky (Uncle Vanya), and his daughter from the first marriage, Sonya, have been toiling for years in order to increase his income. Thinking the world of the professor's fame and learning, Voinitsky has spent the whole of his adult life in serving him—only to discover in the end that the supposedly great man is nothing but an ignorant, puffed-up nonentity. Voinitsky, a weary middle-aged failure, realizes his mistake, but the lost years can no longer be retrieved. To make things worse, he is in love with Elena, who is emotionally too indolent to respond to his advances, or even to those of the younger and more interesting Astrov—still in the process of going to seed. As though lost in his own void, he is frightened of the present and the future. "I am forty-seven. If I live to be sixty, I have another thirteen years. It's a long time. How am I to get through those thirteen years? What shall I do? How am I to fill them up? . . ." In his rancor Voinitsky fires two shots at the pitiably frightened celebrity and, having missed, thinks of suicide. But it all ends peacefully. The learned professor and his wife depart. Life returns to its old routine. Both Voinitsky and Sonya (whose secret love for Astrov is frustrated for good) find an escape—of which they are fully conscious this time—in their accountancy and petty drudgery about the estate.

Three Sisters is written in a similar vein, with an even increased amount of lyrical overtones. Again there is no plot. We are introduced to three sisters—members of the intelligentsia (in this case the cultured higher officers' class in the 'eighties)—who, after their father's death, have remained stuck in a provincial town they loathe. Their determination to return to Moscow, where they were born, only expresses their desire for a full and throbbing life. But the provincial morass is stronger. Neither they nor their brother, who is preparing for a learned career, succeed in extricating themselves. Instead of living, they are compelled only to exist. "I am nearly twenty-four," complains Irina. "I have been working for years, my brains are drying up, I am getting thin and old and ugly and there is nothing, nothing, not the slightest satisfaction, and time is passing, and one feels that one is moving away and being drawn into the depths. I am in despair and I don't know how it is I am alive and have not killed myself yet." It is no fault of theirs that all their efforts are futile and that things go from bad to worse. Their brother, moreover, marries a mean and vulgar *petite bourgeoise* who openly deceives him with another man. And as in *Uncle Vanya,* Chekhov ends the play again *pianissimo,* with the apparent acceptance of the all-round frustrations and blind-alley, camouflaged by hard work.

The tone is somewhat brighter in *The Cherry Orchard*—that dramatized string of comic and semi-tragic incidents. The bankruptcy of the irresponsibly carefree, or rather careless, Ranevskaya and her brother Gayev is here symbolic of the inner as well as external bankruptcy of that gentry-class which not so long ago had dominated the whole of Russian life. Ranevskaya's country-house, together with its magnificent cherry orchard, is bought by the self-made businessman Lopakhin—the son of a former serf; and the first thing the new owner does is to fell the orchard in order to make room for a housing-estate planned out on a most profitable basis. Lopakhin thus emerges as a new social force—a capitalist on a large scale. But the "eternal student" and revolutionary Trofimov has little respect for and less fear of him. "I can get on without you. I can pass by you." He is still young enough to flatter himself with the illusion that he, and not the "practical" money-grabbing Lopakhin, is in the front ranks of humanity even if Lopakhin is the only one who triumphs at the end of the play.

The Cherry Orchard was written specially for Stanislavsky

who regarded it as Chekhov's best dramatic work. Its first performance took place in January, 1904. But its technique was too new and too subtle to captivate the public at once, even the public of the Moscow Arts Theatre.

4.

To sum up that technique in a few sentences is not an easy matter. On the whole, Chekhov stands outside that tradition of Russian dramatic art which goes from Fonvizin (eighteenth century)—via Griboyedov—to Gogol's *Government Inspector,* although Chekhov's farcical pieces are still reminiscent of Gogol. On the other hand, his "belletristic," or perhaps static, method had quite an interesting Russian precedent in Turgenev's *A Month in the Country* which, like *Uncle Vanya,* could be called "scenes from country life" rather than a play in the traditional style. Finally, Alexander Ostrovsky contributed certain elements to the Chekhovian drama, however different Ostrovsky's aims may have been from those of Chekhov. As an innovator Chekhov had several features in common with Ibsen (whom he admired, but again with reservations).

Like Ibsen in his later plays, he too discarded the old-fashioned plot and reduced the external action to a minimum. Yet he replaced the latter not so much by the psychological inner tension à la Ibsen as by an accumulation of that lyrical-impressionistic "atmosphere" which keeps the seemingly disjointed incidents together. The curious similarity between the symbolic use of the seagull in Chekhov's play and that of the wild duck in the well-known drama by Ibsen may, of course, not be purely accidental. Analogies could also be found elsewhere—for instance, between the ending of *Three Sisters* (with the departing soldiers and music in the distance) and that of Ibsen's *The*

Lady of the Sea, not to mention Chekhov's frequent use of the double dialogue, the spoken words of which serve as a mask for what one actually wants to say. On the other hand, there are quite a few differences between these two pioneers of modern drama. For one thing, in his disregard of the conventional plot Ibsen relegated the tragic guilt of his hero to the past (i.e. to the time before the play began) and, therefore, concentrated only on the psychological *dénouement* as seen through the workings of the hero's conscience, tossed as a rule between two contradictory sets of values. The climax is expressed through the hero's inner change due to his sudden perception of a truth which gives a new direction to his will, to his entire personality, even if he may not be strong enough to live up to it, as we see in *Rosmersholm, The Masterbuilder, John Gabriel Borkman,* and *When We Dead Awaken.* In Ibsen's psychological plays the principal character invariably remains in the limelight, while the structure itself is determined by the moral catharsis occurring in his consciousness.

Chekhov proceeds differently. Having discarded the old plot, he does not replace it by a conflict of inner values in the manner of Ibsen for the simple reason that his very point of departure is the bankruptcy of all values. Nor do we find in him that logical and psychological unity in which Ibsen the playwright excelled to the end. On the contrary, Chekhov depicted the casualness of a disintegrating life in that seemingly casual way which Tolstoy once referred to (rather disapprovingly) as a "scattered composition." Yet there was a system in Chekhov's method, as well as an inner unity underneath the externally "scattered" bits and slices of life. It was precisely in the skill with which he achieved this unity that Chekhov proved to be one of the inimitable masters in the whole of European modernism.

5.

In his endeavor to show the tragic nature of ordinary everyday existence by means of the "atmosphere" as the main cementing factor, Chekhov went a long way to abolishing the old method of acting. In this respect his plays are, perhaps, even more difficult to handle than those of Ibsen; but the Moscow Arts Theatre (the beginnings of which are so closely bound up with Chekhov) did full justice to them on the stage: by realizing how much their success depended on nuances and all sorts of psychological imponderables, not to mention the importance of the pauses, of the tempo, as well as of the deeper "symbolic" side of gestures and intonation. After all, it was not for nothing that the impressionist Chekhov was proclaimed by Andrey Bely a precursor of Russian symbolism.

Yet Chekhov's symbolism is more vague and elusive than, say, that of Ibsen. And, perhaps, more organic, too. As it springs not from any calculated literary devices, but from the author's total attitude towards life, it often becomes one of the primary ingredients of the "atmosphere" permeating his works. This "atmosphere" may be tragic enough in itself, but the characters acting and moving in it are either too fatalistic or else too pathetic to be really tragic. In contrast to Ibsen's characters, they have neither enough faith nor enough stamina even to dare to fight for, let alone shape, their own destinies.

This need not be, however, a drawback. Exceptional material lends itself more easily to artistic processes than the apparently uninteresting and drab everyday actuality. The uniqueness of Chekhov is due to the skill with which he proved that the very drabness of life can be turned into great and significant art. But he was able to do this only because of his well-nigh clairvoyant perception of the complexities lurking under the most ordinary crust of life. His principal strength was in his understanding of human weakness. And he showed us that weakness in a subtle, dispassionate light, as well as with that kind of "Chekhovian" understatement, which was itself one of the major contributions to the sensibility of our time.

CHAPTER FIFTEEN

Maxim Gorky

I.

The span of time dividing us from Maxim Gorky's death is now long enough to allow us to see his life-work in its proper perspective from a literary as well as social point of view. In his case it would be rather difficult to separate one from the other, since the pathos permeating his writings was not so much of an aesthetic as of a social and reformatory order, but with a difference. The artist and the reformer were neither antagonistic in him as they were in Tolstoy; nor were they mixed up as was so often the case with H. G. Wells. In Gorky the two propensities converged and, instead of disturbing, seemed to strengthen one another. His very choice of themes was conditioned by his protest against the kind of life he saw around, and he depicted the ugly side of reality in a spirit widely different from that of Gogol and his followers. Instead of feeding on a rancorous negation of life, he permeated his writings with his strongest urge—the urge to turn the whole of existence into something of which human beings need no longer feel ashamed. Gorky's literary work can, therefore, best be understood in conjunction with the rôle he played in the social and political life of Russia during the most fateful transition years in her history. The uniqueness of his rôle was enhanced by the fact that he was the first major Russian author who had started life as a proletarian, indeed as an outcast. Apart from a few months in a shabby elementary school at Nizhny Novgorod, he knew only one other school—that of life. But he made such good use of it that, at the age of thirty, he was already one of the most popular authors in his country, and before long his name became a household word—more, a slogan all the world over.

This alone puts Gorky among the arresting figures of our time. Yet if we want to gauge the full value of his work and personality, we must approach him in the light of the conditions prevailing in Russia at the beginning of the 'nineties of the last century, when he (at that time a railway worker of twenty-four) had his first story printed. The Tsarist Russia of that period was one of the most class-ridden countries in Europe— a state of things which was further aggravated by her rapidly growing industry. The abolition of serfdom in 1861 had made the peasants independent of their former landlords; but as it had not given them enough land to subsist on with their growing families, the landless surplus of the village population began to flood the town-factories, often under the most appalling conditions. The position of the factory workers was rendered more precarious by the lack of adequate organizations among the working masses themselves whose cultural level was still too low for any initiative of this kind. True enough, in Russia there had existed, in the second half of the last century, a peculiar brand of "populist" or agrarian socialism, which had originated in Alexander Herzen and was confined mainly to the intelligentsia. It represented a belated (if somewhat sentimental) effort on the part of the "repentant" intellectuals from among the gentry to atone for the injustice under which the serfs had smarted for generations. This "populism" pinned its faith in a better future exclusively to the peasants tilling

MAXIM GORKY (1868-1936)

the soil, and not to the town-proletarians. It was, moreover, based on the false premise that Russia, in contrast to Europe, could by-pass the capitalist phase and jump, so to speak, from her primitive conditions straight into an agrarian socialist millennium.

Meanwhile, the industrial proletariat in the bigger Russian towns was on the increase. From the 'seventies onwards it slowly began to organize itself—first on a professional and later also on a political and ideological basis. The consolidation of this process coincided with the blossoming out of Gorky's talent. He even became, at the beginning of this century, one of the principal literary and moral forces behind all the activities connected with the working class movement in Russia—activities which reached their first climax in the abortive rising of 1905 and their triumph in the Revolution of 1917. It is the background of these two revolutions, with all the toil which preceded, conditioned and followed them, that can provide us with a reliable approach to such a phenomenon as Maxim Gorky.

2.

Born in 1868 into an artisan family at Nizhny Novgorod, now named after him, Alexey Maximovich Peshkov (Gorky's real name) soon became an orphan and stayed until the age of ten with his grandparents. His grandfather, who had a dye workshop, went bankrupt and the boy was sent to a footwear store, from which he duly escaped. For a while he served as a dishwasher on a Volga steamer, but this was only the beginning of an endless series of other professions: from a sweated worker in a baker's shop to a street pedlar; from a fisherman on the Caspian Sea to a railway worker at some remote god-forsaken stations; from a petty clerk in a lawyer's office to a debutant in literature; and from a provincial journalist to a world-famous author. In the course of all those changes and peregrinations it was in Kazan alone (where he mixed with the radical-minded undergraduates) that Gorky found a congenial atmosphere, but not for long. He had to earn his living, and there were times when he was a regular down-and-out. In 1887 he made an attempt at suicide, but his life was saved by the skill of a hospital surgeon. His frequent companions in those days were social outcasts; yet far from despising them he tried to understand their fate and to fathom through it his own attitude towards life. Years later he confessed to having felt among them "like a piece of iron in glowing coal—every day filled me with a mass of sharp, burning impressions. I saw before me people nakedly greedy, people with rough instincts—and I liked their bitterness about life, I liked their ironically hostile attitude towards everything in the world, and also their carefree attitude towards themselves." There was a great deal of moral and social callousness among them, but Gorky's actively idealistic and reformatory temperament—perhaps the most typical feature of his character—was his surest guide through the vicissitudes of life. He also realized that before taking any part in the fight against the ugliness and cruelty of existence he had much to learn. So he missed no opportunity of making up for the deficiencies of his education. Yet even after his first story, *Makar Chudra,* had appeared in a Caucasian newspaper at Tiflis, Gorky was not quite sure whether writing was his actual vocation. He continued his literary apprenticeship for another few years, working for the most part on the Volga papers, and his talent kept maturing at such a pace that in 1898 he was able to publish the first two volumes of his collected stories. Their success was immediate. Many people were shocked by the novelty of Gorky's themes, by his tone and manner, but they all read him. And they realized there and then that a new literary force had arisen which could be either accepted or rejected, but which could by no means be ignored.

The significance of this force was the greater because the decade preceding Gorky's debut was one of Chekhovian tiredness and disappointment. The resigned melancholy, so typical of Chekhov's stories and plays, is reflected in a number of his older contemporaries: in the writer Garshin (who committed suicide); in the nostalgic poetry of Nadson and Apukhtin; in the paintings of Levitan; in the music of Tchaikovsky. The only thriving proposition in those days was "business" which, from the 'eighties onwards, made rapid strides (especially under the leadership of such a financial wizard as Count Witte) and turned a large portion of the gentry into its votaries. A number of intellectuals hoped to find an escape in Tolstoy's moral perfectionism. Others looked for it in a beefy philistine indifference to everything except comfort and money. Others again shut themselves in "ivory towers" of that decadent art which celebrated its first triumphs in Russia in the middle of the same decade that was so daringly challenged by Maxim Gorky. The whole of Gorky's work can in fact be described as one long challenge. But it was also a tonic potent enough to stir up a new will and a new hope even among those who had never dared to will or to hope.

3.

Gorky's first and second periods, roughly from 1892 until 1901, bore the stamp of romantic defiance to all those forces which tend to cripple life and to dehumanize the vast majority of human beings. For this reason he chose a somewhat loud and often flowery style, charged with the fury of a "stormy petrel," as he was named at the outset. He also introduced into his stories such characters as were likely to express his own defiance and protest. We find among them gypsies, Tatar shepherds, vagabonds, smugglers, thieves, fishermen, ragged proletarians, and people from the "lower depths" in general—people who have never had the slightest reason to be in love with the existing order of things. Resentful, as well as provocative in word and in action, most of them keep to the philosophy of safety last. At the same time they have ideas of human worth which are entirely their own and do not necessarily tally with those of their social superiors, about whom they have no illusions. The consciousness of class-division and class antagonism thus reached in Gorky's characters an acuteness which was itself something new in Russian fiction, and this remained one of his permanent features. Some of Gorky's critics were inclined to see in him, during that period, a kind of Nietzsche from the gutter. But this was a superficial notion. Gorky, who had passed through the gutter and had risen so high above it, was anxious to abolish the gutter of life altogether. In this consisted his strength and his weakness: strength, because such an aim increased his creative *verve;* and weakness, because it imparted to him a didactic and, at times, schematic "purpose." Anyway, he worked in two converging directions. One of these was the way of protest in the name and on behalf of the victims, while the other took the form of a series of pictures of the gutter itself and of the "creatures that once were human beings"—to use his pregnant but untranslatable Russian phrase *byvshie lyudi.*

Most of his early material was taken by Gorky from his own experiences and observations. And like Leskov before him, he keenly appreciated an incident as such, which he imbued with a provocatively romantic and also provocatively didactic strain. This applies even to his pictures of the "lower depths," where his realism of indictment had full sway. For no matter how degraded the people described, he lost no opportunity of stressing the potential excellence of the human material thus crushed and wasted by the prevailing social system. One of his expedients of intensified characterization was the kind of contrast one finds in his early story called *Chelkash*. Its hero, a carefree thief and outcast, has no respect for anybody or anything, yet at bottom he is a broad, generous type—a potential aristocrat by nature. His helper in a somewhat risky adventure is a pious little peasant who in the end turns out to be a worm—capable of murdering his companion in order to gratify his own greed for money. As a result the outcast Chelkash turns out to be much better human material than the acquisitive God-fearing peasant who can think in no other terms except those of property.

Nowhere, however, is Gorky's faith in the latent value of the social outcast stressed to better purpose than in his story, *Twenty-six Men and One Girl,* written in 1899. Twenty-six "creatures that once were men" toil like slaves in a filthy suburban bakery, mercilessly exploited by their boss and despised even by those workers whose pay and social status are slightly higher than theirs. The only ray of light in that squalor is a pretty innocent girl who passes every morning by their den in order to collect some pretzel buns. All the twenty-six slaves fall in love with her—ideally and chivalrously, since she embodies that element of decency and beauty of life which still secretly smoulders at the bottom of their hearts. But even this last illusion is gone when, one day, they find out that she has succumbed to the charms of a swaggering vulgarian, and their brutal revenge only proves the depth of their disappointment.

It was not for nothing that the author of such narratives assumed the nickname Maxim the Bitter (Gorky means "bitter" in Russian). But since his bitterness only increased his fight against the filth and cruelty of life, he could not help being didactic even to the extent of turning many of his characters into mouthpieces of his own ideas. Hence his frequent preachings, his love for sententious formulae, his exuberance and—in contrast to Chekhov—his use of glaring colors. One of the chief faults of his early writings was the overstatement in which he indulged because he naïvely mistook it for strength.

It may have been for this reason that, in a letter, Chekhov referred to Gorky as a deep and thinking author but carrying "much unnecessary ballast—for example his provincialism." In another letter, addressed to Gorky himself (in December 1898) Chekhov expressed his friendly and at the same time severe criticism of Gorky's style in these terms: "In my opinion you do not use sufficient restraint. You are like a spectator in the theatre who expresses his rapture so unreservedly that he prevents both himself and others from listening. Particularly is this lack of restraint felt in the descriptions of Nature with which you interrupt your dialogues; when one reads those descriptions one wishes they were more compact, shorter, put, say, into two or three lines. The frequent mention of tenderness, whispering, velvetiness, and so on, gives to these descriptions a certain character of rhetoric and monotony—and they chill the reader, almost tire him. Lack of restraint is felt also in the description of women and in the love scenes. It is not vigor, nor breadth of touch, but plain lack of reserve." *

This is a fair criticism, especially of Gorky at his worst. But one should not forget that Gorky was a self-made author of a new type who wrote deliberately for a new type of reader,

* *The Life and Letters of Anton Chekhov,* Cassell.

emerging among the working classes themselves. This self-made
reader (if one is allowed to call him so) needed a different approach as well as different food from that offered by the intelligentsia literature of the period. He found both in Gorky's
writings.

4.

Gorky proved a greater stimulus in this respect than any other
Russian author. And when he was at the height of success, he
not only did not dissociate himself from the working masses
but, on the contrary, took a lead in their movement, knowing
that his voice was likely to be heard far and wide. This necessi-
tated, however, an enlargement of his themes, which now included a deeper criticism of society and of the life around
beginning with his first longer work, *Foma Gordeyev* (1899).
The background of this novel is the close-fisted but already
decaying commercial bourgeoisie in a Volga town. Realizing
the emptiness of such existence with its opulent animality, the
principal character Foma, a member of the same class, feels out
of tune with it. One can see in him a not very successful transposition of the "superfluous man" from the gentry to a different
social layer. For Gorky's Foma is the only anaemic character in
the novel. He is certainly much less alive and impressive than
his enterprising father. But to make up for him, the author
brings in some of those dissatisfied characters whose moods and
activities are dictated by a clearer awareness of what they want
and why. Critical realism inspired by a romantic faith and
aiming at a complete renewal of life, now became Gorky's
favorite attitude. This was partly the reason why he tried his
strength in dramatic activities as well. Aware of the influence
that could be exercised from the stage, he wrote in 1901 his

first play, *The Petit-Bourgeois* (*Meshchane*). Here he challenged the philistinism of the more prosperous artisan-class,
the only redeeming feature of which he found in the younger
generation consciously working for a new life and a new
era to come. About a year later, Gorky's second play *The
Lower Depths* (*Na dne*) became a world success, partly because of its subject-matter. The author introduces us here to the
inmates of a dosshouse, yet amidst all the misery and degradation of those "ex-humans" one can still perceive sparks of humanity, strangely mixed with their dreams of a better life. The
indignation permeating the play is social as well as ethical,
and his brutal frankness about the depth of human misery can
have an overwhelming effect, if well acted.

Gorky was by then a member of the Russian social-democratic
party which he joined in 1902. He became something of a
focus for the revolutionary activities before and during the
eventful year of 1905, which did not prevent him, however,
from finishing two more plays, *The Holiday Makers* and *Children of the Sun*. Both were rather topical at the moment: they
treated the old problem of the intelligentsia and the people
from a new angle. Gorky's attitude towards the intellectuals of
his own period was, on the whole, negative. He thought the
bulk of them effete and the more "superfluous" because they
were already despised by the people themselves who could not
help seeing the emptiness of their existence. In another piece,
The Barbarians, the two intellectuals—this time two engineers,
building a railway through a remote provincial town—succeed
in corrupting the whole town as if it had been invaded by a
barbarian horde. The only hope Gorky could see was the new
intellectual arising from the masses and courageously working
for a better future. This, at any rate, is the leading idea of *The*

Holiday Makers, which—let it be said in fairness—is far from being a good play. The problem of the intelligentsia is tackled somewhat differently in *Children of the Sun.* Here we see the elite of the mind; but since this elite is severed from the masses, the danger of it being ousted from life altogether is there and, as Gorky shows, abounds in dreadful possibilities. Finally, in *The Enemies* (1906) he considered the proletariat, in its struggle against capitalism, the principal and perhaps the only guarantee of a better future. Gorky's plays were being successfully staged all over Russia at a time when Chekhov's dramatic art had at last found its proper interpretation in the Moscow Arts Theatre. Even more interesting is the fact that Gorky, whose explosive manner was so different from that of Chekhov, actually adopted Chekhov's technique of a "static" drama. It was a risky step on the part of such a dynamic personality as Gorky. More than once he was in danger of turning Chekhov's delicate lyrical pastel into a didactic oleograph. At his best, however, he managed to get away with it—in his *Lower Depths,* for instance.

5.

Gorky's dramatic works marked a further stage in his endeavor to make literature itself active in clearing away the ballast of the old life. He also became the promoter of the publishing firm *Znanie* (Knowledge) as a gathering point for all those authors who were anxious to preserve the good traditions of Russian realism and yet make their own writings socially significant—in plain defiance of the detached "highbrow" aestheticism just then in the ascendant. The success of this venture surpassed all expectations. A number of talented young

authors—Kuprin, Andreyev, Shmelyov, Veresayev, Bunin—
wrote for *Znanie,* the association with which soon became an
entrance ticket to fame.

Gorky's influence had grown by then enough to make the
authorities perturbed. Having already been in prison on many
occasions, Gorky regarded further experiences of this kind as
a matter of course. After the blood-bath of January 9th, 1905,
when a peaceful procession of workers wishing to lay their
grievances before the Tsar had been massacred by the troops
almost within the precincts of the Winter Palace, Gorky was
arrested once again. His fame was already so great that violent protests followed from all over Europe, under the pressure of which he had to be released. But he remained as incor-
rigible as ever. In October 1905 he founded the socialist paper
New Life which, edited by Lenin himself, existed for some
five weeks before it was clamped down by the police. It was in
this paper that Gorky's series of attacks on the modern bourgeois mentality appeared. He also played one of the leading
parts in the Moscow rising. And when the Revolution of 1905
had proved a failure, Gorky gave all his support to those who
had decided to continue their fight underground. He travelled
in both Europe and America in order to increase the funds of
his party. Then he settled down on the island of Capri where
he worked for a resumption of the struggle and wrote his
revolutionary novel *The Mother* (1907-08)—his first big work
since 1905.

An important social document and a propaganda novel rather
than a work of art, *The Mother* depicts the Russian workers'
struggle for their rights at the beginning of this century. The
events described actually took place in 1902 in the factory district of Sormov near Nizhny Novgorod, and the two leading
characters of the novel—the young worker Vlasov and his

widowed mother—were among Gorky's personal friends. The early chapters, which are the best, show the low level of the old-time factory workers: their sloth, apathy, drunken rows, and hooliganism. Then, gradually, a new set of social values and ideals, with which some of them come into contact, produces an almost miraculous change. The change does not remain mere theory, but is soon translated into an active determination to work for a better future. Gorky makes us follow the various phases of this process. We see how revolutionary organizations are formed from within. Further, we witness the clashes between the workers and the employers; the onslaught of the reactionary powers-that-be. But the struggle goes on, and the tenacity on the part of the workers grows in proportion to their setbacks. The chief impression conveyed by this novel is the incredible vitality of Russian workers once they have embraced a cause in which they believe. Yet it is here in particular that Gorky's didactic propensity asserts itself to the uttermost: propaganda is mixed with, rather than sublimated by, art. In spite of its faults the novel had a tremendous effect upon the working-class consciousness in Russia as well as abroad, notably in France and Germany, at a time when even the liberal bourgeoisie of those two countries had turned against Gorky.

6.

Less than a year after *The Mother,* Gorky published one of his strangest and in its own way fascinating books, called simply *A Confession.* Written in the first person, it reveals a typical Russian roamer: not the anarchic vagabond of Gorky's earlier stories, but an almost Leskovian hero—deeply rooted in his country and united through a kind of *participation mystique* with the eternally toiling, eternally yearning and seeking, "God-seeking" folk masses. Its pages vibrate with that innate love for the land and the people which is a matter of one's deepest instincts rather than any ideologies, and which was so typical of Leskov. Also the beauty of the spacious Russian landscape is conjured up with all its charm. It is Gorky's most poetic book about Russia—probably inspired by nostalgia for his country. The distance which lay between him and Russia made him, however, see and judge also the negative side of Russian life in its proper perspective. This in its turn was responsible for Gorky's increased realism of indictment, as we find it in his narratives, *The Town of Okurov* and *The Life of Matvey Kozhemyakin* (1909-11).

These two works are interdependent. *The Town of Okurov* is called (like Leskov's *Cathedral Folk*) a chronicle. It deals with the same remote provincial Russia as Leskov's famous work, but as it shows only its reverse side, it is more in the line of Saltykov-Shchedrin's scathing invectives. The hero of the narrative is the town itself. There may be a difference between its "respectable" part and its destitute suburb, yet in both life is equally drab, senseless and squalid. The only diversion that now and then interrupts its monotony is crime, or the kind of shabby drama which forms the climax of the narrative at the moment when echoes of the Revolution of 1905 are beginning to stir up even this God-forsaken hole. A typical chronicle is also *The Life of Matvey Kozhemyakin*. Gorky takes here a lower-middle-class inhabitant of the same Okurov and unrolls before us his existence during some fifty years of continuous frustrations. Sapped from the outset, Kozhemyakin is essentially a decent fellow, all the time groping for something worth living for, though without guidance or any tangible results. He feels as "superfluous" in his surroundings as Foma

Gordeyev felt in his, and is equally unable to cope with their crushing effect. His death, which is only the last act of a long and slow process of dying, takes place when the revolutionary outburst of 1905 seems to promise a different era. To quote an entry from Kozhemyakin's own diary shortly before he died: "New workers have now appeared in our life—with hearts full of love for this earth which we have besmirched; they are living ploughs which will furrow God's field deeply, down to its very heart and will make it glow and blossom up with a new sun, warm and kindly to all men, bringing to them a happy life."

After some three hundred pages of "Chekhovian" futility, but depicted with Gorky's ruggedness and indignation, the final note of this work is one of faith and hope. And such an attitude was typical of Gorky even during the stifling era of "Stolypin's collar," * as the noose of the hangman's rope was ironically called at the time. There was, of course, Tolstoy's protest—in his pamphlet *I Cannot Be Silent;* there was a virulent indictment by Korolenko, but nothing could stay the triumph of reaction, which gradually became undermined by its own excesses. Among the major authors Gorky too refused to give in. His criticism of the Okurov Russia became increasingly violent, and so did his insistence on a radical change. Even his most significant literary achievements between the two revolutions, *Childhood* and *In the World*—the first two parts of his autobiographical trilogy—are an indictment of those conditions which can cripple one's tender years as had been the case with Gorky himself. The only bright spot in the nightmare of his early life was his granny, whose portraiture in the book is unforgettable.

---

* The prime-minister Stolypin was regarded as being chiefly responsible for the epidemic of executions after the triumph of reaction in 1905.

Thanks to the amnesty on the occasion of the tercentenary of the Romanovs in 1913, Gorky was allowed to return to Russia where he stayed all through the First World War. But as he was far from enthusiastic either about the war or its behind-the-scenes, his subversive activities continued. In the winter of 1915 he started a big monthly, *The Annals* (*Letopis*), the spirit of which was anti-bourgeois, anti-war, and anti-imperialistic. Then the Revolution of 1917 came which, with all its defects and horrors, seemed at first to promise the very things Gorky had all the time been fighting for. His two bugbears, the decayed capitalist bourgeoisie and the decayed section of the intelligentsia, were swept away by the tidal wave of the upheaval which, at last, opened up as it were the untapped energies of the masses inhabiting one sixth of our globe. To quote Gorky's own words, "Now the entire Russian people is taking part in history—this is an event of cardinal importance, and it is from this angle that we ought to judge all the bad and good things, all our joys and sorrows."

This does not mean that Gorky approved of everything that was taking place in those fateful days. In his resuscitated periodical, *New Life,* he indulged in a series of polemics with the Bolsheviks and with Lenin himself. Appalled by the excesses let loose by the Revolution, he insisted more than ever on raising the cultural level of the masses and, after his reconciliation with Lenin in 1918, he did his utmost to achieve this end. He was one of the principal organizers of help to all writers and savants, regardless of their political allegiance, and this was not a small matter during the general shortage and famine. Gorky also stepped in as a defender of cultural continuity at a time when a number of people were advocating a purely proletarian culture. It was he in particular who turned against such narrow-minded sectarianism and demanded that the best elements bequeathed by the former intelligentsia-culture should be assimilated by the Soviet masses and creatively blended with what they themselves could give to the world. Further, even before the duress of the civil war was over, he set up a far-reaching undertaking, the aim of which was to present the Soviet people with the classical works of world literature, translated and commentated by experts. In this manner he became a bridge not only between the Soviets and the former Russian culture, but also between the Soviets and the culture of the world.

Whether Gorky welcomed or not all the single aspects connected with the birth-pangs of the New Russia does not really matter. What matters is that he fully realized the impact of the new *direction* given to world-history by the Revolution of 1917. After all, Tsarist Russia had been a diseased organism in need of a surgical operation, and the operations performed by history are usually done without anaesthetics. So we must not be surprised that, in spite of repeated squabbles and misunderstandings, Gorky rightly or wrongly threw in his lot with the Soviet system—a step which, several years after, he explained in a private letter as follows: "Do I side with the Bolsheviks who deny freedom? Yes, I do, because I stand for the freedom of all people who work honestly, but I am against the freedom of parasites and harmful babblers. I used to argue with the Bolsheviks and to oppose them in 1917, when it seemed to me that they were unlikely to win over the peasants driven by the war into anarchy, and that a conflict with them threatened to ruin the workers' party itself. Then I came to the conclusion that I was wrong, and now I am fully convinced that the Russian people, however much it be hated by the governments of Europe and whatever its economic difficulties as a result of that hatred, has entered upon the phase of its regeneration."

7.

All these activities on the part of Gorky were so much hampered by his bad health (chronic tuberculosis) that in the winter of 1921 he undertook a cure abroad, first in Germany and later in Southern Italy, whence he returned to Russia in 1928. During that time his literary output remained as abundant as ever and included some of his maturest works: *My Universities,* his novels *The Artamonov Business* and *The Life of Klim Samgin,* as well as his play *Yegor Bulichov.*

My Universities refers to Gorky's hard school of life during his years of adolescence and early manhood. It completes his autobiographical trilogy and (like the first two parts) is crammed with incidents, portraits and descriptions, done without any self-pity and on a high literary level. Like the previous two volumes, it is invaluable for an understanding of Gorky's development and of his personality in general. As for *The Artamonov Business* (1925), the very title of this artistically most perfect novel he ever wrote suggests that, once again, we are taken back to the moneyed bourgeoisie of the old regime. Like *The Forsyte Saga,* it is the history of a big firm spread over three successive generations. Stained by a crime at its beginning, the factory founded by the enterprising ex-serf Artamonov soon expanded into a prosperous concern. But the disintegrating process already set in with the second generation, while in the third the Artamonov dynasty was deposed by the Revolution of 1917. The firm became national property, and a new era began—at least for the workers. A similar motif must have been in Gorky's mind when he planned his unfinished dramatic trilogy of which *Yegor Bulichov* was to be the first part. Here, too, as in *The Artamonov Business,* we see the new era knocking at the door of a prosperous but corrupt firm, only this time the starting point is the chaos prevailing during the First World War and the February Revolution. The cunningly unscrupulous Yegor Bulichov is something of a symbol of the old system and, like the system itself, suffers from a mortal illness. When at last the song of the rising masses bursts from the street into the room of the dying invalid, he knows that his time is up. "What is it? The burial service singing me out of the world!" And so it is. The burial service for the entire historical period represented by him.

There still remains *The Life of Klim Samgin*—the biggest and most ambitious of Gorky's works. It is in four parts, the last of which remained unfinished. At a first glance it may look like a more detailed intelligentsia counterpart of his petit-bourgeois chronicle, *Matvey Kozhemyakin*. But it turns out to be something much bigger: a chronicle of Russian life during some forty years—roughly from 1880 until 1917. Gorky attempted to give here a cross-section of practically all the Russian classes as seen by a typical offspring of the intelligentsia, Klim Samgin. Klim himself serves as the center for an amazing variety of characters, many of them in the course of their development, or else depicted in their reactions to all the phases and crises of Russian history during those years. Particularly good is the first part, showing the early development of a whole generation in a big provincial center. The second and third parts, dealing with the Russo-Japanese War and the events of 1905, may at times be drawn out (by lengthy discussions), but they are of paramount documentary value. The same can be said of the unfinished fourth part, which brings events up to the February Revolution of 1917. Such a long and ambitious chronicle of Russian life is bound to be uneven, but its finest portions show Gorky at his best. The work is a masterpiece of critical realism. Yet however realistic Gorky's method, one feels underneath it—here perhaps more than in any of his former writings—an active idealist aiming at a transformation of the existing pattern of life. Apart from his descriptive passages, Gorky excels here as a portrait painter and psychologist. In no other work did he give such a number of complicated, even "Dostoevskian" characters as here, beginning with the principal hero Klim Samgin, whose life is an abbreviated and somewhat symbolic image of that liberal intelligentsia which was thrown out of its unfulfilled historical mission by the Revolution. It was through him that Gorky tried to analyze not only the external but the inner reasons why it was that during the most crucial period of Russian history the intelligentsia proved unable to lead the country and the nation through the crisis. This is why it was necessary to show—in retrospect— the entire development of the generation represented by Klim. We see him first as a child growing up in a family with "populist" traditions. After his Grammar School years in a provincial town, we follow him as a student to Petersburg, to Moscow, then as a lawyer to the provinces, as a tourist abroad (mainly in Paris), finally again to Petersburg where he watches the Revolution of 1917 and becomes one of its victims. He is a most interesting summary of the bourgeois intelligentsia in its process of Hamlet-like doubts and disintegration. We watch how, step by step, everything goes to seed in that particular circle: family, love, sex, culture, literature, politics, while the happenings in Russia seem to go on as though urged by an irresistible logic of their own. The final issue is, in fact, Intelligentsia and the Revolution. It is an answer, or at least Gorky's answer to the question why the intelligentsia could not help being so cruelly eliminated by the cataclysm of 1917.

8.

Even a brief survey such as this should not omit mentioning Gorky's pamphlets, diaries, articles, essays, and especially his excellent reminiscences of Tolstoy, Korolenko, Chekhov, and Andreyev. Those of Tolstoy are among the shrewdest things ever written about that complicated genius. As though emulating Leskov, Gorky gives us here not analysis, but only a string of anecdotes and impressions, organized in such a manner as to present Tolstoy without the slightest hagiographical touch—intensely human and intensely alive.

Last but not least, Gorky was the initiator and the first theoretician of socialist realism, which is at present the only legitimate current in the literature of Soviet Russia. The actual aim of this current, which has undergone considerable changes since its birth in 1932, was or should have been eventual integration not only of the individual and society, but also of literature and life. In Gorky's opinion socialist realism "presents Being as action, as creation aimed at the unbroken development of the finest individual traits of man, that he may triumph over the forces of nature, that he may realize the joy of living on earth, which by his ever-increasing requirements he is induced to transform into a splendid place for all mankind united into a single family."

This active type of realism in the name of a new life involved by its very nature what might be called socialist humanism, which indeed was closely connected with Gorky's name. A society founded on the struggles and the hatred of classes necessarily requires countless victims and personal frustrations, by virtue of which the individual willy-nilly regards himself as an enemy of society. This feeling of hostility and general uprootedness grows together with the callous and destructive brand of pessimism. As Gorky himself pointed out, "in the twentieth century pessimism degenerated into a philosophy of complete social cynicism, into a complete and decisive denial of 'humanitarianism' of which in former times the bourgeois of all countries boasted so much." He saw the only remedy in a society based on a pattern which would form a synthesis of socialism and humanism. A synthesis of this kind was for him the great problem of today and of tomorrow. Here literature, as Gorky thought, could be a powerful corrective. This is why, only two years before his death, he said in one of his talks: "I want literature to rise above reality and to look down on reality from above, because literature has a far greater purpose than merely to reflect reality. It is not enough to depict already existing things—we must also bear in mind the things we desire and the things which are possible of achievement." This last sentence could be used as a motto for Gorky's work as a whole. In a number of his writings he proved to be the very embodiment of socialist humanism with its respect for human personality—not isolated and self-centered personality, but one directed towards, and consciously working for, its integration with society. No wonder that he became the idol of the new readers as well as the new intellectuals from among the Russian working classes, whose tastes and requirements differ considerably from those of the former intelligentsia.

The success of this trend in particular can be judged by the astronomical sales of his writings. According to the *Literary Gazette* (June 15th, 1946) Gorky's works have appeared, between 1917 and 1946, in sixty-six languages and have sold in 42,000,000 copies. It is doubtful whether any author anywhere else on earth could dream of such sales. Even the fateful years which have passed since Gorky's death in 1936 do not seem to have impaired his stature. Having come from the people, he is still regarded as the people's author in the truest sense. And lastly, his own will and vitality seem to be symbolic of a nation which has shrunk from no labors, no sacrifices, and even no mistakes in order to shape a life different from its past ordeals. It will be for history to say whether this task is to succeed or not.

CHAPTER SIXTEEN

Leonid Andreyev

I.

In each literature there are authors the symptomatic significance of whose works is often greater than their artistic value. Typical not so much of their own epoch as a whole but rather of some of its conspicuous single facets, they are usually overrated during their life-time, and underestimated once they are dead. Such, at any rate, was the fate of Leonid Andreyev (1871-1919) who, between 1902 and 1910, was one of the most discussed writers in Russia and, for a time, rivalled in popularity even Gorky himself. Nor is it without interest that the first literary successes of Andreyev were partly connected with Gorky's name, although he later became hostile to everything Maxim Gorky stood for. While Gorky worked for a new era, a new community and a new set of readers, Andreyev preferred to hitch his talent to the decaying bourgeois intelligentsia in order to reflect, as in a magnifying and also somewhat crooked mirror, their consciousness during the last few years before their passing out of history. Roughly from the middle of the 'nineties onwards, the spirit of despondence was being gradually replaced by more hopeful moods, at least on the part of those intellectuals who saw the *raison d'être* of their existence in paving the way for a final clash with the forces of reaction. But when, in 1905, the clash took place, the reaction won a victory so brutal and yet so complete that most of the bellicose intellectuals were hurled, once again, into the slough of despond; or into a vacuum, where the demand for all kinds of dopes and escapes—aesthetic, "mystical," or even grossly sensuous—was on the increase. Andreyev seized the opportunity and became, overnight as it were, one of the most successful authors in Russia. But he was not the only one ministering to those particular needs of the defeated and defeatist intelligentsia. There were other modernists who, on different levels, played a similar part: Sologub, for instance, or Artsybashev.

Fyodor Sologub, a "highbrow" decadent and symbolist, differed from the rest in so far as he did not cater for popularity. Keeping away from public life, he shut himself in his private ivory tower, where he indulged in an aesthetic or would-be aesthetic cult of death and of weird necromantic phantoms. But even before reaching that stage, he had made—in his novel *A Petty Demon*—a formidable onslaught on that philistine vulgarity, the fight with which was considered almost a duty by every Russian author from Gogol onwards. The hero of Sologub's novel—a paranoiac schoolmaster—outstrips even Gogol's examples of intensified vulgarity and, like the characters in *Dead Souls,* he is symbolic in his realism. But whereas Sologub was concerned with the elite, Artsybashev wrote for the rank and file of the demoralized intellectuals; for those in fact who were on the look-out for cheaper means of escape, even if this meant a surrender to sexual looseness, such as is preached in Artsybashev's sensational novel *Sanin*. He must have cashed in well on it; yet even in the heyday of his popularity (or notoriety) his success could not compare with that of Andreyev whose work falls, roughly, somewhere between that of Sologub and Artsybashev.

Apart from his early stories, the majority of Andreyev's writings deal with rather "big" subjects, treated in that hasty quasi-modernist style which, for all its pretentious garb, is generally accessible and therefore likely to flatter the vanity of the less tutored readers by giving them the illusion of being "highbrows." But this alone would hardly have brought him to the pinnacle of fame and prosperity, had he not sponsored some of those sensational themes which were bound to appeal to the intellectuals of the post-1905 period.

2.

As a son of a petty official in the provinces Andreyev could not boast of a background spacious and cultured enough to give him that sureness of taste without the guidance (whether conscious or unconscious) of which even a great literary talent is likely to go astray in an age so full of experiments and vagaries as the one he lived in. On finishing his University studies, he became a lawyer's assistant—a profession he gave up when he discovered (from 1897 onwards) that he could make a living as an author. In his early stories the echoes of Chekhov, Korolenko, and Gorky are noticeable. Soon the influences of Dostoevsky and Tolstoy were added, and later also that of Edgar Allan Poe. The writings of his early period are realistic, with a social or humanitarian undercurrent, but invariably ending in a minor key. The final note of his *Little Angel* (1899), for instance, is one of gloom and disillusionment. So is the ending of *Petka in the Country* (1899)—a pathetic story of a boy of ten slaving as a barber's assistant in Moscow. For the first time in his life he is taken for a holiday in the countryside; but when his impressionable mind has opened to all the beauties of nature, he is forced to go back to his tedious drudgery in the Moscow slums.

Even when Andreyev became a member of Gorky's publishing firm *Znanie* (Knowledge) he made hardly any concessions to the social or humanitarian optimism of that group. One of such concessions is his story *In the Basement,* obviously implying—like Gorky's *Twenty-six Men and One Girl*—that even the hearts of the "ex-humans" still retain some sparks of true humanity which may flare up if given a chance. Two of Andreyev's best early stories, *Once there Lived* (1901) and *In the Fog* (1902) were partly inspired by Tolstoy—the first by *The Death of Ivan Ilyich,* and the second by *The Kreutzer Sonata.* *Once there Lived* takes place in a clinic where there are several patients knowing that they are doomed, but the atmosphere of death is handled with Chekhov's technique and, what is more, with Chekhovian understatement—a rare thing in Andreyev's writings. A different propensity is noticeable in *In the Fog.* Here Andreyev tackled the tragedy of awakened sex in a schoolboy who has contracted a venereal disease and eventually murders a prostitute and commits suicide. The story caused much uproar and can serve as a proof of the author's growing hankering for sensational themes, worked out in a dramatic (or melodramatic) manner. This was particularly the case when he came under the spell of Dostoevsky's themes and problems. As the latter were often much bigger than his talent, he tried to make up for it by raising his tone and filling his pages with would-be symbolistic *clichés,* designed to surprise, or rather to stun his readers also by means of paradoxical logic. This brought, however, a forced, not to say false note into his writings, and its pretence increased in the ratio in which he abandoned the straightforward realistic method for the sake of stilted pseudo-symbolism. This genre was clearly anticipated in stories such as *Silence, The Wall, The Tocsin, The Abyss,* and *The Thought*—all of them written between 1900 and 1902 in a mood of futility. Chekhov's pathetic blind-alley was taken up by Andreyev with relish, but he turned it into a substitute for religion, with its theology of "mystical anarchism," its solemnly hollow rites and incantations, the only genuine element in which was his fear of life. The apotheosis of this fear became Andreyev's "purpose" (one could almost say—moral purpose) which he piously cultivated as the very essence of his own aesthetic modernism.

Always an individualist, Andreyev was strongly attracted by the heroic pose of a modern anti-philistine. But as he felt more and more the fascination of Dostoevsky's metaphysical rebels, he too became one of them without even believing in metaphysics. He prostrated himself before the principle of negation which he pushed to the verge of grotesqueness. Like some of Dostoevsky's heroes he saw (or forced himself to see) in life only a "vaudeville of the devils"; but instead of searching for something beyond it, as Dostoevsky did, he derived from the very hopelessness of such a disposition—into which he often worked himself by means of alcohol—a peculiar and almost ecstatic pleasure.

3.

One of his first successful longer stories, imbued with this kind of nihilism, was *Life of Father Vasily Fiveysky* (1903). The problem here tackled is the eternal problem of evil, only the questioner in Andreyev's story is a village priest whose unconditional faith in God is being gradually undermined by the horrors of life he sees around. Like a modern Job, Father Vasily passes through a series of personal and family misfortunes, including the birth of an idiot son. He first looks for comfort in the Christian faith, but his reiterations of the formula, "I believe, O Lord, I believe," are answered only by the imbecile laughter of his stinking little idiot and by an all round increase of evil—personal and otherwise. Outraged in his moral sense of justice, the priest hurls at last a mad challenge to God, but here he himself is crushed by the weight of the emptiness in a Godless and senseless world.

Senselessness is further canonized in Andreyev's story, *Phantoms* (1904)—obviously a literary descendant of Chekhov's *Ward No. 6,* with the action taking place in a lunatic asylum. The author analyzes the imaginary phantom existence of the inmates in whose minds the boundary line between the normal and the abnormal has been obliterated. But life outside the asylum (especially in the fashionable night-club, where the doctor in charge spends most of his free time) is implied to be equally phantom-like; so there is not much to choose between the two. Or take *The Red Laugh* (1905)—a crudely pretentious monologue of an officer who lost both legs in the Russo-Japanese War, the "madness and horror" of which continue to haunt him in his invalid bed at home. In Andreyev's allegorical narrative, *Thus Was It and Will Be* (1905), the futility of revolutionary upheavals is marked by the clock of time and its indifference to the happenings on earth, the history of which remains the same blood-stained farce, no matter what antics and atrocities may be performed by the human Yahoos. With no less emphasis Andreyev stresses in another story, *My Memoirs* (1908), the nothingness of freedom and—by implication—of the fight for freedom. To crown it all, his turgid *Lazarus* (1906) brings such a nihilistic attitude to a head. Lazarus, resurrected by Christ, is more like a walking corpse, paralyzing all those with whom he comes into contact, since he reminds them by the mystery peering out of his eyes that life itself is only a form of death.

Yet if his "metaphysical" themes often outstrip his talent, Andreyev fares much better when concentrating mainly on psychology. One of his best stories of this kind, *The Governor* (1905), is told with restraint and with almost Tolstoyan matter-of-factness. The hero of the story is the governor of a province who in the turmoil of the revolution ordered that a gathering of workers should be shot at. As a consequence he receives an intimation from the local terrorists that they have sentenced him to death, and the certainty of impending doom hangs over him like fate itself, until the inevitable happens. As psychologist Andreyev had learned a great deal from Dostoevsky. At his best he also succeeded in skilfully combining psychological observations with some deeper thought which added to the value of the story. In his *Christians* (1904), for example, he unmasks with unflagging irony the hypocritical character of our Christianity, seen from the angle of a prostitute who obstinately refuses to take a Christian oath, to the indignation of the no-less-prostituted but otherwise respectable and respected citizens—a mark of Tolstoy's influence.

More involved in its subject-matter is the story, *Darkness* (1907). Once again, Andreyev attacks morality, but this time from an unexpected and in its own way supra-moral angle. A revolutionary terrorist, whose whole life has been one long struggle for freedom and justice, is hiding from the police. The circle of his pursuers has grown so narrow that the only refuge where he still feels relatively safe is a house of ill-fame. As he has never been in such a place before, he is staggered by the filth and degradation he finds there. In his struggle for a better world he had kept pure and never touched a woman. Now, too, he would have nothing to do with the prostitute in whose room he is hiding. But having guessed who he is, and feeling offended by his purity, she asks him rather impertinently what right he

has to be moral while she and millions of other human beings
cannot help wallowing in filth. The problem unexpectedly sinks
into his mind and, step by step, produces a strange reaction.
Unable to behave like a "saved" moral prig amidst so much
squalor around him, he begins to feel uneasy about his own
"white robes" until he is actually ashamed of them. In the
end he becomes conscience-stricken on account of his chastity,
in which state of mind he is impelled by a strangely twisted
moral impulse to degrade himself, and to fall so low indeed that
even the gendarmes, who at last get hold of him, are disgusted
—without suspecting the actual cause of his "immorality."

<h1 style="text-align:center">4.</h1>

Andreyev can be good, even excellent, only when he is less
preoccupied with his nihilistic outlook than with the story as
such, provided he tells it without affectations. The two of his
longer though widely different narratives of this kind are
Judas Iscariot and Others (1907) and *The Seven that Were
Hanged* (1908).

The first of them is rather ambitious not only because it is
connected with the Gospel, but on account of the mysterious
personality of Judas himself. What were the motives behind his
betrayal of Jesus Christ, since greed alone is too paltry an
explanation? Did he want to protect Jesus, hoping that while in
prison He would be beyond the reach of the infuriated Jews?
Or was he anxious that Jesus should fulfil His mission without
vacillating and thus proclaim His own glory to the world?
Without bothering about any previous explanations of the motives, Andreyev took a provocative line of his own. His Judas is
something of a self-divided modern misanthropist whose double
nature is marked by the very shape of his ugly head. Endowed

with far greater intelligence and knowledge of life than all the other disciples put together, he is suspicious and cynically scornful of human beings. He does not think much of the noisy plebeian Peter or of the smugly virtuous John, let alone the weak-minded simpleton Thomas. But he knows how to conceal his spite, as well as his cruel wisdom, behind the mask of a clown. There is only one person before whom he bows unconditionally and with fanatical devotion, namely Jesus. Judas the cynic would not question for a moment the Master's moral and spiritual greatness. The point about which he felt skeptical though was the assertion of Jesus that He was the Son of God, since the clever doubter Judas could hardly presume the existence of a God behind such a senseless world. He was puzzled by it to the point of actually betraying Jesus Christ in order to arrive at some certainty at least with regard to this matter. For if God exists at all, He would not allow the scoundrels to triumph over His beloved Son, and a miracle was sure to happen, proclaiming the Savior's glory to the world. But even if God does not exist, the Master's hour of trial might still become an hour of triumph, because the mob, callous though it was, could not but recognize in Him the noblest being that ever trod the earth.

This was why the betrayal took place. Insults were piled on Jesus. He was ridiculed, maltreated, tortured, spat upon, yet God remained silent: no miracle happened. And the howling mob, which not long before had shouted Hosanna in the streets of Jerusalem, now clamored for the malefactor Barabbas to be set free instead of Jesus. During the Master's agony Judas, too, went through a crucifixion of his own. With anguish past endurance he watched the last hours of Jesus at a time when all the other disciples, prudently hiding, were able—to Judas's disgust—to eat and even to sleep. But of what account were the disciples now that everything had crumbled to pieces! The only thing left was to fling the money back into the faces of the pompous worthies responsible for the Master's fate and then clear out of a world in which such things were possible. Which he did.

The Seven that Were Hanged is much more topical. It was written during the worst days of the Stolypin regime, when hangings of the revolutionaries were a daily occurrence. Andreyev obviously wanted to join Tolstoy and Korolenko in their vigorous protest, only instead of a pamphlet he presented the world with a gruesome and in its own way intensely moving story about seven people—five revolutionaries and two ordinary criminals—condemned to die on the gallows. The thoughts, moods and emotions of each of them, from the sentence of death to the moment of their execution, are described with powerful directness and with warmth, although even here Andreyev is interested in the revolutionary personalities rather than in the revolution as such. Anyway, this time he paid due tribute to the fighters who sacrificed their lives for the sake of that better world about which he himself was so skeptical.

The dilemma of a selfless terrorist forms the backbone of Andreyev's only real novel, *Sashka Zhegulyov* (1911). Sashka is a young intellectual who, in the years of upheaval, joins the revolution from sheer altruism. He forms a band of terrorists, but in their practice criminal and revolutionary motives become so intermixed that in the end it is impossible to tell one from the other. Under duress the band dissolves, while its few remaining members are surrounded and killed. The novel bears the mark of Andreyev's weakening talent. The same can be said with greater justice about his *Satan's Diary* (1917) even if its idea of the devil (embodied in an American multi-millionaire) being out-deviled by human malice and base-ness is not bad at all. As though feeling that his narrative zest was subsiding, Andreyev turned, from 1908 onwards, more and more to the theatre and the drama.

5.

He began writing plays after the success of Maxim Gorky's *Lower Depths.* As he was at that time considered—in popu-larity at least—a rival of Gorky, it was natural that he should have emulated him also on the stage where he soon became more prolific than Gorky himself. From 1912 onwards he wrote practically nothing but plays. Like his stories, these can be divided into a realistic and a philosophic group, with the addi-tion of a few pot-boilers of the kind that are sure to please the public. And like his stories again, they all reflect Andreyev's problem-hunting and nihilism *à outrance.*

In his first dramatic work, *To the Stars* (1905), he tackled the Nietzschean problem of one's love for the "far ones" as being something incompatible with the love for one's neigh-bors. His realistic *Savva* and his abstractly "expressionist" mor-ality-play, *The Life of Man* (both written in 1906), testify to an even greater despair over man and life than his stories. "I survey with my eyes the earth," says Savva, "and I see that there is nothing more terrible than man's life." *Savva* is soaked in that negative revolutionary mood which wants to destroy mainly for the sake of destruction. Since history and civilization have proved such a flop, then the best we can do is to scrap the whole of it and start afresh—perhaps with more success. Also the drama, *King Hunger,* is revolutionary in its protest against the capitalistic minority. The enslaved workers who rebel are crushed by the technocratic (or for that matter—

LEONID ANDREYEV (1871-1919)

"managerial") elite, but the muffled threats of the slain to come back do not augur well for the future of that elite. On the whole, this is one of Andreyev's weakest plays. As in *The Life of Man,* or even more so, he mistakes here allegory for symbolism, especially in the last scene the forced artificiality of which is positively painful.

In *The Black Masks* (1908) the Dostoevskian theme of self-divided personality crops up once more—this time in the shape of a "surrealist" nightmare, taking place in a brain which is already in the grip of madness. *Anathema* (1909), on the other hand, belongs to the "titanic" genre. It is a pretentious allegorical melodrama on a Faustian scale, with all the faults of Andreyev the author underlined. Vaguely allegorical is also *He Who Gets Slapped* (1915). Here a former intellectual luminary has become a circus clown, celebrated on account of the prodigious number of slaps he is able to endure. Intellect itself (in the garb of a clown) lustily slapped in a circus to the delight of a gaping and laughing mob—such is the ulterior allegorical meaning of this melodrama.

Among Andreyev's plays intended for the public at large the two pot-boilers, *The Days of Our Life* (1908) and *Gaudeamus* (1910), about the life of the students, were great box-office successes. In the much more spicy *Anfissa* (1909), he piled up certain morbid elements, including incest, to the extent of verging on a naturalistic parody. *Katerina Ivanovna* (1912), *Professor Storitsin,* and *Thou Shalt not Kill* (1913) record the low and vulgar mentality of an epoch in which there was little room for the values of a higher order. A new departure in the direction of humorous satire was Andreyev's play, *The Pretty Sabine Woman* (1912)—a somewhat heavy skit on the opportunism of the Russian liberals of the period. One of Andreyev's last plays, *Samson in Chains,* tackles once again the drama of self-division, though more convincingly than in *The Black Masks*.

During the First World War Andreyev, for all his previous nihilism, suddenly became a patriotic bourgeois liberal and, after the Revolution of 1917, developed a violent hatred of the Bolsheviks. About two years later he died in his lonely villa in Finland. But had he lived longer, he could not have added anything to what he had said. As the mouthpiece of that layer of the intelligentsia which was already decayed to the extent of revelling in its predicament, and even in the prospect of its own historical death—waiting round the corner, he could not but share the same fate, once the old order was swept away by the Revolution. No modern author of his potential caliber has paid such a heavy price for success as Andreyev. If we want to see a drama (instead of a melodrama) lived by a sensitive Russian of that period, we must turn from Andreyev to the poet Alexander Blok.

CHAPTER SEVENTEEN

Alexander Blok

I.

One of the striking features of modern Russian literature is its alternation between poetry and prose. The Pushkin period, for example, was essentially one of poetry. Then from the 'forties to the beginning of the 'eighties monumental prose prevailed. But in the 'nineties a wave of modernist verse set in and reached its climax in Russian symbolism proper (notably in the work of Vyacheslav Ivanov, Andrey Bely, and Alexander Blok) during the first decade of this century. The early stage of this trend was frankly "decadent." Its appeal lay in an excessive "art for art's sake" attitude on the one hand, and in an exaggerated egotism—taken for the most part from Nietzsche—on the other. Its ingredients were similar to those of the "decadent" currents in Western Europe from which they had been largely derived. In Russia the escapist "ivory towers" of aestheticism and neo-romanticism were, perhaps, even more tempting than anywhere else, since her political realities were often too crazy to be endured. Yet as creators of a new compensatory reality in the realm of fancy and beauty the modernist poets prided themselves on their exclusiveness, on being different from ordinary mortals, and were therefore anxious to write not for the crowd but for the elect. The gap between the "highbrow" reader and the mass reader thus could not be avoided. Certain

267

aspects of the modernist movement actually demanded too
great an artistic and literary culture to be accessible to all.
They appealed the more to the exclusive circles of readers.

This led to sterile sectarianism and to an equally sterile detachment from life. Once aware of the danger, several Russian
poets began to champion a more vital conception of poetry
which, instead of turning away from reality, would provide a
deeper interpretation and affirmation of life. Efforts of this kind
had to pass through numerous literary and philosophic ven-
tures before they crystallized, during the first decade of the
present century, into a definite school of Russian symbolism—
as distinct from French symbolism, for example, which was
concerned above all with the new methods of poetic expression.
The principal Russian symbolists, while accepting those methods, were anxious to go beyond "mere" literature and were
keenly interested in the genesis of a new consciousness, of a
new man. Such speculations brought them, however, into contact with the writings of Dostoevsky and with those of Vladimir Solovyov.

Solovyov was the most conspicuous figure in the religious-
philosophic thought of Russia towards the end of the last century. His aim was to work out an active synthesis of philosophy,
religion, art and life. He dreamed of a universal regeneration of
man and the world through Love (in a religious sense) as well
as through that "integral fullness of existence" in which he saw
the only alternative to universal anarchy and chaos. Unfortunately, he was not always immune from the fallacies of those
romantics who, instead of integrating intuition, thought, art,
philosophy and religion, only mixed them up and blurred the
boundaries between them. Deeply versed in European and
Eastern thought, in the teaching of the gnostics, as well as
in Christian mysticism, Solovyov was both a philosopher

and a poet. To his belief that "all transient things are but symbols" he added his vision of a new man and a new earth, and may therefore justly be called the first important representative of Russian symbolism proper. He partly anticipated it in a poem affirming that—

> All that about us lies
> Is but the shade, the mirrored image,
> Of things not seen with eyes.

Such an attitude towards the world eventually served as the starting point for the greatest and in his own way the most tragic figure among the Russian symbolists—Alexander Blok (1880-1921).

2.

It sounds like a paradox that Blok had only vague ideas of modern poetry before he was eighteen. The favorite authors of his youth were the dreamy Zhukovsky and those German romantics with whom he felt a certain affinity. It may have been due to their influence that his own early poems were imbued with a hazy medieval flavor, while Solovyov's work was responsible for the trend and perhaps even for the final awakening of Blok's poetic genius. Like Solovyov, he accepted the immanent mystical "World-Soul" (or the gnostic "Sophia" —the feminine hypostasis of divinity) as the Eternal Feminine, from which he hoped for a transfiguration of all life with a fervor strong enough to blend his religious and his erotic impulses in one powerful flame. His awakened sex turned entirely within, to the symbols and phantoms of his poetic imagination. He not only imagined—he actually felt Love to be the key to the mystery of the Universe. What in an ordinary

talent might have resulted in dreamy sentimental outpourings
was thus transformed by Blok's genius into his first accomplished book of poems—*Verses About the Lady Fair* (1905).

In these poems, typical of his early period (roughly between
1897 and 1904), Blok combined Solovyov's yearning for the
miraculous with the erotic dreaminess of a Novalis, and the
music of Shelley with the tenderness of Dante's *Vita Nuova,*
while yet imparting to them a style and a texture entirely his
own. Evocative in a musical and magical sense, many of them
sound like ardent prayers of a troubadour extolling the Eternal
Feminine, symbolized in his own vision of the Lady Fair. But
the distance between her and him is so immense that an approach is unthinkable. All he dare look forward to are a few
fleeting moments in which her presence, with the glory of a
different realm, would descend, like God's grace, upon him. As
if unaware of the world around, Blok sings—at this stage—like
a man in a trance, or like a medium, whose very passivity
increases his poetic intoxication. His images, for the most part
vague, are yet imbued with an uncanny "aura," radiating in
each line. His language may still be reminiscent of Solovyov,
but the melody and the "touch" are his own. And as for the
wealth of his rhythms, his new musical and prosodic devices,
they are enough to drive frantic even the most experienced of
translators.

The guardian spirit hovering over Blok's poetry of that
period was Solovyov the visionary and the mystic, even if Blok's
raptures were not always as innocent as they looked. The
prayer-like tone of his early poems (he wrote about eight
hundred of them before he was twenty-five) was often disturbed by flashes of the opposite depth: that of spiritual descent, blasphemy, and rebellion. This ambivalent element
assumed for a while the form of fear, of ominous forebodings.

> I am afraid of my double-faced soul,
> And I carefully conceal
> My diabolical and wild countenance
> Underneath this sacred armor.

The awareness of the danger made him cling all the more to his mystical Beatrice. But he knew that descent was impera-tive, even inevitable in so far as he realized that he had no right to serve his ideal apart and away from life. And since he, too, was a man and not a ghost, he could not but wonder what would become of his vision on the plane of life as it is and not as it presents itself to a poet's imagination. His misgivings came out in this poem addressed at one of such moments to his Lady Fair:

> I have foreknown Thee! Oh, I have foreknown Thee. Going
> The years have shown me Thy premonitory face,
> Intolerably clear, the farthest sky is glowing,
> I wait in silence Thy withheld and worshipped grace!
> The farthest sky is glowing: white for Thy appearing,
> Yet terror clings to me: Thy image will be strange,
> And insolent suspicion will arouse upon thy nearing,
> The features long foreknown, beheld at last will change.
> How shall I then be fallen!—low with no defender:
> Dead dreams will conquer me, the glory, glimpsed will change,
> The farthest sky is glowing! nearer looms the splendor,
> Yet terror clings to me. Thy image will be strange.*

3.

What happened before long was a complete change of "her" image. Having heard the summons of life, he had no right to

---

* Translated by Babette Deutsch and Avraham Yarmolinsky in *Modern Russian Anthology*, Harcourt, Brace & Co., M. Lawrence.

ignore it. But once he had abandoned the realm of idealistic heights, he had to be ready for any shock in the realm of facts. To follow this second period (1904-07) means to watch the first act of the tragedy between Blok the man and Blok the poet, when his spiritual maximalism of "all or nothing" came into collision with the world as it is. In a somewhat flowery essay written in 1910 (i.e. during the growing crisis of Russian symbolism), Blok gave a veiled explanation of what had taken place. He deals in it with his inner experiences only. As these are treated in terms of his poetic activities on the one hand, and of life around on the other, he touches upon the problem of Art and Life in some of its acutest aspects, but, of course, from an entirely personal angle. On the plane of concrete earthly love and earthly existence there certainly was no room for such a symbol as the Eternal Feminine. Here his Beatrice was a romantic phantom, a myth, which, instead of bridging the gap between the actual and the transcendental, only widened it. The two worlds—the world of spiritual values and visions, and the world of facts—proved incompatible. One seemed to exclude the other. There was even no guarantee that his previous ecstasies had not been mere indulgence in subjective fancies rather than flashes of intuition with a higher reality behind them.

In this state of doubt and bewilderment, Blok was assailed by a swarm of "doubles" which had been dormant in him as an antithesis to his former aspirations. A further disappointment may have been due to his married life, from which he probably expected miracles that never happen.* Be this as it may, he found himself cut off from the "streaming light" of those regions where his imagination had soared before. His Lady Fair became a ghost, a doll, and all turned into a tragi-comic

* His wife Lyubov was the daughter of the famous scientist Mendeleyev.

puppet show in which he and his likes were but actors and buffoons, whether they knew it or not. "Had I made a picture," he confesses in the essay mentioned, "I would have depicted it in this manner: in the lilac dusk of an endless world there sways an enormous white catafalque, and on it lies a doll whose face is dimly reminiscent of the countenance which once had shone through the heavenly dawns. . . . And so all is finished: my miraculous world has turned into an arena of my personal acting—into a puppet show in which I myself am only one of the company of my strange puppets. In other words, my own life has become art. . . . I stand before it all without knowing what to do either with the show, or with my life turned into art; for in my immediate presence there lives my own phantom-creation: neither alive nor dead—a blue ghost. . . . It is here that arises the problem of the curse of art, of a return to life, of service to the community."

This was complicated by the fact that having lost his former romantic faith, Blok preserved his romantic temperament, which now began to play havoc with him. When such an incurable idealist is faced with the facts and conditions of real life, he cannot but react to them in Blok's manner. Romantic irony and indictment play the principal part in it as they did in Blok's poetry which, from now on, became a strange psychological document and a confession in one—a record of his own inner drama. His lyrical play, *The Puppet Show* (*Balaganchik,* 1905), was one of the first attempts to ridicule his former visionary phase by means of buffoonery. From the angle of life as it is, the whole of that phase now appeared to him a tragic farce. And if his Lady Fair was but a doll or a ghost, then his own acts of devotion, as well as those of similar romantic Pierrots, were no more real than the gestures of puppets made of cardboard. In another little play, *The Stranger* (*Nez-*

nakomka), he lets his Beatrice—symbolized as a star—fall down onto our earth, where she becomes an ordinary prostitute. Romantic irony thus passed into romantic blasphemy. But the old nostalgia was there and it still pursued him in haunting visions. In a poem under the same title, *The Stranger,* Blok wants to forget "her" by means of alcohol, but "she" hovers around him even in the dingy surburban restaurants, where amid unspeakable vulgarity drunkards show their true nature, while emptying their bottles of wine. It is here that every night—

> At a certain hour infallibly,
> (Or is this but a dream of mine?)
> A girlish shape in silken draperies,
> In the dark window seems to shine.
>
> Always slowly and companionless,
> Through drunken crowds she is seen to glide,
> And in a cloud of fragrant loveliness,
> She sits down at the window's side.

Spellbound by her presence, her shape, even by the nodding ostrich feathers in her hat, the poet is transferred for a moment to the hazy "magical shore" of the world he had been familiar with. And as his own drunkenness increases, he is ready to believe in the truth and reality of that world, knowing full well that this illusion, too, will disappear once the effect of wine is over.

> Now I am lord of deepest mysteries,
> The sun of another world is mine,
> My soul is glowing with its radiance,
> Filled with the bitter spirit of wine.
>
> The ostrich feathers nodding dreamily,
> Sway in my heart for evermore,

Those fathomless blue eyes are flowering
Upon a wondrous distant shore.

In my soul there's hidden a treasury,
It has one key—the key is mine,
Yes, you are right, tipsy monstrosities—
Now I know, there is truth in wine.*

Having become something of a Don Juan, Blok looked in his love-adventures, too, as he did in wine, for an escape from the drabness of existence. But even in the hectic love poems, in which he sings of the real women who had loved him, there vibrates the repressed nostalgia for his vanished Beatrice:

Yes, I have loved. And the mad glowing
Of love's drunk pain is at an end,
The triumph and the overthrowing,
The name of "foe," the word of "friend."

There have been many . . . are all fleeting?
Mere memories and shades of dreams,
Strangely I call them up, repeating
The golden music of their names.

There have been many, but a single
Charm bound them all in unity,
One frenzied Beauty made them mingle:
Its name is Love and Life to me.*

4.

Aware of his "puppet show," Blok was now ready to face reality, while yet refusing any compromise with it. The "respectable" normal course of existence was outside his ambitions;

* Translated by V. de Sola Pinto. In the original the first and third lines are also
  rhymed.
* Translated by C. M. Bowra in *A Book of Russian Verse*, Macmillan.

worse—outside his taste. Life meant to him above all intensity
of experience, intensity at any price. And when he could no
longer procure it through the ecstasies of the heights, he
plunged into those of the depths—into the emotional chaos of
the Unconscious, of the "psychics," tinged with his own pessimism and tedium. But even on this level Blok could not continue without a substitute for his former Beatrice. He had to
find a new beloved, but a more tangible one, upon whom he
could again project his yearnings, his faith, his passion for the
boundless. This new beloved of his was now Russia—not the
"holy" but the irrational Russia of endless spaces, winds and
blizzards; of flying *troikas;* of maddening nostalgia, drunkenness, and chaos.

> I will listen to the voice of drunken Russia
> And I will rest under a tavern roof.

Snow-Mask is the title of his most typical book of that period,
and its main note is one of intoxication with the blizzards, with
wine, with passion. The delight in self-annihilation rings in the
accents of his sensual *Faina.* In the more virile verses of another
section, *Enchantment through Fire,* his wish to come to terms
with life flared up, but only for a moment. What followed was
a new surrender to psychic drugs, but soon he could not rely
on them either he had to look upon the world with a sobered
mind and with more than sobered eyes.

The prevalent mood of that phase (from 1908 until 1917,
that is, between the two Revolutions), can best be defined as
spiteful apathy. The filth and vulgarity of existence over-
powered him to such an extent as to make all effort appear
futile. The title of a collection of poems written in those years
is itself significant—*The Loathsome World.* In *Iambi* he tried
to kindle his crushed faith in life; in his romantic drama in

verse, *The Rose and the Cross* (1912), even his one-time devotion to the Lady Fair was revived. Yet the fire that was now burning came too much out of the ashes. The same can be said of his cycle *Carmen,* with its temporary outburst of carnal passion. The world seemed "loathsome" in all its aspects. But the more deeply he felt the futility of things the more intense became he as a poet. Having abandoned his trance-like vagueness and music, he adopted a vocabulary which was tersely realistic and at the same time symbolic. These two short poems, both of them written in 1912, convey his moods and his method during that period. The theme is *Night in Petrograd.* And this is what Blok has to say about it:

> Night: the street, a foolish lamp giving
> A dingy light, a druggist's store:
> For a quarter of a century go on living,
> No escape. All will be as before.
>
> You die: afresh you start life boldly,
> Just as of old each detail repeat.
> Night, the canal rippling so coldly,
> The druggist's store, the lamp, the street.*

In the second poem the condensed big-city nightmare is rendered as follows:

> An empty street: light in a single window gleams.
> The Jew apothecary is moaning as he dreams.
>
> Before the cupboard labelled "poison" he can see,
> Intently bending down on ghastly creaking knee
>
> A skeleton wrapped in a cloak, who all the while
> Searches for something, twists his black mouth in a smile.

* Translated by V. de Sola Pinto.

Finding it, he stumbles unaware and makes
A noise, then turns his death-head while the sleeper wakes,

Screams and rises in his bed, and falls on the other side,
But the visitor beneath his cloak can hide

The accursed phial for two noseless women there,
Waiting outside beneath the street lamp's cold white glare.*

An even more typical example of Blok's symbolic realism
is the first poem of his *Danses macabres* which we quote in a
paraphrased version (done by R. M. Hewitt):

It's hard for a corpse in this world of men,
Better remain apart, alone,
You have to mix with them now and then
Or you'll never succeed in your career.
But oh! the fear that they might hear,
The rattle of bone on bone.

Live men still sleep when the dead man rises.
His thoughts are black as the day is long,
Plods to the office, bank or assizes,
Where quills whisper a welcome-song.

Hour by hour must the dead man labor;
At last he's free and puts on his coat,
Wags his haunches, grins at his neighbor
And feeds him a bawdy anecdote.

The rain has smeared with a nameless liquor
Houses and churches and humans grimy;
But the dead man drives where the mud is thicker,
Knowing a place that is still more slimy.

A gilded hall with mirrors about it.
Imbecile hostess and husband fool

* Translated by V. de Sola Pinto.

Are glad to see him, who can doubt it?—
His evening suit was made by Poole.

Corpse, be brave now, raise thanksgiving:
They can't hear the rattle against that band:
No easy work to prove you are living,
But go round briskly, shake their hand.

Who is that by the distant column?
His eyes light up, for she too is dead,
Under their patter, with faces solemn,
Words that are real words are said.

"Weary friend, it's cold and strange here."
'The tomb is cold, as I can tell.'
"It's midnight now." 'Since there's no danger—
Dance with that girl, she likes you well.'

And over there with senses reeling,
Waiting alert, her blood on fire,
The virgin stands, her eyes revealing
The ecstasy of life's desire.

With fluent malice more than human,
He murmurs into her ear alone,
Just as a live man woos a woman.
"How clever he is, how kind and dear!"
But somewhere near she can faintly hear
The rattle of bone on bone.

Another longer poem (or rather a cycle of poems), *The Life of My Friend,* is written in the same vein. In his beautiful *Garden of Nightingales* Blok the dreamer emerged again with all the magic of his verbal art, but one of his recurring motifs during the whole of that period was his thought and his love of Russia. When everything else had disappointed and betrayed him; when he was tormented by forebodings about the "cold and gloom of the days to come," his love for Russia never faltered, although he was profoundly aware of her failings, enumerated in a poem which begins (1914):

> To sin unashamed, to lose, unthinking,
> The count of careless nights and days,
> And then, while the head aches with drinking,
> Steal to God's house, with eyes that glaze. . . .

There follows a long list of vices and transgressions, depicted in all their ungainliness. But as if aware of something different and deeper underneath it all, Blok exclaims in the end:

> Dearer to me than every other,
> Are you, Russia, even so.*

5.

The mixture of disgust and despair, so much in tune with the atmosphere which followed the abortive rising of 1905, was only the reverse side of Blok's incurable idealism, of his yearning for a total change of man and life. This yearning was shattered in him, now and then, but never destroyed; which explains his secret hopes that an elemental catastrophe would come at last and cleanse the earth of its quagmire. His hopes turned into prophetic forebodings and even into certainty, especially with regard to Russia. These he uttered in a number of poems (*On the Field of Kulikovo, The Voice from a Chorus,* etc.), one of which, *Russia in 1914,* deserves to be quoted in full.

> They do not remember the paths they have taken,
> These children of a peaceful hour:

* Translated by Babette Deutsch and Avrahm Yarmolinsky in *Russian Poetry*, M. Lawrence.

ALEXANDER BLOK (1880-1921)

We are born of a Russia by terror shaken—
To forget the past is not in our power.

O years that crumble away into ashes,
Bringing madness or hope's bright dreams?
From freedom's flame or war's dire flashes
A blood-red light on men's faces gleams.

Dumbness—and then the tocsin ringing:
Each mouth is sealed and so we wait;
In hearts that once with joy were singing,
There's now an emptiness charged with fate.

And when the crows in the sky shall hover,
Above us lying beneath the sod,
May there be better men to look over
This Thy kingdom, O God, O God.*

Only an attitude such as this can explain why Blok was one of the first to greet the Revolution of 1917 with demands and expectations of his own. At last the gap between his "art" and the "service to community" was likely to disappear so far as he was concerned. He sensed a deep symbolic meaning even in the horrors of those years: it was a new Apocalypse in the very compass and intensity of which there was hope. Far from being perturbed by it, he identified it with that elemental "spirit of music" which—according to him—is at the bottom of all creative revolutions. What he actually meant by it was analogous to Nietzsche's "Dionysian spirit." Both Nietzsche and Blok saw the cause of the *one-sided* development of European mankind in our "Socratic" rationalism—severed from that irrational spring of life which Nietzsche labelled with the name of Dionysos and Blok with the "spirit of music." The divorce between Reason and Nature as well as the Cosmos itself was,

* Translated by V. de Sola Pinto.

in their opinion, at the root of all the aberrations characteristic of modern man and civilization. Having lost his sense of the irrational, the infinite, the timeless, man has been deprived of his true focus and narrowed down to his petty rationalism and even pettier egoistic concerns, without suspecting that life, real life begins only where such bondage ceases and the sway of the timeless "music of the universe" begins. This is how Blok explains it in his essay *The Downfall of Humanism* (1919):

"There are two kinds of time, one historical according to the calendar, and the other 'musical,' without date or number. In the consciousness of civilized man the first kind alone is immutably present: but it is only when we realize how near we are to Nature, only when we abandon ourselves to the wave of music issuing from the chorus of the Universe, that we live in the second. For life in days, months, and years no balance of our powers is necessary. And this absence of necessity for effort soon reduces the majority of civilized people to the state of mere dwellers upon the earth. But balance becomes indispensable as soon as we live near the 'musical' reality of the world— near to Nature, to the elemental. For this we need above all to be well-ordered both in body and spirit, since it is only with the complete body and the complete spirit acting together that the 'music of the universe' can be heard. Loss of balance between the bodily and the spiritual inevitably makes us lose that music. It makes us lose the ability to escape from the time of the calendar, that is, from historical days and years, into the other time that cannot be calculated. Epochs in which this balance is not destroyed may be called epochs of culture, in contrast to those when an integral perception of the world is beyond the bearers of an outlived culture, owing to the influx of melodies up to that time unfamiliar and unknown, which overcrowded the hearing. The influx may be slow if measured by

the calendar, for new historical forces come into the consciousness of humanity gradually. Yet that which takes place slowly
according to the laws of one kind of time can be completed
suddenly according to the laws of the other. The movement of
the one directing baton is enough to turn into a hurricane the
drawn-out melody of the orchestra. The mistake of the inheri-
tors of humanistic culture, the fatal contradiction into which
they fell, originated in their exhaustion. The spirit of integrity,
the 'spirit of music,' abandoned them, and so they blindly put
their trust in historical time. They failed to see that the world
was already rising at a signal from a movement which was
entirely new. While continuing to believe that the masses were
acquiring freedom within the individualistic movement of civilization, they naturally could not see that those very masses
were bearers of a different, of a new, spirit."

The old romantic in Blok thus came out in his attitude towards the Revolution, but this time with a definite view about
the creative value of the hurricane which brought into history,
so dramatically, a "different new spirit." Carried away by the
sway of this spirit, he felt a stirring of new hopes and visions.
It was in January, 1918, that is, during the cruellest civil war
and havoc, that he wrote his *The Twelve* and *The Scythians,*
both echoing the Revolution in a quasi-Apocalyptic strain and
spirit.

6.

The first of them is the high watermark of Blok's poetry. Incredibly simple yet full of ingenious rhythms and new devices
(including phrases taken from the street jargon and the factory
ditty), it seems to defy all attempts at an adequate translation.
But even those who can read it in the original will miss a

great deal if they fail to see in it a work in which all the
ingredients of Blok's poetry meet as though in a knot. The
romantic, the realist and the symbolist collaborate here on
equal terms. So does his hatred of the old world; his tedium
and bitterness; his love of the "mad" irrational Russia with
her wind-swept spaces; his revelling in the immensity of events;
and finally, his fantastic vision of a new world arising out of
chaos and destruction.

> The wind reels, the snow dances;
> A party of twelve men advances.
> Black rifle-slings upon their backs.
> And flame, flame, flame upon their tracks.
> With crumpled caps, lips smoking fags,
> All should be branded as prison lags.

This is how the poet introduces the twelve Bolshevik guards,
patrolling the streets of Petrograd, at night, during the worst
days of the revolutionary turmoil. The poem has twelve parts,
each of them composed in a different rhythm and with different contents. The language is appropriate to the "prison lags"
and the situation. It is the language of the street, interspersed
with half-digested revolutionary slogans and clichés.

The narrative incident itself is crude and could have been
taken from any police chronicle. One of the twelve patrolling
soldiers, infatuated with the street-girl Katya (whose stockings
are "packed with Kerensky notes") shoots her dead uninten-
tionally—while aiming at his own rival in love. Throughout
the poem we can follow his reactions to the crime, but this
personal drama is cunningly interwoven with the chaos of a
bleak northern winter and of the Revolution. The tension of
the conflicting social strata is suggested by the rhythm, the tone
and the accent of each verse, as well as by Blok's own sallies
against the old "bourgeois" order:

> The bourgeois, where the roads divide,
> Stands with his nose sunk in his fur;
> And, hairy, shivers at his side
> With drooping tail, a poor whipped cur.
>
> Like the dog, stands the bourgeois, hungry,
> A silent question to the sky;
> The old world, like a homeless mongrel,
> With tail between its legs stands by.

Nothing that belongs to the old world matters any longer. Even the "Holy Russia" of yore can be blasphemed, and, hooligan-fashion, trampled underfoot for the sake of a new era:

> Don't shrink, comrade, get your rifle out;
> Give Holy Russia a taste of shot.
>> At the wooden land,
>> Where the poor huts stand,
>> And her rump so grand!
> Aha, but no Cross!

The fury of destruction, with "no Cross," fills the air. But however un-Christian its external ravages, a revolution in the name of justice and brotherhood may, perhaps, be based on a Christian impulse, which in the end must win—provided the revolution itself is imbued with that "spirit of universal music" of which Blok spoke in his essay. This is where the creative element of the revolution comes in, no matter whether the participants are aware of it or not. So "the twelve" (a distorted reflection of the twelve Apostles) march on. And in the midst of all the desolation, crime and chaos they are suddenly joined by an apparition which confers upon the poem a final message and meaning:

> On they march with sovereign tread,
> With a starving dog behind,

With a blood-red flag ahead—
In the storm where none can see,
From the rifle bullets free,
Gently walking on the snow,
Where like pearls the snowflakes glow,
Marches rose-crowned in the van
Jesus Christ, the Son of Man.*

7.

The Twelve, now world famous, is pervaded with the pathos
of revolution and yet remains elusive enough to be interpreted
in a number of ways. Christ as the leader of the twelve Bolshevik guards may appear to some people a blasphemy, to others
a *deus ex machina*—the more so because nothing in the poem
makes one expect such a denouement. On the other hand, He
can be explained as a Messianic symbol of that creative side of
the cataclysm which ought to follow upon the Inferno of
suffering, blood and destruction. A revolution devoid of inner
meaning remains only a calamity which has not been deepened
into a purifying tragedy, and a mere calamity is always crushing and sterile. Blok knew that an event of such magnitude as
the cataclysm of 1917 could not be without a meaning, and
he said so. *The Twelve* was a final attempt on his part to regain
his faith in humanity and in life—an attempt expressed in
strains of which only great poetry is capable.

Less elusive and somewhat programmatic is his other poem,
The Scythians. It was written during the peace negotiations at
Brest-Litovsk and represents a platform counterpart to *The
Twelve.* Here Blok challenges the luke-warm "bourgeois" West
to join the universal brotherhood inaugurated by the Revolu-

* Translated by C. M. Bowra in *Horizon,* July 1944.

tion, or else—to tremble before a barbaric invasion to come. In a spirit redolent of both the "populists" and the neo-Slavophils, he reproaches the Western nations as a revolutionary and as a Russian:

> Yes, you have long since ceased to love
> As our cold blood can love; the taste
> You have forgotten of a love
> That burns like fire and like fire lays waste.

> Yes, Russia is a Sphinx. Exulting, grieving,
> And sweating blood, she cannot sate
> Her eyes that gaze and gaze and gaze
> At you with stone-lipped love for you, and hate.

This "stone-lipped love and hate" in one with regard to Europe forms another link between Blok and the Messianic Slavophil Dostoevsky. Only Blok's Messianism has nothing to do with the past—it is turned to a future growing out of the Revolution. Hence his appeal to the skeptical and reluctant West:

> Come unto us, from the black ways of war,
> Come to our peaceful arms and rest,
> Comrades, while it is not too late,
> Sheathe the sword! May brotherhood be blessed.

And in case the Western nations should refuse to join, he threatens them with the "Asiatic face" of Russia, as well as with her indifference to their fate.

> We will not move when the ferocious Hun
> Despoils the corpse and leaves it bare,
> Burns towns, herds cattle in the church
> And smell of white flesh roasting fills the air.*

---

* Translated by Babette Deutsch and Avrahm Yarmolinsky in *Russian Poetry*, M. Lawrence.

Little did he suspect that the "smell of white flesh roasting" would—in a few years—be practised not by the savage Asiatics, but by the civilized inhabitants of the heart of Europe. In the year of grace 1918 history was not yet "fantastic" enough to make the death-factories of Auschwitz, and of other equally "efficient" places, look probable.

8.

"Life is only worth living when we make immense demands upon it," Blok wrote (quite in the spirit of Gorky's socialist realism) in an essay at the time of his two revolutionary rhapsodies. "All or nothing! A faith, not in what is not found upon earth, but in what ought to be there, although at the present time it does not exist and may not come for quite a while." Approaching the Revolution with such an attitude, he saw its scope in nothing less than a gradual remaking of the world. "A true revolution cannot aim at anything less, though we cannot yet say whether this aim will be accomplished or not. Its cherished hope is to raise a universal cyclone which will carry to the lands buried in snow the warm winds and the fragrance of orange groves, and will water the sun-scorched plains of the south with the refreshing rain from the northern regions. *Peace and the brotherhood of nations* is the banner under which the Russian Revolution marches on its way. This is the tune of its roaring flood. This is the music which he who has ears to hear should hear."

Such was Blok's idea of the great "cyclone" which he, an intellectual, joined without hesitation. At the same time he turned bitterly against those members of the intelligentsia who had not followed his example (and they were the majority). His own maximalist demands made him impatient to see the economic and political upheaval completed by an adequate inner change in man himself, but this change was either absent, or else different from what he had expected. It must have been the discrepancy between the external and the inner revolutions—a discrepancy which assumed rather ugly aspects during the ravages of the Civil War, the famine, and the Cheka —that eventually damped Blok's hope and enthusiasm.

Disappointment, apathy, and illness closed upon him, and practically silenced him during the last two years of his life. He died in 1921, at the age of forty-one.

Blok's death coincided with the disintegration of that symbolist school in Russia of which he was the acknowledged leader. But quite apart from this, he was and still remains one of the most significant poets in the whole of European modernism.

CHAPTER EIGHTEEN

Sergey Esenin

I.

Russian symbolism reached in Alexander Blok not only its climax but also its crisis. A reaction against its vagueness and mistiness was therefore inevitable. It began soon after 1910 and took, on the whole, three directions. The so-called acmeist group, led by Gumilyov (executed in 1922), Anna Akhmatova, and Sergey Gorodetsky, was all out for concreteness and clarity. The second group consisted of the futurists who, despite such gifted poets as Khlebnikov and Mayakovsky as their leaders, were at first looked upon too much as literary freaks to be taken seriously. More successful was the third group—that of stylized village poets who, in a way, lined up their poetry to the work of Koltsov and Nekrasov, but with a new method and a new accent. The earlier representative of this trend, Nikolai Klyuyev (1887-1926), was still connected with the symbolist school, and so was, for a while, Sergey Esenin (1895-1925). It was during the decay of that school that Esenin emerged on its fringes as one of the strongest and most promising young talents.

He on the one hand, and Mayakovsky on the other, are the two dominant figures among the crop of the poets who came into their own during the first decade of the Soviet regime. Yet what a contrast between these two gifted youths, both of whom ended eventually by suicide! While Mayakovsky became the poetic voice of the rising proletarians, Esenin preferred to turn his enormous gift into a lament for the old peasant Russia, and he could hardly have made any other choice. Born and brought up in the depths of rural Russia (the district of Ryazan), Esenin was so much steeped in the soil and the peasant lore that he was never able to detach himself from them, not even when he did his best to fit into the life of the capital, or into the spirit of the Revolution. It would be a mistake, though, to regard his rural poetry from the angle of mere village folk-lore or local color. It goes deeper. In a way it could be defined as poetic self-assertion of the "eternal peasant" against the encroaching machine and the mentality of the industrial town. The village in its primeval quintessence, sifted through his individual temperament, found in Esenin's verse one of the most poignant expressions in modern poetry. It was and remained the basic and perhaps the only source of his inspiration.

This modern village poetry assimilated quite a few technical devices taken from the symbolist movement. It even looked at first as though it would impart a new vitality to symbolism itself at a time when the latter was already on the decline.

No wonder Klyuyev was so quickly promoted to the rank of an outstanding poet. A true Russian moujik, who yet remains at his shrewdest when pretending to be most humble and simple, Klyuyev is worth studying as a character. And he is certainly worth studying as a poet, since his verse bears the authentic stamp of the peasantry from which he sprang. It was this current that reached its peak in Esenin whose path to fame began soon after his arrival in Petersburg in 1916.

Esenin, like Klyuyev, knew how to conceal at his debut a great deal of peasant cunning behind the pose of a "gentle shepherd swain," all of which was taken for the real thing by the Petersburg intelligentsia. His one-time friend, the poet Mariengof, tells us in a book about him that Esenin used to put on an embroidered blouse (the kind he may not have worn even while staying in the village), a peasant cap and top boots, after which he would play on the accordion village tunes—to the satisfaction of the highbrows who thus came into touch with the "people" without needing to leave their comfortable drawing rooms. Esenin, who had made good use of such comic-opera masquerades, probably chuckled at his audiences with no less amusement than the "little moujik" Klyuyev must have done during his own first steps towards fame. But apart from that, Esenin—like Klyuyev—was of the stuff true poets are made. Gorky goes so far as to proclaim him, in an article, the greatest lyrical genius since Pushkin. More authentic in his poems than in his peasant blouses, top boots, and accordions, Esenin sang with a poignancy born out of his very nostalgia for the cornfields he had left behind.

> O fields of corn, O fields of corn,
> An orphan's grief is mine;
> Heavy on my heart lies yesterday,
> But in my heart you shine.
>
> The fleeting miles whistle like birds
> About my horse's mane
> And the sun is sprinkling lavishly
> Her holy healing rain.
>
> O land of floods and agony
> And gentle spring-tide powers,
> Under the masters Dawn and Stars
> I passed my schooling hours.
>
> While in the Bible of the winds,
> I pondered o'er the words,

> Isaiah came and walked with me
> To keep my golden herds.*

Esenin's pastoral motifs, far from being a repetition of hackneyed old melodies, vibrate with such freshness and sincerity that, in spite of his calculated experiments in poetic technique (new rhythms and forms), they sound as if extemporized. He often achieved surprisingly original texture and inflection by the manner in which he used peasant imagery and peasant idioms as one of his expedients. Religion, poetic superstition, naïve animism, and pantheism seem to vie with each other to make him produce that intimate yet strangely remote atmosphere which permeates the poems of his early period. But this was only one facet of Esenin's work. Its second and for a while hidden aspect was that potentially anarchic spirit of the steppe which, lurking in their unconscious, was perhaps more typical of the pre-revolutionary Russian peasants than were their seeming quietism and submissiveness. Whereas in the West the word freedom is associated with society, in Russia it used to be inseparable from the idea of the boundless spaces where everything seems to be on a bigger and more lavish scale than in Europe. This spirit in particular was responsible for all kinds of inner restlessness, as well as for a truly "Russian" excess in everything: in piety and sacrilege, in meekness and cruelty, in active idealism and anarchic destruction. Esenin—an "essential" peasant from those spaces, stretching into the heart of Asia—actually confessed in one of his lyrics: "I cherish my secret purity of heart; but still I may murder someone to the whistle of the autumn wind. . . ." It may be that the same unruly spirit rather than any con-

* Translated by R. M. Hewitt in *A Book of Russian Verse*, edited by C. M. Bowra, Macmillan.

victions made him hail the revolution even while he, too, expected from the latter a renewal of life. The sentimental-idyllic and the turbulent elements were intertwined in him as in a fugue, out of which emerged some of his most remarkable melodies.

2.

Unhampered by education or excessive reading, Esenin relied, like Nekrasov before him, on the sureness of his poetic instinct which made him glean the right kind of words, metaphors and images in the depths of the folk-genius itself. Most of his symbols, especially in his early poems, were connected with the archaic life of the village, and he enlarged them now and then—in a mythological sense—to cosmic dimensions. The people's saints are treated by him as something inseparable from the fields, the seasons, and the cattle. God is referred to as a grey elder sowing stars like winter corn. Esenin's landscape has the meek eyes of a cow. The dawn over the cornfields reminds him of a cow licking her newly born calf. The moon is a golden puppy, or else a "curly lamb gambolling in a blue meadow." He also knows how to combine his peasant vision with unexpected up-to-date similes and associations. One of his early poems consists of these four lines:

> Where dawn is watering the cabbage rows,
> Splashing red pails upon her mighty jamb,
> A little nuzzling maple reaches up,
> To suck the full green udders of its dam.*

In another poem he compares the Russian autumn to a chestnut mare cleaning her "rough mane."

---

* This and the next two poems are taken from *Russian Poetry*, translated by Babette Deutsch and Avrahm Yarmolinsky, M. Lawrence.

Her hooves' blue clatter sounds above the bank,
Of the still river where the reeds are rank.
The monkish wind steps lightly, and retrieves
With idle fingers handfuls of dry leaves,
And where a rowan blooms he stoops to lean
And kiss the red wounds of a Christ unseen.

Or take these few characteristic lines:

In the clear cold the dales grow blue and tremble,
The iron hooves beat sharply; knock and knock.
The faded grasses in wide skirt assemble
Flung copper where the wind-blown branches rock.
For empty straths, a slender arch ascending:
Fog curls upon the air and, moss-wise grows,
And evening, low above the wan streams bending,
In their white waters washes his blue toes.

The "essential" peasant was so strong in Esenin that he could not shed him even after he had turned to other themes and interests. While piling up laurels and disillusionments in the two Russian capitals, he still regarded the hut and the corn-fields of his childhood as his only home. And when the Revolution came, Esenin welcomed it in a spirit which was entirely different from that of Blok or Mayakovsky. He hailed it neither as a dissatisfied intellectual who thought he had found an outlet in the new Apocalypse; nor as a proletarian, dancing on the ruins of the old world, but exclusively as a peasant and a villager. It was the turbulent yet Utopian villager in Esenin that made him write, in 1919, the revolutionary paean *Inonia* —a peasant counterpart to Blok's *The Twelve*.

3.

Inonia is, together with Blok's famous poem, Klyuyev's *Lenin,* and Andrey Bely's *Christ Has Risen,* among the most outspoken Messianic affirmations of the Russian Revolution on the part of the still lingering symbolists on the one hand, and the village poets on the other. Louder and more exuberant than *The Twelve,* Esenin's *Inonia* expresses the vision of a millennium ruled, not by the proletarians and their machines, but by the peasants inhabiting a free and universal Arcadia: quite in the style of those "populists" who once dreamed of a Russia untainted by the horrors of industrialism. Revolutionary in its tone and language, the poem thus seems to be anti-proletarian by its very subject.

If *The Twelve* can be likened to a disciplined and almost fettered ecstasy, *Inonia* is delirium passing into emotional and rhetorical debauch. As though intoxicated with his own words and visions, Esenin here lets loose not only his Utopian moods, but also his latent turbulence, verging on spiritual hooliganism. The result is a strange torrent of poetry and of verbal hysteria. "I will shear the blue firmament like a mangy sheep of its wool," he shouts almost with foam on his lips. "I will bite through the Milky Way. I will raise my arms as high as the Moon and will crack her like a nut. . . . With my firm hand I am ready to turn upside down the whole world. . . . Eight wings are splashing in stormy blizzards from my shoulders." And so on—one "colossal" simile hurled upon another. Forgetting the meek peasant Saviour of his former days, Esenin now yells in a raucous voice: "The body, the body of *Christ* I will spit out of my mouth." But what he offers instead is his vague Arcadian idyll "where the Deity of the living resides";

SERGEY ESENIM (1895-1925)

where there is faith in power, and Truth is to be found only in man himself. The worn old phrases, repeated in a new fortissimo.

This poem is a landmark between Esenin's early lyrics and his "imaginist" experiments, the limitations of which he recognized soon enough. Russian imaginism (analogous to, but not identical with, Anglo-American imagism) was ushered into existence in 1919 with a manifesto which proclaimed images the means as well as the aim of poetry, and therefore something self-sufficient to the extent of dispensing, when necessary, even with logic or coherence. In their search for original images, the adepts of this current often strained their fancy to the point of grotesque obscurity and distortion. Otherwise the movement hardly showed much vitality. But for the fact that Esenin happened to be one of its temporary members, it might have passed unnoticed, and even he cleared out of it before long. "Imaginism was a formal theory we wanted to affirm," he wrote in a subsequent autobiographical note, "but it had no ground under it and died, leaving the truth behind that only organic images are of value." But whether in or outside the group, Esenin had his fill of the excesses which the bohemian and the underworld Moscow of the NEP period could still provide.

4.

Associated with a few other turbulent though less talented poets, Esenin must have felt strangely out of place in the turmoil of the Soviet capital. Yet he forced himself to fit into it and to satisfy at least the unruly element in him. He did all he could to outdo the bohemians on their own ground, in which he seems to have succeeded. Jeeringly he walked about—

his "head unkempt and like an oil lamp," glad to welcome any scandal, any escapade. Night brawls, prostitutes, taverns, police stations, hospitals, irresponsible marriages and divorces—such was his record of those riotous years. To make things worse, he met the famous dancer Isadora Duncan who, at the request of the Soviets had come to Moscow in order to conduct a dancing school for children. Esenin, handsome and still in his prime, proved so irresistible that Isadora and he soon got married, both of them knowing full well how unsuitable they were for anything even remotely connected with married life.

The consequences could have been predicted. In due course Esenin grew tired and irritated. In his fits of retrospective jealousy he often treated his easy-going wife *à la moujik,* until a time came when the only thing to do was to part. But even this was not done without scenes, a glimpse into which is provided by this passage, taken from *Isadora Duncan's Russian Days* by Irma Duncan and Allan Ross Macdougall (Gollancz): "Some time later, one afternoon when Isadora sat in her room with some callers Esenin came again to demand his bust. He demanded it loudly and instantly, and finally forced his drunken way into the room. The bust, which Konienkov had genially hacked out of a huge block of wood, stood atop a high bric-a-brac cabinet in one corner of the room. When Isadora refused to give him the bust and asked him to come back again some time when he was more fit to carry it away, he dragged a chair over to the corner and with shaky legs mounted it. As he reached the bust with feverish hands and clasped it, its weight proved too much for him. He staggered and fell from the chair, rolling head over heels on the floor, still clasping tightly to his breast his wooden image. Sullenly and shakily he rose to his feet; and then reeled out of the room to wander later about the byways of Moscow and lose the encumbering bust in some gutter. That was the last view Isadora Duncan had of her poet and her husband, Sergey Alexandrovich Esenin."

But there was despair in his excesses. His buffoonery was that of a sentimental-romantic peasant boy who came too soon into the bedlam of a big city and was crushed by its grip. Unable either to adapt himself to it, or to rise above it and escape, he wanted to drown his despair in the mire which he probably loathed yet without which he would have felt even more isolated and out of place, since his instincts and the very roots of his being had remained in another and totally different pattern of existence. He was born much too late to fit into the age and the conditions he lived in, let alone the chaotic turmoil of the period. A prey to his own sensitiveness, he would, perhaps, have collapsed sooner, had he not found a temporary refuge in cynicism, in alcohol and scandal. And when the trend of events took the direction of industrialism on a gigantic scale, Esenin—with his ideal of a rural Arcadia—felt more dismayed than ever. Crushed by the depths of his own frustration, he arrived, in his tavern poems, at the conclusion that, together with him, everything else was also doomed. The following verses convey aptly enough what he meant:

> The little thatched hut I was born in
>   Lies bare to the sky,
> And in these crooked alleys of Moscow
>   I am fated to die.
>
> No hope have I now of returning
>   To the fields where I played,
> Of hearing the song of the poplar
>   As I lie in the shade.

The city is senile and dingy,
    And drab, yet I love it!
The golden somnolent East
    Is brooding above it.

And at night when the moon is a-shining
    (A hell of a moon!)
I lurch through the slums till I come to
    My favorite saloon.

There all the night through there is riot,
    And babble and sin,
I read out my verses to harlots
    And treat them to gin.

Still fiercer and quicker my heart beats,
    This is all I can say:
"I am lost, you are lost, we are all lost,
    I don't know the way."

The little thatched hut I was born in
    Lies bare to the sky,
And in these crooked alleys of Moscow
    I am fated to die.*

In moods such as this Esenin called himself the "last of the village poets" and predicted that rapid mechanization of the land which, according to him, was to destroy all the romance of patriarchal life he had known and loved in his boyhood:

I am the last of village poets;
A plank bridge croons but modest songs.
I celebrate the requiem mass
Of censer-swinging leafy birch.

The iron guest will soon appear
And pace the paths of azure fields,

* Translated by R. M. Hewitt.

His swarthy hand will snatch away
The oaten sheaves spilled out by dawn.

O hands, your touch is lifeless, strange,
These songs won't live within your reach.
And only ears of corn, like steeds,
Will grieve and mourn their master old.

And, dancing requiem dances, winds
Will suck their mournful quivering neighs.
The moon will strike its wooden hours
And snore my twelfth and final hour.*

Provocative in his manners and in his verses, Esenin paraded, at times, words and expressions which are banned from civilized intercourse. As he could no longer rely upon his inspiration, he often piled up images some of which were tiresomely labored. Yet his tavern poems have a genuine tragic ring and produce, now and then, the effect of lived hallucinations.

5.

It was during those years of riot and scandal that nostalgia for his lost and therefore poetically embellished Arcadia became particularly painful. One can feel it in his *Confessions of a Hooligan* (1920), and somewhat differently in his *Return Home* (1924), where the encroachment of the new Soviet village left little or no room for his old dreams.

Rain with arrows in a crowd
Has convulsed my home with clod,
Mowed the blue bud from the land,
Trampled down the golden sand,
Rain with arrows in a crowd.*

* Translated by G. Reavey in *Soviet Literature*, Wishart.
* Translated by C. M. Bowra. Op. cit.

Even his sister, a fresh peasant girl, pored "as if it were a Bible," over Marx's *Capital*. The idyllic Russia was gone. All that she left behind was the nervousness of a transition period, alien to his simple peasant instincts. For, with all his puzzling ways, Esenin was much too simple for the age and the conditons he was compelled to live in. Having tasted of glory and adulation; of riot and scandal; of travels (together with Isadora Duncan) in America, Germany, and France, he yet remained inwardly tied to the village—inert and "partriarchal" because of its very inertia. But while refusing to outgrow it, he suddenly saw himself stranded and left behind by the new sovietized village which he refused to accept. Hence his aimlessness and bewilderment. And as for his premature fame, it only unbalanced him like strong adulterated wine indulged in by a child.

Too sensitive and much too weak to face the unpleasant realities, he remained hanging in the air—a stranger to the world in which there was no room for his archaic dreams and ideals. So he took revenge upon life as well as upon himself through a kind of moral *harakiri,* and revelled as it were in his gradual self-destruction. It is true that during the last two years of his life he had a few quiet intervals, but it was the quiet of tiredness and of surrender to his own disgust. Even in those rare moments when he was inclined to "accept all without yearning for anything" he still yearned: for his squandered youth; for a different kind of life; for the rural Atlantis submerged by the Revolution. A last visit (after his parting from Isadora Duncan) to the haunts of his early years only made things worse. Instead of recovering his paradise lost, he felt that he himself was a walking anachronism—out of joint with everybody and everything, his native village included. All he could do was to translate his sorrow into lyrics, or else stifle it in riotous night life.

With regard to form he now underwent another change. Having abandoned the "imaginist" eccentricities, he chose for his model the lucid genius of Pushkin. Once more he sang in simple intimate strains. In his *Persian Themes* he even caught something of Pushkin's serene insouciance which lasted, however, only during his wanderings in the East. On his return home he was plunged into the former welter, but this time the gap between fancy and reality was steadily widening. It was no use drugging himself with wine, women, and scandal. Besides, he already felt too tired for such expedients. At the age of thirty he was like an old man who had nothing to hope for, nothing to work for, nothing to look forward to. A victim of hypochondria, disgust, and self-disgust, he saw only one way of escape and he took it. A juvenile melodramatic touch was lent to his death by the fact that he wrote his last poem in his own blood.

Such was the literary career of the poet whose personal fate was in a way symbolic of the transition period between the two Russias—the old and the new; between the agricultural pattern of existence on the one hand, and the birth-pangs of the industrialized Soviet society on the other. The inner conflict involved by this change found in Esenin a pathetic voice which, in its turn, appealed to thousands of readers and was responsible for his vogue during and immediately after the Revolution. It was his pastoral nostalgia that found a ready response in all those contemporaries who regretted the passing away of the old rural Russia, and they consisted by no means of mere *kulaks*.

As it happens, each period has its own swan-song. The gentry period of Russian life found it in Turgenev's work; the intelligentsia period—in Chekhov; and the archaic peasant Russia— in Esenin. Suspended over the gulf of the vanishing past and the as yet much too complicated and therefore problematic future, he could not help reacting in the way he did. Suicide became only the last act of his own line of least resistance. Some five years later he was followed in this by another young poet, Vladimir Mayakovsky, whose personal fate had however been much more closely and more actively connected with the Soviet system than that of Esenin.

CHAPTER NINETEEN

Vladimir Mayakovsky

1.

Apart from being the most prominent poet of the revolutionary period proper, Vladimir Mayakovsky is something of a land-mark in Russian poetry as a whole. Like his rival, Sergey Esenin, he achieved both fame and notoriety before the cataclysm of 1917, yet the source from which he drew his inspiration was widely different from the one that appealed to the pastoral trend of Esenin. While Esenin clung to the pattern of the old peasant Russia, Mayakovsky was a hater of any settled patterns of existence, a breaker of rules and taboos. So instead of looking back to the past, he devoted his talent to the shaping of the future. He had started his poetic career under the banner of futurism. But it would be wrong to lump the small futurist group of Russian poets together with the Italian futurists who had their heyday between 1910 and 1915. The Italian move-ment under that name, initiated and led by Marinetti, was a noisy reaction to the weight of too great a cultural heritage. An excess of humanistic tradition was felt to be a drawback, a brake, in an age of technique, of speed and machines. Conse-quently an attempt was made to ignore that tradition and to turn art itself into a glorification of the mechanical values of life. Marinetti's revulsion from Italy's over-rich humanistic past was so complete indeed that he tried to drag, with a hysterical impetus, not only literature but also painting and the plastic arts from the plane of culture to that of an up-to-date technical civilization, imbued with the spirit of a Darwinian struggle for existence and the survival of the fittest. It was Marinetti who anticipated (*via* d'Annunzio and a semi-digested Nietzsche) all the elements of fascism and of the "dynamic" mailed fist. What that tendency was like can be gathered from the *Initial Manifesto,* issued during the exhibition of Italian futurist art in London, in 1912. Here are some of its pronouncements:

"Literature has hitherto glorified thoughtful immobility, ecstasy, and sleep; we shall extol aggressive movement, feverish insomnia, the double quick step, the somersault, the box on the ear, the fisticuff.

"We wish to glorify War—the only health-giver of the world—militarism, patriotism; the destructive arm of the Anarchist, the beautiful ideas that kill, contempt for woman.

"We wish to destroy the museums, the libraries; we fight against moralism, feminism, and all opportunistic and utilitarian meannesses.

"Set fire to the shelves of libraries! Divert the courses of the canals to flood the cellars of the museums! Oh! may the glorious canvases drift helplessly! Seize pickaxes and hammers! Sap the foundations of the venerable cities!

"We stand upon the summit of the world and once more cast our challenge to the stars!"

The frothy rhetoric of these sentences speaks for itself. A psychologist can easily detect in it the fury of a vain but sterile mind, anxious to lay the blame for its own sterility on the excessive culture of the past. In Russia, however, where there was little evidence of an over-ripe cultural heritage, the position as well as the task of the futurists was essentially different.

A new poetic technique, more appropriate to our modern pace and manner of life, *was*—as in Italy and elsewhere—one of its aims. But otherwise the overwhelming tradition of the past was not one of culture, but of autocracy and political oppression. This means that a fight for the future had to start with a fight against those evils. Hence the curious paradox that while in Italy futurism degenerated into a staunch supporter of fascist tyranny, in Russia it switched over to the Revolution, which indeed found its principal bard in Mayakovsky.

2.

It goes without saying that the technical innovations introduced into poetry by Mayakovsky were directed above all against symbolism, especially against its "feminine," or perhaps effeminate, characteristics. He demanded a clearer, more concrete and at the same time more robust and warlike poetry —a poetry which would not shrink from any harshness of thought and expression. Hence his challenge—

> My words
> > are not used
> > > to caressing ears;
> nor titillate
> > with semi-obscenities
> maiden ears
> > hidden in hair so innocent.
> I open on parade
> > my pages of fighters,
> pass in review
> > their lineal front.
> My verses stand
> > in lead-heavy letters

> ready for death
> and for deathless glory.*

The small group of the Russian futurists, led by Mayakovsky and consisting of lower middle-class bohemian *déclassés,* thus started their activities in a warlike mood. Defying the traditional public taste, they tried to revolutionize Russian prosody, word-formation, syntax, and made some interesting excursions (especially in the case of Velemir Khlebnikov) into the realm of the so-called pristine word. Some members of the group invented a "translogical" language of their own, based on the suggestiveness of sound and rhythm, going even further in this respect than, say, James Joyce during his last period. Mayakovsky's experiments were less eccentric. In his attempt to create a new type of poetry designed especially for the platform, he freed the verse from meter and based it on intonation. His rhythmic system was thus divorced from the old lyrical melody. He was concerned with the dynamic and dramatic value of single words instead, which now tended to become independent units. This involved a new rôle on the part of pauses, inflections, and also punctuation. The so-called spatial punctuation—with its peculiar pattern of printed words extending over the whole page—had been started by the symbolists, notably by Andrey Bely and Alexey Remizov. But Mayakovsky adopted it for his own purposes and brought it to perfection.

Having abandoned the former melodious and symmetrical verse, he proceeded to work out his loud and essentially rhetorical platform-technique by means of which a poem was often reduced to the equivalent of a poster or a cartoon—with such a mixture of planes as to achieve a maximum of *striking* expressiveness. In contrast to the symbolists, who were concerned

* Translated by George Reavey in *Soviet Literature,* Wishart.

with the inner reality, he concentrated on an intensified rendering of external things as such. Hence the harsh "palpability" of his poetic language, of his metaphors, similes, unexpected parallelisms and associations. He indulged in assonances in rhyme and also in his invariable staccato manner. As if taking tips from Nekrasov, he continued to depoetize poetry—through slang, through street and tavern-jargon while making deliberate use of hyperbolisms on a colossal scale. (In one of his poems he depicts himself walking about with the sun as his monocle and holding Napoleon on a leash like a terrier.) Yet Mayakovsky's depoetized verse tends to be poetry of a new and forcefully suggestive kind. The *Prologue* to one of his longer poems may serve as illustration.

> Your thought
> that muses on a sodden brain,
> as a fattened lackey on a green couch,
> I shall taunt with my heart's bloody tatters;
> satiate my insolent, caustic contempt.
> Not a single grey hair streaks my soul,
> not a trace of grandfatherly fondness!
> I shake the world with the might of my voice,
> and stalk—handsome,
> twenty-two year old.
>
> Gentle souls!
> You fiddle sweet loves,
> but the crude club their love on a drum.
> Try, as I do, and wrench
> yourself inside out and be just engulfing lips!
>
> Come and be lessoned—
> prim graduates of the angel league,
> from boudoirs lisping in cambric!

You who tranquilly finger your lips
as cooks page a cookery book.

. . . .

I do not believe in flowery Nice!
I sing once again
men crumpled as hospital beds
and women as trite as a proverb.*

Colloquial bonhomie, combined with satire, parody, and a grotesque mythology of his own in which a mixture of the trivial and the comically grandiose plays the principal part, is one of Mayakovsky's frequent devices. Among his Parisian poems, for example, there is one in which he chats with the Eiffel Tower, trying to make it leave "this Paris of prostitutes, poets, bourse, the gap-yawning boulevards" and emigrate to Soviet Russia where it would presumably feel more at ease, and ends with the promise to get it a visa. Or take this *Most Extraordinary Adventure,* which "happened to me, Vladimir Mayakovsky, at the Rumyantsev Summerhouse, Mount Akula, Pushkino, on the Yaroslav Railway." On a hot July day, the poet—in a joking mood—invited the Sun himself to come down for a while and have a cup of tea with him. But the Sun took the invitation seriously and began to descend—

Coming of his own free will,
Striding with great flaming rays
Across the field
And down the hill.
I don't want to seem afraid,
So I take a few steps back.
Now his eyes are in the garden,
He's coming up the garden path.

* Translated by George Reavey. Op. cit.

Through the windows
And the doors,
Through every crack
In the walls and the floors
The great flaming bulk
Of the sun's body pours
And pours.
And a very big breath he draws,
And in a deep voice makes this exclamation:
"I have turned my fires back you see
For the first time since creation.
I heard you calling me.
So here I am.
Come on, you poet, hurry up with that tea,
Come on, and I want some jam!"
Tears were pouring out of my eyes,
With the heat.
I was quite unsteady.
But I got to work
And soon had the samovar ready.
"All right" I said,
"Come on, old Shiner, and take a seat."

It must have been the devil
Who gave me the cheek
To yell out that invitation.
There I sat sadly
On the edge of the bench
In the greatest trepidation.
You see I was very scared
That things would turn out badly.
But from the sun
A strange brilliance flared
And I soon forgot
My shyness.

And gradually I got into conversation
With his celestial highness.

I began to chat
Of this and that,
I was calling him, "old boy,"
And I clapped him on the back.
And the Sun said: "See here,
You and I, comrade,
Are a pair, that's clear.
Come, poet, come with me,
We'll soar and we'll sing,
And defeat the world's dingy curses,
Over all that trash my beams I'll pour,
You'll flood it with your verses!"

.   .   .   .

To shine—
No nonsense, I say,
That's the sun's slogan,
And it is mine.*

3.

Whatever subject Mayakovsky took on, he filled it with his
own vitality, as well as with his sonorous voice, which seemed
to be created expressly for the platform and mass meetings.
In handling the word as such he certainly had no equal.
One of the contemporary Russian critics, Roman Jakobson,
goes so far as to say that the "word of Mayakovsky is quali-
tative and different from anything that preceded him in the
Russian verse, and no matter how many genetic links we
may try to establish—the pattern of his poetry remains pro-

* Translated by V. de Sola Pinto. The poem is quoted with considerable omissions.

VLADIMIR MAYAKOVSKY (1893-1930)

foundly original and revolutionary." But if so, it is the more interesting to watch how and why he eventually dedicated the whole of his talent to the cause of the working classes and of the Soviet experiment. Not that such a thing happened all at once, or that there was no other side to his being. On the contrary, it is enough to compare his poetry before 1917 with the verses he wrote after the Revolution in order to see that there were at least two Mayakovskys whose interrelations were very much dependent on the peculiar circumstances of his life.

Born in 1893 in the Caucasus, where his father was a forest-ranger, he did not know poverty until 1906, about which year we read in his brief autobiography: "Father died. End of prosperity. After father's funeral we had three roubles left. Instinctively, feverishly, we sold our chairs and tables. Moved to Moscow. Why? Not even acquaintances there." * In Moscow he settled, together with his mother and his two sisters, to a precarious semi-proletarian existence. In 1908 he became a member of the Russian Social-Democratic Party, was arrested, and spent eleven months in prison, where he started writing verse. The same year is marked by the following passage: "Entered School of Painting, Sculpture and Architecture. Only place that did not ask for a certificate of good conduct. Worked well. Was amazed to find imitators petted and original minds badgered. My revolutionary instinct stood up for the badgered ones."

In the Art School Mayakovsky developed his talent for drawing posters—an occupation which he continued (also in his poems) until his death in 1930. It was here that he met another dissatisfied youth, David Burlyuk, who appreciated Mayakovsky the poet before any of his verses were published.

* Translated by Herbert Marshall in *Mayakovsky*, Pilot Press.

An amusing example of the shock-tactics this friend employed occurred once after Mayakovsky had read to him, for the first time, some of his poems. "In the morning, Burlyuk, introducing me to someone, trumpeted: 'Don't you know him? My genius friend. Famous poet Mayakovsky.' I tried to stop him. Burlyuk was adamant. Leaving me, he bellowed: 'Now write or you will make me look a regular fool.'"

Although a poor man himself, Burlyuk gave Mayakovsky half-a-rouble daily so that he could write poetry without starving. Before long he introduced him to two other youngsters who, together with them, formed the nucleus of Russian futurism. But let us quote Mayakovsky's reminiscences once again. "Khlebnikov in Moscow. His quiet genius was at that time completely overshadowed by the roaring David. Here, too, was Kruchonykh—futurist, jesuit of words. After a few lyrical nights we gave birth to a joint manifesto. David collected the material, copied it, christened the manifesto and published *A Slap at Public Taste*." * This juvenile venture was followed by a series of lectures and scandals in the two capitals and also in some bigger cities in the provinces. Then the year 1913 was suddenly marked by the brief "tragedy in verse," *Vladimir Mayakovsky,* which was actually performed (by amateurs) in one of the parks at St. Petersburg.

4.

As the narcissistic title indicates, this work is a "grandiose" self-dramatization, natural enough in a youth of twenty and a gate-crasher in the temple of fame into the bargain. At the same time it is Mayakovsky's own equivalent of *Une Saison en Enfer*—with the world as its setting and with the humans

* Translated by Herbert Marshall. Op. cit.

teeming around like "bells on the fool's cap of God." It is also his first display of defiance born of despair. Like Gogol, Mayakovsky too (to use his own words) "crucified on a cross of laughter his own tormented groan." But whereas Gogol's method reminds one of Hogarth, that of Mayakovsky is more like a mixture of Picasso with the wildest fantasies of H. Bosch. Among his dramatis personae there actually appear (as allegorical accessories to Mayakovsky himself) an old man—thousands of years old—with dried-up black cats; a man without an eye and one foot; a man without an ear; a man without a head—all this in the same "expressionist" poster-like style which he adopted also in his next three longer poems: *A Cloud in Trousers, The Backbone Flute,* and *War and Peace.*

The original title of the first of these three works was *The Thirteenth Apostle,* but it was not passed by the censor. It is a vociferous poetic document in which, as in a fugue, Mayakovsky's frustrated personal love is combined with his social indignation raised to the point of rebellion against the world-order itself. In a preface to the second edition of this book (in 1918) he referred to it as a catechism of present-day art, but this can only be applied to it in a negative, destructive sense. "Down with your kind of love! Down with your kind of art! Down with your system of life! Down with your religion!" Such are the slogans of its four parts. Its "colossal" metaphors are deliberately heavy; and however strange it may appear at times on the surface, the inner association of the externally incongruous things is there. For all its extravagances, this is a most effective work, in which Mayakovsky's pathos of despair is expressed by an adequate new tonality and a new technique.

This pathos is even more intense in his *Backbone Flute,* which is inwardly connected with the previous poem, or rather with the previous two poems. In the teeth of all the rules of Marinetti's futurism, the tragedy of his own love is again one of Mayakovsky's *leitmotifs,* alternating or else running parallel with his social-political theme. Here his unrequited passion is treated as a curse, a punishment, torment and self-torment, the only result of which is inner devastation. Such a note, aggravated by a definite foreboding of his own tragic end, prevails also in his anti-bourgeois poem, *Man* (1917), whereas in *War and Peace* (written, in 1916, under the impact of the First World War) the social momentum is stronger—probably under the influence of Gorky in whose periodical, *The Annals,* he wrote at the time. Mayakovsky gave here another poetic poster, interpreting the world in terms of the blood-stained arena in the Roman Colosseum. Anti-militaristic in the extreme, it ends with the dream of a better and united world, inhabited by a new species of man.

> And such day has dawned
> That Andersen's tales
> Were crawling at its feet like puppies.

5.

During the whole of that period Mayakovsky's source of inspiration was above all his unhappy love* which he "clubbed on a drum" with the chaotic world around as its background. He was a revolutionary by temperament rather than by any definite aims or convictions. Yet when the Revolution of 1917 broke out, it provided a supra-personal aim and outlet which he adopted the more eagerly because he was not rooted either in the intelligentsia tradition like Blok and Bely, or in the peasant tradition like Esenin and Klyuyev. He embraced the

* He was in love with a woman (Mme. Brik) who was married to one of his friends and early publishers.

tasks of the Revolution in their entirety and became the poet of the rising masses—even if his voice and manner were often those of a poetic "boss" rather than a servant of the Revolution. But the very fervor with which he now voiced its cause may have been prompted by his wish to "crush under foot" the melody of his personal love-drama which had only been pushed aside rather than sublimated. Hence the over-loud character of his propaganda poems, beginning with his play, *Mystery-Bouffe* (1918, a revised edition in 1921).

This deliberate parody of the old mystery-plays is called by Mayakovsky a "heroic, epic, and satirical picture of our epoch." It is done in the style of a spectacular cartoon and, like all cartoons, it lacks depth, however amusing the very coarseness of its surface. The poet's familiar patting of the cosmos passes here into music-hall jokes and blasphemies about God, and the whole allegory is typical of the author's attempt to "restore to the theatre its spectacular character and to turn the stage itself into a platform." The figures include the Unclean ones (the proletarians), the Clean ones (the bourgeoisie), mixed up with God, the angels, and the devils. After the flood has destroyed the old earth, the Unclean rebel against the Clean ones and relegate them to Hell. Then they visit the heavenly Paradise which does not impress them at all. In fact, they leave it with scorn and go back to the ravaged earth which they want to transform into the Promised Land of happiness, of plenty and of universal comfort. The finale is similar to the one in Mayakovsky's *War and Peace,* but this time the stress is laid on the working class which—through the triumph of socialism, work and technique—has become the ruler of the world. It all ends, poster-like, with the paraphrased *Internationale:*

> All memory of the past shall perish;
> The bourgeois rule is crushed and lost.

The earth we hold and aye shall cherish.
We, soldiers of the toilers' host.
From fields and factories ascend,
Come from the towns both great and small.
The world is ours from end to end,
We who were nought, today are all.*

Mystery-Bouffe is Mayakovsky's counterpart and polar contrast of Esenin's *Inonia*. He would hear of no idyllic peasant paradise on earth. Nor is he afraid of the machine, of technique, provided that man shall be its master and not its slave. It is all rather simplified, yet in the years of Civil War it must have served its purpose well. No less simplified is his long allegorical poem, "150,000,000." Written in 1919, it represents the moujik Ivan in single combat with President Wilson—the champion of capitalism. The issue of the duel is, of course, a foregone conclusion.

Such loud and poster-like poetry required no strain on the part of the audiences in so far as it was offered with the flavor of smart journalism. The bulk of Mayakovsky's work after 1917 is actually a deliberate mixture of the two. Even his travel poems (1924-25) about France, Mexico, and America are journalistic *feuilletons* in verse—full of quick observations, irony, and political harangues. "In my work I am consciously becoming a newspaper man," Mayakovsky said at a time when he was pouring out countless propaganda limericks, rhymed slogans, and "agitkas" or agit-verses (his favorite genre), exhorting the Soviet citizens to perform their daily tasks and duties. He also asserted that "meetings, speeches, front-line limericks, one-day agit-prop playlets, the living radio-voice and the slogan flashing by on the trams—are all equal and sometimes valuable examples of poetry. To crown it all, he eventually defined his

* Translated by G. R. Noyes and Alex. Kaun, Appleton.

own verses as Com-Party poems and did not mind calling himself an "agitator, loud-speaker-in-chief." Here is an extract from his "agitka" *Hands off China* (1927):

> War,
>   daughter of imperialism,
> stalks,
> a spectre through the world.
> Workers roar: Hands off China!—
> Hey, Macdonald,
>   don't meddle
> in leagues and muddle speeches.
> Back, dreadnoughts!
> Hands off China!—
> In the embassy quarters
>   kings meticulously
> sit, weaving a web of intrigues.
> We'll brush away the cobweb.
> Hands off China!*

6.

Such was the character of Mayakovsky's poetry (or whatever you call it) when the social-political element prevailed in it. Yet even his loudest voice was not loud enough to suppress in the long run that personal dilemma of his which he had tried to eliminate, or at least to silence. It kept troubling him even during his most active propaganda period. In his poem *I Love* (1922), for example, he confessed—

> In others I know the heart's abode
> is in the bosom as we all know.
> But on me
> anatomy has run amok,

* Translated by George Reavey in *Soviet Literature*, Wishart.

> I am nothing but heart
> tingling all over.

A year later another poem, *About That,* reminiscent of his pre-war poetry (especially of *The Backbone Flute*), contained the following motif:

> "He" and "she" is my ballad.
> The terrible thing is that "he" is I
> and that "she" is mine.

The constructive years that came after the civil war was over, were inspiring enough to fill him with social enthusiasm to the exclusion (a temporary one) of disturbing personal problems. That period was responsible for his longest and best propaganda poem, *Vladimir Ilyich Lenin* (1924), on the occasion of Lenin's death. Despite its detailed passages about Marx etc., the poem reads like a paean to the Revolution and its leader whom, with a sudden flair for hero-worship, Mayakovsky relegates to the sphere of the great historical symbols.

> He is earthly—
> > but not of those
> > > whose nose
> delves only into
> > their own little sty.
> He grasped the earth
> > whole,
> > > all at one go,
> saw that
> > which lay hidden
> > in time.

And in his diatribe against the modern super-capitalist as seen from Soviet Russia, Mayakovsky comes to the characteristic conclusion:

> . You can't
>   jump over him,
>   no how you dodge past,
>   Only one way out—
>   explode! *

Between his propaganda poem, *Very Good* (1927), commemorating the tenth anniversary of the Revolution, and his personal confession, *At the Top of My Voice,* written in 1930 (that is, in the year of his suicide), Mayakovsky finished two satirical comedies, *The Bedbug* and *The Bathhouse.* The first is a "fantastic" satire—in nine pictures—on the eternal Philistine who emerged in many a Soviet citizen during the NEP period. We see a drunken NEP wedding, in the course of which a fire breaks out and burns all the revellers to death. Fifty years later one of them is resurrected (exactly as he was) by a special scientific method and he proves to be such a mean and vulgar insect in human form as to cause regular panic. *The Bathhouse,* in six acts—"with a circus and a display of fire-works"—is a grotesque buffoonery directed against the bureaucratic careerists in the new Soviet State: a tendency which was welcomed during the party purge in 1929. In this case the "fantastic" element is provided by a time-machine which can transfer one into the future, and during one of such journeys the principal character (a cut-and-dried Soviet bureaucrat) is left behind together with his piled-up luggage. None of these works contains as much as a hint of the poet's personal secret. But in one of his last poems, *At the Top of My Voice,* the social and the personal motifs are mingled, once again, in such a significant manner that the only thing to do is to quote this extract from its beginning:

* Translated by Herbert Marshall. Op. cit.

Highly respected
                    comrade posterity,
grubbing
          in our present-day
                              petrified dirt,
studying the darkness of our generation,
You,
    it may be, will inquire about me,
And
   it may be that one
                      of your erudite scholars,
Cutting short with his learning
                            the stream of questions,
will say: Once there lived
                          a boiling hot singer,
a violent enemy of cold water.
Now Professor,
              take off your optical bicycle,
I'll tell you in person
                      about my times
                                    and about myself:
I was a sanitary man
                    and a watercarrier,
I was mobilized,
                called up by the Revolution,
I went to the Front
                    from the lordly estate
Of Poetry—
          a capricious old lady.

    .   .   .   .

Yet I'm
        utterly fed up
                      with propaganda:

Yes I'd have liked
to strum
love songs to you,
They bring in good money
and they're delightful.
But I
conquered myself
and stamped
On the throat of my own song.
So listen here,
comrade posterity,
Listen to an agitator
a wild bawling ranter.*

The last few lines have often been interpreted as a proof of Mayakovsky's disappointment with the Revolution, which is nonsense. They prove only one thing: that his enthusiastic work for the Revolution was not enough to save him from the complications of his intimate personal dilemma. But if he deliberately chose to flee from it, to "stamp on the throat" of his own song, then even his revolutionary activities looked like escapism from himself, whether he was aware of it or not. Unable either to solve or to crush his personal dilemma for the sake of the bigger social cause, he must have been haunted by the idea of suicide even while writing some of his most spirited "agit-verses." The irony of it all was that he committed suicide at a time when he was universally regarded as the embodiment of socialist optimism. Worse—he gave away his secret in a farewell letter by this simple statement: "For me there are no outlets."

* Translated by V. de Sola Pinto.

7.

It is, perhaps, too early to assess Mayakovsky's place in Russian literature, yet one thing remains clear: he made a brave attempt to revolutionize not only the technique but the very rôle of poetry. One of the outstanding Soviet poets, Boris Pasternak, does not hesitate to ascribe to him (in his *Safe Conduct*) the greatest poetic destiny. "Whenever afterwards our generation expressed itself dramatically, lending its voice to a poet, be it Esenin, Selvinsky, or Tsvetayeva, in precisely those ties which bound them to each other and to their generation, that is, in their appeal from their times to the universe, the echo of Mayakovsky's consanguineous note was heard. I say nothing regarding masters such as Tikhonov and Aseyev, because I am linking myself to this dramatic tendency." *

Pasternak, who is a chamber poet *par excellence,* obviously refers here above all to Mayakovsky's personal poetry. But as for his numerous propaganda verses, the question still remains open in how far they are poetry if measured by our existing standards. To call them so wholeheartedly would mean to revise our definition of poetry in more respects than one. As though sensing the thorny side of this dilemma, the younger generation launched (especially after 1937) the slogan "back to Pushkin," as a corrective. While making use of all the technical innovations introduced by Mayakovsky, several of the Soviet poets aim again at that lucid and restrained simplicity which was typical of Pushkin. Moreover, "back to Pushkin" means also a return to the broad, tolerant humanism represented by him.

The convergence between socialism and humanism is, be-

* From *Boris Pasternak. The Collected Works,* Lindsay Drummond.

yond doubt, among the vital issues of our time. So vital indeed that, unless the new socialist society is founded on a broad humanistic basis—with its respect for individual rights and liberties, then socialism itself may become totalitarian. And totalitarianism from the left can in the end be as ruthless as that from the right. How far have the Soviet writers been aware of such a danger? How far have they been compelled to ignore it? A brief survey of the Soviet novel from its beginnings to the present day may provide us with some clues in this respect.

CHAPTER TWENTY

A Pattern of the
Soviet Novel

I.

In Soviet Russia, too, as everywhere else, the novel became and remained (as far as possible) the chief literary vehicle for the moods, trends, and realities of the age. It is true that the cataclysm of 1917 was followed by a prolonged gap in printing; but once the civil war was over, the novel came into its own again. Many of the old authors, including Bunin, Remizov, Zaitsev, and Kuprin emigrated abroad where they continued to write in the three centers of Russian émigré literature—Paris, Berlin, and Prague. Others became "internal émigrés" for whom silence was the best or perhaps the only policy. Others again adapted themselves to the new regime, no matter whether they felt enthusiastic about it or not, and made the best of it.

Needless to say, the Revolution and the civil war produced a crop of young authors who were both overawed and fascinated by the scale of the happenings they had witnessed. These they began to depict in a spirit of romantic exaltation regardless of the fact whether they themselves belonged to the "fellow-travellers" (as Trotsky had labelled them) or to the proletarian writers proper. The members of the first category were largely of gentry or "bourgeois" origin, and their education had followed the old intelligentsia tradition. Regarding art and culture as something which stands above class-ideologies, they were anxious to preserve above all their creative freedom. This was particularly true of the so-called Serapion Brotherhood (1921-24)* which included some of the best talents of the budding Soviet fiction. The "proletarians," on the other hand, insisted from the outset on a class culture and literature. Entrenched in organizations, such as the "October," "On Guard," "Smithy," many of them advocated that all the remnants of the former "bourgeois" culture, the writers included, should be thrown overboard. Fortunately, a sounder counsel prevailed. In literature at any rate continuity persisted, and as time went on most of the great "bourgeois" authors of the 19th century were rehabilitated and even reprinted.

The unexpected rise of the Soviet prose was due above all to the "fellow-travellers": Boris Pilnyak, Konstantin Fedin, Vsevolod Ivanov, Leonid Leonov, Yury Tynyanov, and a score of others. Moreover, the critic Voronsky, who was editing at the time the Soviet monthly, *Red Virgin Soil* ("Krasnaya Nov"), had the good sense to include a number of non-proletarian authors among his contributors, thus raising the periodical to a surprisingly high level. Another lucky coincidence was that during the NEP (New Economic Policy), roughly from 1922 until the inauguration of the First Five-Year Plan in 1928, there was a considerable amount of intellectual freedom. As long as the authors did not try to undermine the party-line, they were allowed to choose a fairly wide range of themes and subjects. There was enough room, say, for such a nihilistic satire on civilization as *The Extraordinary Adventures of Julio Hurenito*

---

* The "Serapion Brothers" took their name ostentatiously from one of the most romantic narratives by E. T. A. Hoffmann.

(first published in Berlin in 1922) by that prolific journalistic
and literary virtuoso Ilya Ehrenburg (b. 1891); for the detective novels, with an ideological lining, by Marietta Shaginyan
(b. 1888); or just for fantastic novels and stories of adventure
far removed from past or present by A. Grin (Alexander
Grinevsky, 1880-1932), not to mention a few other extravagant
writings. The NEP period was sufficiently tolerant for all that
—an attitude which was amply repaid by results.

2.

Even a quick glance at that early phase of Soviet fiction is
enough to make one see its main features. Its principal mark
was fermentation after the chaos. The process of groping for
the values of a new era was full of queries and baffled wonder
in the elderly writers, and of elation in the younger ones—
whatever their "ideological" adherence. Among the older authors it was Alexander Serafimovich (1863-1949) who in his
Iron Stream (1924) gave a fine description—in fact a Soviet
classic—of the red partisans fighting in the Caucasus during
the civil war. Other well established authors such as V.
Veresayev (Vikenty Smidovich, 1867-1946), Count Alexey N.
Tolstoy (1882-1945), and Sergey N. Sergeyev-Tsensky (b. 1876)
were anxious to depict the process of transition above all from
the angle of the doomed intelligentsia. Veresayev's *Deadlock*
(1924), as well as his much later novel *The Sisters* (1933), is
among the fairest and quietest disquisitions of this kind. More
agitated is Alexey Tolstoy's ambitious trilogy, *The Path of
Suffering,* with its panorama of Russia on the eve of the First
World War, during the war and the Revolution, as it affected
the consciousness of two members—a man and a woman—of

the old intelligentsia. The same period was tackled on a broader scale by Sergeyev-Tsensky in a series of novels the first of which, *Valya,* appeared in 1923. The series was to be known under the general title of *Transfiguration.*

If the surviving layer of the intelligentsia seemed to be puzzled and bewildered by what they had gone through, the young Soviet authors saw in the revolution no longer a problem but an accomplished fact the magnitude and the import of which were beyond questioning. The awareness of this seemed to have affected their very style. The majority of them drew their material from the revolution and the civil war the episodes of which they often described in a jerky, dithyrambic, and "dynamic" prose full of daring technical experiments. Both can be found in *Bare Year* (1922)—the first major work by Boris Pilnyak (Boris Wogau, b. 1894). This is a nervous, ornate, and as if eruptive narrative about the effects of the revolution in the country-side which was suddenly invaded by hordes of town-dwellers in a frantic search for food. Like the poet Esenin, Pilnyak dreads the machine and the advent of industrialism. His hero is the primitive peasant mass as such, with all its rough vitality, rootedness, and the interplay of primeval instincts. The bulk of Pilnyak's early writings are flavored with semi-mystical populism and a patriarchal pre-Petrine flavor. He would have felt much more at home in the times of Avvakum than in those of Lenin and Stalin.

Similar to Pilnyak's "new" prose, but even more colorful in its idiomatic ruggedness is the prose of Vsevolod Ivanov (b. 1895)—a Siberian who had started his literary career under the guidance of Maxim Gorky. He, too, is fond of primitive, elemental characters who are all of a piece. What interests him most, however, is their beastliness and inhumanity released

by the anarchy of the civil war. His early narratives and novels
deal with the red guerilla exploits in Siberia and Turkistan.
Neglectful of the plot, he makes up for it by exotic settings
or by the unusualness of situations. His three early novels
in particular, *Armoured Train No. 14-69, Colored Winds,* and
Blue Sands, all of them published in 1922-23, show the verve
of a man who is in love with life even if he has no respect for
human beings.

Different from both is Konstantin Fedin (b. 1892). His quiet,
lucid prose has more in common with the tradition of Turgenev,
Chekhov, and Bunin than with the "dynamic" somersaults
of Pilnyak or Ivanov. His novel, *Cities and Years* (1924), is
an excellent piece of psychological realism extracted from the
turmoil of the war and the revolution. It also represents an
experiment in structure—at least in its disregard for the chron-
ological sequence of time. Its hero, the student Startsov, is a
former civic internee in Saxony where he was able to see the
war from the German angle. Repatriated after the peace of
Brest-Litovsk, he tries to take an active part in the Revolution,
but he is too much of a Russian Hamlet-like intellectual to
merge wholeheartedly with any cause. After a number of
emotional and other adventures he comes to the conclusion (like
Nezhdanov in Turgenev's *Virgin Soil*) that he is a "superfluous revolutionary." In the end he is shot as a traitor by his
German artist-friend Kurt Wahn who, during his captivity in
Russia, has become a fanatic of communism.

What surprises a student of Soviet literature during the NEP
period is the fact that even such a novel as *The White Guard*
(1924) by Mikhail A. Bulgakov (1891-1936), eulogizing the
chivalry of the patriotic white officers during the Ukrainian
terror in Kiev, met with no objections. On the contrary, its

dramatized version, *The Days of the Turbins,* was produced by the Moscow Arts Theatre. Equally surprising was the publication of his book, *Devilry* (1925), full of satirical sallies against Soviet bureaucracy and the Soviet pattern of existence.

3.

Whereas Fedin linked up the early Soviet fiction to Turgenev, the tradition of Dostoevsky was followed by Leonid Leonov (b. 1910), and that of Tolstoy by Alexander A. Fadeyev (b. 1901) and Mikhail A. Sholokhov (b. 1905). After an experimental period, Leonov published in 1924 his Dostoevskian short novel, *The End of a Small Man.* This is a nightmarish narrative of how a world-famous scientist perished during the famine and the *sauve-qui-peut* period in the post-revolutionary Petrograd. Leonov's psychological bent found an outlet also in his rather stylized civil-war novel, *The Badgers* (1925), presenting the eternal antagonism between town and country. Frankly Dostoevskian again in his bulky novel, *The Thief* (1927), which will be discussed later.

As for Fadeyev, his first real success was a remarkable narrative, *The Rout* (1927), describing the exploits and the debacle of a red guerilla detachment during the civil war in a far-off corner of Siberia. The author had certainly learned from Tolstoy how to combine vivid physical portraiture with psychological analysis and how to intensify life without giving the impression of exaggerating it. The same method was applied by him in his long unfinished work, *The Last of the Udéghé* (begun in 1928). Planned for six volumes, this novel depicts the effect of the revolution on the inhabitants, civilized and primitive, of a region in the Russian Far East. But the canvas

proved too broad for Fadeyev's brush. In any case, the saga
(or whatever one calls it) is too drawn out. A more impressive and lasting example of Tolstoyan tradition is Sholokov's
Quiet Flows the Don (1928-31, with another volume added in
1940). This Soviet counterpart of *War and Peace* is an epic of a
Cossack community during the First World War and the Revolution. Following Tolstoy's lead, Sholokhov conjures up a wide
panorama full of characters—each of them alive as an individual yet fitting into the picture as a whole. The only disturbing point is the author's frequent propensity towards naturalism
of a somewhat sensational kind.

Judging by these standards, the proletarian authors' contributions to the early Soviet novel, albeit conspicuous, were on
a more modest scale. Fyodor V. Gladkov (b. 1883), a writer of
peasant origin, made a hit with his *Cement* (1925)—a bracing
piece of work which, for all its faults (occasional melodrama,
pretentious style, etc.) has the ring of sincerity. Its subject-
matter is the reconstruction of a cement plant in Novorossiysk
amidst the aftermath of the civil war. But against this background an inner drama, too, is taking place which leads to a
revaluation of sex and marriage according to the new moral
code. Alexander Malyshkin (1890-1938) gave a spirited picture
of the Bolshevik victory at Perekop—the key to the Crimea,
in his novel, *The Fall of Dair* (1924), whereas Yury N. Libe-
dinsky (b. 1898) aroused much attention by his novels dissecting
high-ranking communists both as private individuals and members of the party. Finally, there was an excellent documentary
narrative, *Chapayev* (1923), by Dmitry A. Furmanov (1891-
1926) about a peasant who during the civil war became a most
efficient leader of the partisans in the Urals. Furmanov's *Revolt*
(1925) describes with the same verve the civil war in Central
Asia.

4.

At the risk of omitting several authors (Isaac Babel, Lydia Seyfullina, Alexander Neverov, etc.) whose works had left a mark in the early Soviet prose without deviating from its general trend, we can now pass to some of those writers of the NEP period who were primarily interested in the realities of Soviet life, once it had begun to settle down. The transition from the civil-war chaos to a more normal existence in the still abnormal conditions led to all sorts of contrasts and problems—some of them pathetic, others grotesque and ridiculous, others tragic. Leonov's novel, *The Thief* (1827), for example, took up the problem of a former commissar and hero of the Revolution who, after the exciting years he had gone through, was unable to adapt himself to the routine of a quiet existence. So he became leader of a criminal gang and drifted morally and socially from bad to worse. But after a number of shocks he became aware of his better self and finally left for the country with something like a promise of a moral renewal. A similar theme was attempted by Mikhail Slonimsky (b. 1897) in his *The Middle Prospect* (1927) which is structurally less complex than Leonov's novel.

Several authors were content, however, to depict the Soviet *byt* in its single aspects just as they saw them. Mikhail Zoshchenko (b. 1895) began pouring out humorous as well as satirical anecdotes, snapshots and feuilleton-like sketches, mostly in the form of the *skaz*. Boris Lavrenyov (1892), too, who first wrote romantically colored stories about the Revolution and the civil war, turned in his *Crazy Tales* (1926) to descriptions of Soviet life. And so did Vladimir Lidin (V. G. Gomberg, b. 1894) in his narratives which were partly modelled on

Chekhov.* The best products of this kind are, however, such picaresque novels as *The Embezzlers* (1926) by Valentin Katayev (b. 1897), or *Twelve Chairs* (1928) and *The Little Golden Calf* (1931) by the joint authors Ilya Ilf (1897-1937) and Evgeny Petrov (E. Katayev, 1902-42).

The heroes of *The Embezzlers* are two irresponsible Soviet clerks in Moscow. Having stolen a considerable sum of government money, they escape, and keep wandering and hiding, until they are both caught and brought to justice. This simple motif is worked out with amusing freshness, while the errands of the two heroes introduce the reader to all sorts of vagaries of Soviet life in the provinces. Humor, satire, and adventure permeate also the two novels by Ilf and Petrov. The astute but broadminded rogue Ostap Bender (a very "Russian" character) who figures in both is a product of the post-revolutionary conditions, but knows how to exploit these to advantage. Whether in search for the diamonds hidden by their former owner in one of the twelve chairs long disposed of, or on a more straightforward blackmailing mission, the sympathy of the readers is inclined to be on his side rather than on the side of the authorities whose rules and laws he proceeds to break with such a light-hearted gaiety, indeed with a perfectly good conscience.*

Among the narratives and novels about Soviet life *The Crime of Kirik Rudenko* (1928) by Nikolai Nikitin (b. 1897) deals with the demoralized young factory workers in the countryside. The literary circles in Leningrad are vividly described by Venyamin Kaverin (V. A. Zilberg, b. 1902) in his novel, *The*

* Those who are interested in the Soviet school life during that period will find the documentary *Diary of Kostya Ryabtsev* (1928) by N. Ognyov most interesting.
* The two authors gave later on (1936) a witty and satirical account of their visit to the U. S. in their joint book, *One-Storied America*. Among their short stories the one about Columbus landing in our days at New York and finally victimized by Hollywood is full of irrepressible amusement.

Troublemaker (1928), while Mikhail Kozakov's (b. 1897) *Adameyko the Philistine* (1927) is an exciting detective and psychological novel in one. Social student life again is tackled in Vladimir Lidin's novel, *The Renegade* (1928). The last two works actually bring us to another genre of Soviet fiction during the NEP period: the psychological novel proper.

5.

The psychological novel, which had played such an important part in Russian literature from Lermontov's *The Hero of Our Time* onwards, had a strong enough tradition to assert its rights also during the Soviet regime. Of the older writers it was Panteleimon Romanov (1884-1940) who combined certain moral problems—those of sex and marriage—with a psychological approach to Soviet youth and the new type of intellectuals. A balance between the Soviet *byt* and the psychology on Dostoevskian lines was struck in Leonov's *The Thief*. Other authors, too, such as Olesha, Savich, Budantsev, and also Kaverin, shifted the attention to the "inner man" whom they approached from a cautiously irrational angle.

In Olesha's short novel *Envy* (1927), for instance, one can feel the author's rebellion against the mechanized and rationalistic straitjackets imposed upon life. The book is a vindication of the free human personality as such with its right to love, hate, hope, weep, pity, and forgive in the very teeth of all prefabricated rules and norms of human behavior. Another Soviet novel, *The Imaginary Interlocutor* (1928) by Ovadiy Savich, has its ancestry in Tolstoy's *The Death of Ivan Ilyich*. Its hero is a minor Soviet official in the provinces. Amidst the humdrum of his so-called life something goes suddenly wrong with him. In a fit of mental aberration he mechanically steals some government money—a transgression for which he is forgiven. He is granted a leave of absence during which his illness grows worse. He suffers from hallucinations, sees his own double (with whom he converses), feels alienated from everyone, and finally dies. All this in the setting of provincial officialdom with its pettiness, drabness and its dull, mechanical efficiency.

Even during the first Five-Year Plan one can see traces of relative freedom in such a narrative as *A Tale of The Suffering Mind* (1929) by Sergey Budantsev (b. 1896) or Venyamin Kaverin's *Artist Unknown* (1931). The first is a psychological dissection—full of reminiscences—of a young Russian scientist of the 1860's. He lives in a respectable Swiss pension where he is going blind and tries to find an escape from his ordeal in two attempts at suicide—both of them frustrated. Kaverin's novel, on the other hand, is a spirited defense of artistic freedom, as well as of those old ethical values which are threatened to be swept away by the tide of streamlined materialism.

The literary pattern of the NEP period would not be complete without the mention of another genre the vogue of which began in 1925 and continued in an ever increasing wave, namely the biographical and historical novel.

6.

This genre, properly modernized and brought up-to-date, was given a good start by Yury Tynyanov (1894-1944) with his novel *Kyukhlya*. Such was the nickname of Pushkin's friend, the poet Kuechelbecker, a queer but lovable personality who had been involved in the "Decembrist" rising of 1825 and ended his days in Siberia. Both the portraiture and the historical background of the period are rendered by the author with consummate skill. The same can be said of Tynanov's *Vazir Mukhtar* (1929)—a novel about the dramatist and diplomat Alexander Griboyedov. The author follows Griboyedov's career up to his death in 1829, when he had been murdered by the incited Persian mob at Teheran. Excellent though it be, *Vazir Mukhtar* is less compact as a whole than Tynanov's previous masterpiece.

Often it is impossible to draw a line between the biographical and the historical novel.* There is a large margin where the two overlap, since both of them are concerned with real characters and periods of the past. In Soviet Russia this particular genre began to grow for two widely different reasons. One of them was the tendency to escape from the strenuous transition period back to a less hectic past; the second and perhaps more frequent reason was the wish to explain the happenings of the present by those of the past, or at least to find some analogies or points of contact between the two.

The progress of this type of historical novel reached its highwater mark in Alexey N. Tolstoy's monumental *Peter the First,* the three volumes of which appeared in 1929, 1933 and 1945 respectively, while an unfinished fourth volume was added after the author's death (1945). Alexey Tolstoy sees history mainly in terms of agitated dramatic moves and movements. His treatment of Peter I and of his *entourage* is on the whole fair and competent. So is his description of Russia during those eventful years. The idea which gradually emerges in the novel and corroborates, as it were, one of the principal Soviet tendencies after Lenin's death, is the idea of the centralized State to which everything else should be sacrificed. No wonder a

---

* In 1937 (the anniversary of Pushkin's death) Tynanov published the first volume of his third and longest biographical novel, *Pushkin*, which is too meticulous in details and rather slow in its pace for a novel.

Soviet critic called this work an "approach to our present epoch from its distant rear."

Another writer of the older generation, Olga Forsh (b. 1875) gave in *The Contemporaries* (1927) a biographical novel about Gogol in Rome. An even stronger piece of work is her *Clad in Stone* (1927), dealing with the revolutionary activities among the young intellectuals of the 1860's, with the terrorist Beideman as one of the central figures and Karakozov's attempt upon the Tsar's life in 1866 as its climax. The heroes of her other novels are Radishchev, the semi-mad Tsar Paul I, and (not without malice) the literary figures of the symbolist and the early Soviet periods.

Without touching upon analogous contributions by Ilya Ehrenburg, Artyom Vesyoly, Alexey Chapygin and others, a brief mention should be made of the novels by Anatoly Vinogradov (b. 1888). In one of them, *Three Colors of Time* (1930) he gave a full-size portrait of Stendhal, with a lively description of the French retreat from Moscow in 1812, in which Stendhal took part. *His Black Consul* (1931) is about Toussaint l'Ouverture, the leader of the Haiti rebels against the French. One of his novels deals with the Masonic movement in Russia at the beginning of the 19th century (*The Tale of the Brothers Turgenev,* 1932); another with the famous Russian scientist Mendeleyev; and another even with the life and fate of Paganini. This kind of novel not only continued but actually flourished during the first Five-Year Plan. It was taken over also by the subsequent period of Socialist Realism.

7.

After Stalin's victory over Trotsky, the triumph of the idea of "socialism in one country," as an alternative to universal revolution, could not but lead to a number of successive Five-Year Plans whose aim was the industrialization of Soviet Russia, as well as her consolidation from within and from without. The first of these plans began to operate in 1928; and since literature, too, had to be drawn into the process, there began to pour in all sorts of "social commands" which soon put an end to the relative freedom enjoyed by the Soviet authors during the NEP period. For one thing, the communist party now felt strong enough to impose its brakes upon any ideas and activities which deviated or threatened to deviate from the prescribed party-line. Critics of the dogmatic Marxian persuasion (Averbakh, etc.) came into their own. So did the proletarian authors. Even the "fellow travellers," many of whom had by now gone a long way to being on good terms with the regime, were expected to make their contributions. Some of them did so sincerely, others less sincerely. In either case they had to hitch their narratives, novels, and plays to the intentions of the powers-that-be. Literature thus ran the danger of being turned, step by step, almost into applied literature.

Among the countless Five-Year Plan novels the voluminous *Bruski* (1930) by Fyodor Panfyorov (b. 1890) was among the first to make due impression. The whole of it is about the collectivization of a village community on the Volga, with the obvious note of propaganda on behalf of such a process. The author's knowledge of the conditions and the peasants cannot be denied. Yet the novel is badly constructed, rather drawn out, and often garrulous. Its sincere enthusiasm at first appealed to communist readers. Later, however, the author was attacked on account of his bad craftsmanship.

Some of the best literary contributions to the Five-Year Plan came from such "fellow-travellers" as Pilnyak and Leonov. Pilnyak, who had already had several misunderstandings with the authorities, evidently came to the conclusion that the saftey-first policy was not such a bad thing after all. Anyway, he con-formed, as far as he could, to the prescribed literary recipe in his otherwise excellently written novel, *Volga Flows into the Caspian* (1930). The theme is the building of an enormous dam in the Moscow region. The workers and the technicians are of course enthusiastic about it. But there are villains as well, wreckers, and reactionaries. Finally, there are mental and emo-tional complications arising among the engineers in charge of the dam. But virtue is bound to triumph in the end, and triumph it does. Pilnyak's style is more sober this time than usual. He indulges, though, in too many technical and scientific digressions.

On as high a level as Pilnyak's novel but equally encumbered with technical details are Leonov's *Sot* (1931) and *Skutarevsky* (1932). In the first he makes a whole epic out of the foundation of a huge paper mill in the forests of northern Russia. We see all the phases of the work, the eager personnel, the wicked sabo-teurs, and the success of the enterprise once the numerous diffi-culties have been overcome. *Skutarevsky,* on the other hand, is centered above all on a famous scientist and "bourgeois" intel-lectual whose gradual conversion to the service (if not to the ideology) of the Soviets is the *leitmotif* of the novel. The por-trait of the somewhat angular, cut-and-dried but otherwise solid professor, who is entrusted with the electrification of a vast area, stands out as a memorable figure amidst the atmosphere of that early endeavor to build up a new Russia. Also Sholokhov's *Virgin Soil Upturned* (begun in 1931) was a success. This well written novel about the collectivization of the land brings the readers back to the same Don Cossacks to whom they had been introduced in *Quiet Flows the Don.* Always an acute observer, the author yet remains dispassionate enough to prefer truth to propaganda. Katayev's *Forward O Time* (1932) is interesting on account of its cleverly applied film technique rather than because of its naive optimism and apotheosis of the machine—the action takes place in a huge combine at Magnitogorsk. But the appearance of this novel already coincided with the rise of a new phase of Soviet literature—a phase which went under the banner of socialist realism.

8.

Socialist realism was inaugurated after the formation of the "General Union of Soviet Writers" (Russian and non-Russian) in 1932 and has become since the only recognized literary trend in the Soviet Union. It is often referred to as realism plus party optimism, but it would probably admit a few other "isms" as well. Its actual creator, Maxim Gorky, had once defined the trend as an "accurate description of reality in so far as this is necessary for a deeper and clearer understanding of all that we must abolish and of all that we must build up." Gorky's intentions were to combine in this trend socialism with what can be called new humanism. In practice, however, it only amounted to a stronger grip of the party ideology on literature. And since the ideology itself found it expedient to change from time to time its views and tenets, the authors now had to keep pace with it accordingly.

The only permanent tenet seemed to be that the Soviet regime, the most "perfect" regime in the world, should not be criticized. At the same time there was a gradual tendency to build up a Stalin cult and Stalin myth which for many observers amounted to nothing less than a kind of paternal Tsarism from the other end. Moreover, with Hitler's accession to power in 1933, and Japan's warlike preparations in the Far

East, the remnants of Soviet internationalism vanished overnight. The new slogan was patriotism, which soon demanded
a thorough revision of books and textbooks on history. Official
approval was now with the writings capable of bolstering up
the Soviet peoples' morale, as well as the patriotic pride in their
achievements.

Among the books which served this double purpose the autobiographic novel, *How the Steel was Tempered* (1935), by
Nikolai Ostrovsky (1904-36), deserves a special mention. Its
author, a proletarian by origin and by convictions, was so badly
crippled during the civil war that he later became paralyzed
and blind. Yet by dint of sheer defiance of his fate he wrote a
book about his past—a book which was full of courage, of faith
in life and read like a testament for the younger generation. It
sold in millions of copies.*

With all its restrictions (one of them being a veto on any
pessimism or doubt), socialist realism has produced, amidst a
morass of indifferent and dull novels, some good ones, but
their authors are for the most part our old "fellow-travellers."
Thus Kaverin's *Fulfilment of Wishes* (1934-5) combined, like
the rest of his works, an exciting plot with certain moral and
psychological questionings apropos the relationship of the individual and society. Plenty of psychological disquisitions can
be found also in Leonov's novel, *The Road to the Ocean* (1935),
which is something of a *tour de force* in style and structure.
This time his hero is a convinced communist holding a responsible post on a railway system. He suffers from an incurable
disease which affects in its own peculiar way both him and his
relations with other human beings—a regular feast for Leonov.
Vsevolod Ivanov gave a most unusual transposed autobiography

---

* Ostrovsky's second novel, *Born in Storm* (1937), about the struggle of the Ukrainian
    workers, against the Polish landlords during the revolution, remained un-
    finished.

in *The Adventures of a Fakir* (1935). Katayev scored a success with his fresh and simple *Lone White Sail* (1936) which takes one back to the rising of 1905, with two Odessa urchins and a rebellious sailor as its main characters.

A purely documentary book of great interest is *An Educational Epic* (1934)* by Anton Makarenko (1888-1939). It is a moving narrative of how a crowd of young delinquents and "orphans of the storm" had been turned into decent citizens simply by humane treatment. Among the numerous novels about reconstruction in the various parts of Russia the one about the Urals, *People from the Backwoods* (1938), by Malyshkin is excellent reading. Glimpses of reconstruction in Siberia, together with an imaginary but quite exciting war between Japan and Soviet Russia, can be obtained from the novel *In the East* (1937) by Peter A. Pavlenko (b. 1899). The author's militant communism is here combined with that intensely patriotic spirit which had by now invaded also the historical novel of Soviet Russia.

9.

This spirit reached its climax just before and during the second world war. As soon as Hitler had invaded the Russian territory in 1941, the historical novel became in fact one of the principal weapons on the "literary front." The great figures of the Russian history were conjured up in order to spur on the patriotic zeal, as well as the hatred of the invader. Even that ruthless "gatherer of the Russian lands" Ivan the Terrible had to be whitewashed and shown in the light of a great patriot and statesman. This was done, and very ably too, by Valentine Kostylyov (1888-1950) in his trilogy *Ivan the Terrible* (1941-

---

* Its English title, as well as the title of the filmed version, is *The Road to Life*.

45), whereas Sergey Borodin (Amir Sergidzhan) tackled a much earlier period in his *Dimitry Donskoy* (1942), showing the first victory of the Russians over their Tartar masters on the Kulikovo Field in 1380 under the leadership of the Moscow prince Dimitry. The descriptions of the historical atmosphere, of the *byt,* and of the cautious preparations for war are both vivid and competent. V. Yan's (Vasily Yanchevsky's) trilogy about the Mongolian invasion, *Ghenghis Khan, Batu Khan,* and *Alexander the Uneasy* * (1941-45) takes us even further back in history. The author seems to be familiar not only with the historical facts he describes but also with the oriental literary sources and documents upon which he draws to great advantage. The cunning arrière-pensée behind this trilogy is the parallel between the Mongol savagery and that of Hitler.

One of the most popular books during Hitler's invasion was Leo Tolstoy's *War and Peace.* Monographs of the great Russian generals of 1812, whether in the form of biography or fiction, also became great favorites. Other wars which aroused interest were the Crimean Campaign and the First World War. Both were dealt with in some of Sergeyev-Tsensky's novels. His *Ordeal of Sebastopol* (1937-38), describing the climax of the Crimean Campaign, was much read during the German occupation. So was his *Brusilov's Break Through* (1943) and *The Guns Forward* (1944), both of them depicting certain heroic episodes of World War I.

10.

While Hitler's hordes were being fought and eventually driven out of Russia, anti-German and anti-fascist propaganda was the

---

* This was the nickname of Alexander Nevsky, the prince of Vladimir (1220-63) whose policy helped a great deal to ease the Tartar yoke upon the Russian population.

order of the day. Journalistic reportage, sketches from the front, patriotic plays, poems, stories, and novels—all had to serve one purpose only: victory over the enemy. When in 1943 Zoshchenko had begun to print in a periodical (*October*) a series of introspective reminiscences of his childhood and boyhood— *Before Sunrise,* he was promptly reminded that such "irrelevant" things should not have been brought forward at a time when the very existence of the nation was at stake. The author's crime was not forgotten even when the war was over, and in 1946 he was duly "excommunicated" by Zhdanov.

The majority of poets, especially Nikolai Tikhonov, Konstantin Simonov, Pavel Antokolsky, Vera Inber, Margarita Aliger, Olga Bergholz, and even such an individualist as Boris Pasternak, did what they could to help the war effort. The same was true of the playwrights, which does not mean that their plays were necessarily good.* As for the novels, they ranged from the sensational piling up of German war horrors in *The Rainbow* (1942) by Wanda Wassilewska to the less emotional but more solid narrative, *The People Immortal* (1943), by Vasily Grosman, with its refreshing portraits of Soviet officers and soldiers. The workers' resistance in the Kuban region during the German occupation found an adeqaute treatment in Boris Gorbatov's novel, *The Unconquered Ones or the Taras Family* (1943), whereas Konstantin Simonov depicted the gruesome epic of Stalingrad in his *Days and Nights* (1944). Captain Saburov, the chief character of this novel, is in the tradition of the unassuming Russian heroes, and his modesty about his own exploits only makes the actual horrors of the siege of Stalingrad appear the more authentic. A good but purely documentary work about Leningrad is Fadeyev's *Leningrad in the Days of*

---

* *The Russians* (1942) by Konstantin Simonov achieved considerable success on the stage also in London.

the Blockade (1944). Vera Inber's diary, *Almost Three Years* (1945), deals with the same blockade but from a personal angle.

Among a legion of propaganda novels, *The Struggle for Peace* (1945) by Fyodor Panfyorov can be mentioned. It describes how a whole factory was transferred by the workers to the safer Urals where it continued to help the war effort. As for the more artistic narratives, Leonov's *The Taking of Veliko-shumsk* is impressive by its cleverly worked out contrast between the deadly tank-machines on the one hand, and the human element represented by the soldiers on the other. The title of Sholokhov's contribution, *They Fought for Their Country* (1944), does not sound promising, but the narrative is at a high level. It is an episode of the Cossack resistance to the Germans, and reads like a promise of a much longer work to come. Yet no sooner had the hostilities ceased than new slogans and directives were on the way. Zhdanov's ruthless "purge" of literature in 1946 left no doubt about this. "Socialist realism" underwent some further modifications.

II.

During the first few years after the war, novels connected with war activities continued. Some of them, such as Boris Polevoy's *Tale of a Real Man* (1947), were simple and straightforward accounts based on actual facts. Others—Pavlenko's *Happiness* (1947) for instance, dealing with the Yalta conference—incorporated certain disturbing elements in which the cult of Stalin went hand in hand with a growing anti-Western attitude. The "cold war" thus penetrated into literature as well. Ilya Ehrenburg, who can be regarded as a thermometer of the moods and intentions of the high-ups, made this quite clear in his novel, *The Storm* (1948), in which he is hardly fair to the allied armies in France. But there were also less biased novels about the war in retrospect. Vera Panova described in her *Travel Companions* (1947)* the life in an ambulance train, with a subtle analysis of the relations—emotional and otherwise —between the various members of its personnel.† Also Katayev's recent novel about the underground activities in Odessa, *For the Power of the Soviets* (1949), has something of the freshness typical of his *Lone White Sail*. In fact, its principal characters are the same two boys—now men of an advanced age.

Parallel with this there were some good books which had nothing to do with the war. Fedin's *First Joys* (1946) and *Unusual Summer* (1948) are transposed memories of the author's boyhood and youth in a Volga town before 1914. Gladkov's *Story of my Childhood* (1949), on the other hand, is a piece of straightforward autobiography—a simple, sincere, and pathetic narrative which can be regarded as that author's best work.

Despite single exceptions of this kind, the general run of the Soviet novel since 1946, i.e. since Zhdanov's "purge," has been mediocre and dull. The gist of his decrees amounted to nothing less than a complete subjection of literature to the party control. This implied quite a number of ready-made motifs and solutions. Obligatory Stalin worship and an enforced anti-Western attitude were only two of its facets. Others consisted in a certain juvenile optimism, in the "Stakhanovite" cult of work, in the boosting and boasting of what was being done by collective farms or factories, and in the final truimph of communist virtues whatever their names. The writings in the more tolerant days of the NEP period must certainly have pre-

---

* The title of the English translation of this novel is *The Train*.
† Her two subsequent novels, *Kruzhilikha* (1948) and *The Serene Shore* (1949) are about post-war reconstruction.

supposed a higher mental age in the readers than was now the case. But in the war against man's inner and external freedom literature is often one of the first casualties.

The regrettable fact is that Moscow has assumed once again its old rôle of the "third Rome," only this time in an infallible anti-religious sense. The "iron curtain" between Russia and western culture in general and literature in particular was thus bound to grow. Not so many years ago the Western world was eagerly following and translating Soviet authors. All that interest is now gone. But the "other," i.e. the European face of Russia, may emerge once more and lead to some *modus vivendi* between her and the rest of the world. The initiative will have to come, though, from the elements which lie outside literature. A rapprochement in the politico-economic field would almost inevitably be followed by one in culture and literature as well. The benefit derived from it would be invaluable for Russia and the West. Indeed for the whole world.

Conclusion

Literature of Russia, from its beginnings to our times, had an evolution quite in keeping with the erratic ups and downs of that country's history. After a promising start in Kiev, under the auspices of Byzantine Christianity, there set in a prolonged gap due to Tartar domination. Things began to improve during the Moscow period, although at that time literature remained predominantly in the service of Church and State. Moreover, from the middle of the thirteenth century onwards Russia had few contacts with the West and Western civilization. Her attitude toward both was one of diffidence if not open hostility. That secularization of culture, which in the West had taken place under the impact of the Renaissance, began in Russia—roughly—as late as the second half of the seventeenth century. It was accelerated, though, and brought to a climax by Peter the Great—the actual promoter of the Petersburg period in Russian history and culture.

The process which he thus tried to carry out was the grafting on of European influences in all spheres of life, literature included. But once Russia's apprenticeship had been sufficiently advanced, the foundations for a national literature were laid down by Pushkin and Gogol. Having blended Western literary methods with Russian themes and spirit, the subsequent Russian authors reached a level of excellence which had to be reckoned with all the world over. Their works indeed began to pay back Russia's debt to Europe and to influence the much older Western literatures. The period of monumental Russian prose had its heyday during the 1860's and 1870's. In the 1880's there was a recession; but by the middle of the 1890's a new impetus was given to literary activities—notably to poetry—by the symbolist movement which became the dominant trend during the first decade of this century and culminated in the work of Alexander Blok.

The Revolution of 1917 led to a political and "ideological" cleavage between the Soviets and the West. Once the Russian capital had again been transferred back to Moscow, the old Muscovite intransigence, too, was revived. Yet the peak of Soviet literature, while trying to assimilate the new social and political climate, preserved, as far as it could, its allegiance to the best nineteenth century traditions. It also showed originality and vigor—at least in the 1920's, when the interference of the "party-line" still left a considerable margin of creative freedom. It was only with the growing pressure from above, especially after the introduction of socialist realism as something obligatory, that the general level of Soviet literature began to deteriorate.

During Hitler's invasion there were signs of a renewed cultural and political rapprochement with the West. But once the war was over, difficulties arose again on both sides. During the subsequent "cold war" things were allowed to drift from bad to worse. This does not mean, however, that such a situation is bound to last. Now that Stalin is dead there certainly is room for new changes and possibilities. After all, regimes as well as "ideologies" come and go, but man's creative spirit remains. And in the end it will prevail, whatever the obstacles put in its way.

Short Bibliography of Works in English and French

CHAPTER ONE

The Lay of Igor's Campaign. Tr. S. H. Cross, in *La Geste du Prince Igor,* 1948.
The Tale of the Armament of Igor. Tr. L. A. Magnus, 1915.
Le Slovo d'Igor, by A. Mazon, 1940.
History of Early Russian Literature, by M. K. Gudzy, 1949.

CHAPTER TWO

The Life of the Archpriest Avvakum, by Himself. Tr. Jane Harrison and Hope Mirrless, 1924.
Avvakum et les débuts du raskol, by P. Pascal, 1938.
A History of Russian Literature from the Earliest Times to the Death of Dostoyevsky, by D. S. Mirsky, 1927.
History of Early Russian Literature, by M. K. Gudzy, 1949.

CHAPTER THREE

The Choice of a Tutor, by D. I. Fonvizin, in *Five Russian Plays.* Tr. C. E. Beechhofer, 1916.
The Young Hopeful, by D. I. Fonvizin, in *Masterpieces of the Russian Drama.* Tr. G. Z. Patrick and G. R. Noyes, 1933.

CHAPTER FOUR

The Captain's Daughter and Other Tales. Tr. Natalie Duddington, 1933.

The Russian Wonderland. Tr. B. Brazol, 1936.

The Works of Alexander Pushkin. Ed. by A. Yarmolinsky, 1936.

Eugene Onegin. Tr. D. Prall Radin and F. Patrick, 1937.

Evgeny Onegin. Tr. Oliver Elton, 1937, 1943.

A Book of Russian Verse. Ed. by C. M. Bowra, 1943.

Pushkin's Poems. Tr. Walter Morison, 1945.

The Fairy Tales. Tr. T. Pancheff, 1947.

Pushkin, Lermontov, Tyutchev. Poems. Tr. V. Nabokov, 1947.

Biographies and studies in English: by D. S. Mirsky (1926) S. H. Cross (1937), E. Simmons (1937), J. Lavrin (*Pushkin and Russian Literature,* 1947). In French: *A Pouchkine,* 2 vols. by H. Troyat, 1949.

CHAPTER FIVE

The Works of Gogol, 6 vols. Tr. Constance Garnett, 1922-28.

Tales from Gogol. Tr. R. Portnova, 1945.

Diary of a Madman, Nevsky Prospect. Tr. B. Scott, 1946.

The Government Inspector. Tr. D. J. Campbell, 1947.

Dead Souls. Tr. George Reavey: 1948.

Tales of Good and Evil. Tr. D. Magarshack, 1949.

Biographies and studies in English: by V. V. Nabokov (1944, 1947), Janko Lavrin (1952).

In French: by Louis Léger (1914), B. de Schloezer (1932), D. S. Merejkovsky (*Gogol et le diable,* 1939).

CHAPTER SIX

A Hero of Nowadays. Tr. S. Phillimore, 1920.

A Hero of Our Time. Tr. R. Merton, 1928.

A Hero of Our Own Times. Tr. E. and C. Paul, 1940.

The Demon. Tr. G. Shelley, 1930.

A Song about Tsar Ivan Vasilyevich, His Body-Guard and the Valiant Merchant Kalashnikov. Tr. J. Cournoss, 1929.

A Book of Russian Verse and *A Second Book of Russian Verse.* Ed. by C. M. Bowra, 1943 and 1947, respectively.

CHAPTER SEVEN

A Book of Russian Verse and *A Second Book of Russian Verse.*
Ed. by C. M. Bowra, 1943, 1947.
Pushkin, Lermontov, Tyutchev, Poems. Tr. V. Nabokov, 1947.

CHAPTER EIGHT

The Novels of Ivan Turgenev, 17 vols. Tr. Constance Garnett,
1919-23.
The Plays of Ivan Turgenev. Tr. M. S. Mandell, 1924.
Three Plays. Tr. Constance Garnett, 1934.
Fathers and Children. Tr. R. Hare, 1947. Another translation
(*Fathers and Sons*), by G. Reavey, 1950.
Smoke. Tr. Natalie Duddington, 1949.
A Sportsman's Notebook. Tr. C. and N. Hepburn, 1950.
First Love. Tr. I. Berlin, 1950.
Rudin. Tr. A. Brown, 1950.
On the Eve. Tr. M. Budberg, 1950. Another translation by G.
Gardiner, 1950.
Turgenev in England and America, by R. A. Guttmann, 1941.
Biographies and studies in English: by E. Garnett (1917), A. Yarmo-
linsky (1926), J. A. T. Lloyd (1942), D. Magarshack (1954).
In French: by E. Haumant (1906), A. Maurois (1931).

CHAPTER NINE

Who Can Be Happy and Free in Russia. Tr. J. M. Soskice, 1917.
Poems. Tr. by J. M. Soskice, 1920.
Nekrasov l'homme et le poète, by C. Corbet, 1948.

CHAPTER TEN

A Common Story. Tr. Constance Garnett, 1917.
Oblomov. Tr. C. J. Hogarth, 1915. Another version by Natalie
Duddington, 1929.
Un maître du roman russe, Ivan Goncharov, by A. Mazon, 1914.
Goncharov, by Janko Lavrin, 1954.

CHAPTER ELEVEN

The Storm. Tr. Constance Garnett, 1898. Another version by C. J. Holland and M. Morley, 1930.

Plays (Four). Ed. by G. R. Noyes, 1917.

The Forest. Tr. C. W. Winslow and G. R. Noyes, 1926.

Easy Money and Two Other Plays. Tr. D. Magarshack, 1944.

The Diary of a Scoundrel. Adapted by K. Ackland, 1948.

Ostrovsky et son théatre de moeurs russes, by I. Patouillet, 1912.

CHAPTER TWELVE

The Novels of Fyodor Dostoevsky, 12 vols. Tr. Constance Garnett, 1912ff. A new edition began to appear after World War II.

Stavrogin's Confession. Tr. S. S. Koteliansky and V. Woolf, 1922.

The Diary of a Writer, 2 vols. Tr. Boris Brazol, 1949.

Crime and Punishment. Tr. D. Magarshack, 1951.

The Devils. Tr. D. Magarshack, 1953.

Letters of F. F. Dostoevsky to his Family and Friends. Tr. C. Mayne, 1917.

Biographies and studies in English: by J. Middleton Mury (1916), A. J. Meier-Graefe (1928), A. Yarmolinsky (1935), Janko Lavrin (1943), Zernov (1944), J. Lloyd (1946), J. C. Powys (1947), L. A. Sander (1948), E. J. Simmons (1950), V. Ivanov (1952). Two of the French studies, one by André Gide and the other by H. Troyat (1940), are available in English.

Centenary Edition of Tolstoy's Works, edited by Aylmer Maude, 21 vols. 1928-37. Tolstoy's single works are obtainable in numerous other editions in English, as well as in all other European languages.

There is also an enormous collection of books on Tolstoy and his works. As for studies and biographies in English, we can mention those by H. Faussett (1927), Aylmer Maude, in two vols. (1929-30); A. I. Nazarov (1930), L. Dillon (1934), L. Derrick (1944), J. Lavrin (1944), E. Simmons (1946), Alexandra Tolstoy (1954). One of the most stimulating short books on the subject is Maxim

Gorky's *Reminiscences of Tolstoy* (see Bibliography to Chapter XV). As for Tolstoy's views on history, *The Fox and The Hedgehog*, by I. Berlin (1954) is as amusing as it is illuminating.

CHAPTER THIRTEEN

The Cathedral Folk. Tr. I. F. Hapgood, 1924.
Tales of Leskov. Tr. N. Norman, 1944ff.
The Enchanted Pilgrim. Tr. D. Magarshack, 1946.
The Lady Macbeth of the Mtsensk District. Tr. Walter Morison in *Representative Russian Stories,* 1946.
The Amazon and Other Stories. Tr. D. Magarshack, 1949.

CHAPTER FOURTEEN

Plays by Anton Chekhov. Tr. A. Fell, 1915.
Tales of Chekhov. 13 vols. Tr. Constance Garnett, 1916-22.
Select Tales of Chekhov. Tr. Constance Garnett.
Plays by Anton Chekhov. Tr. Constance Garnett.
Biographies and studies in English: by W. Gerhardi (1923), W. H. Bruford (*Chekhov and His Russia,* 1948), Nina Toumanova (1937), L. Avilova (*Chekhov in My Life,* 1950), Ronald Hingley (1950), D. Magarshack (*Chekhov the Dramatist,* 1952).

CHAPTER FIFTEEN

Foma Gordeyeff. Tr. I. F. Hapood, 1901.
Tales from Gorky. Tr. R. N. Bain, 1902.
My Childhood. Tr. G. M. Foakes, 1915.
In the World. Tr. G. M. Foakes, 1917.
Bystander (the first volume of *Klim Samgin*). Tr. B. G. Guerney, 1930. The other three volumes were translated by A. Bakshy: *The Magnet,* 1931; *Other Fires,* 1933; *The Specter,* 1938.
Down and Out. Tr. G. R. Noyes and A. Kaun in *Masterpieces of the Russian Drama,* 1933.
Reminiscences of Tolstoy, Chekhov and Andreyev. Tr. S. S. Koteliansky and Leonard Woolf, 1934.

The Last Plays. Adapted by Gibson-Gowan, 1937.

Best Short Stories. Ed. by A. Yarmolinsky and M. Budberg, 1939.

Seven Plays. Tr. A. Bakshy, 1945.

The Artamonov Business. Tr. A. Brown, 1948.

Unrequited Love and Other Stories. Tr. M. Budberg, 1949.

Mother. Tr. M. Wettlin, 1950.

Autobiography (including *My Childhood, In the World, My Universities*). Tr. I. Schneider, 1953.

Biographies and studies in English: by E. J. Dillon (1902), A. S. Kaun (1932).

CHAPTER SIXTEEN

Plays. Tr. L. Meader and F. N. Scott, 1915.

The Red Laugh. Tr. A. Linden, 1915.

The Little Angel and Other Stories. Tr. H. Bernstein, 1916.

The Crushed Flower and Other Stories. Tr. H. Bernstein, 1916.

When the King Loses His Head and Other Stories (including *Judas Iscariot* and *Life of Father Vasily*). Tr. A. J. Wolfe, 1920.

Satan's Diary. Tr. H. Bernstein, 1920.

His Exc. the Governor. Tr. M. Magnus, 1921.

He Who Gets Slapped. Tr. Y. Zilborg, 1922.

The Dark. Tr. L. A. Magnus and K. Walter, 1922.

Samson in Chains. Tr. H. Bernstein, 1923.

Sashka Giguleff. Tr. L. Hicks, 1925.

Professor Storitsyn. Tr. I. Minkoff, J. R. Noyes and A. Kaun in *Masterpieces of the Russian Drama,* 1933.

Judas Iscariot. The Christians. The Phantoms. Tr. W. Morison, 1947.

The Seven Who Were Hanged. Tr. E. Schimanskaya and M. E. Gow, 1947.

Leonid Andreyev, by A. S. Kaun, 1924.

Dostoevsky and Andreyev, by H. King, 1934.

Reminiscences of Tolstoy, Chekhov and Andreyev, by M. Gorky. Tr. S. S. Kotzeliansky and Leonard Woolf, 1934.

CHAPTER SEVENTEEN

The Twelve. Tr. Babette Deutsch and A. Yarmolinsky, 1920, 1931.

A Treasury of Russian Literature. Ed. by B. G. Guerney, 1943.

A Book of Russian Verse (1943) and *A Second Book of Russian Verse* (1947). Ed. by C. M. Bowra.

The Spirit of Music. Tr. I. Freiman, 1946.

A Treasury of Russian Verse. Ed. by A. Yarmolinsky, 1949.

The Frenzied Poets: Andrey Biely and The Russian Symbolists by Oleg Maslenikov, 1952.

In French: *L'univers poétique d'Alexandre Blok,* by S. Bonneau, 1946. *Blok et son temps* by N. N. Berberova, 1947.

CHAPTERS EIGHTEEN AND NINETEEN

Soviet Literature. An Anthology. Ed. by G. Reavey and M. L. Slonim, 1933.

Mystery-Bouffe. Tr. G. R. Noyes and A. Kaun in *Masterpieces of the Russian Drama,* 1933.

A Treasury of Russian Literature. Ed. B. J. Guerney, 1943.

Mayakovsky and His Poetry. Compiled by Herbert Marshall, 1942, revised edition, 1945.

Soviet Poets and Poetry, by A. S. Kaun, 1943.

An Outline of Modern Russian Literature (1880-1940), by E. J. Simmons, 1943.

Soviet Literature Today, by George Reavey, 1946.

Soviet-Russian Literature, by Gleb Struve, 1951.

In French: *De Marinetti a Mayakovski* by G. Lehrmann, 1942.

CHAPTER TWENTY

Practically all the Soviet authors mentioned in this chapter are available in English translations, whether published in America or in Great Britain. A good and comprehensive bibliography of translations, as well as of works on Soviet literature, can be found in *Soviet-Russian Literature,* by Gleb Struve, 1951. A selected bibliography is given in the chapter on Soviet literature by Prof. J. Simmons in *A Handbook of Slavic Studies,* edited by I. Strakhovsky, 1949. *A Bibliography of Soviet Russian Literature* was published by the University of Oklahoma in 1950. The readers interested in the earlier controversy of the Soviet critics should consult *Literature and Marxism,* edited by A. Flores, 1938. Brief but valuable is Mr. Francis J. Whitfield's additional chapter on Soviet literature in the abbreviated edition of D. S. Mirsky's most valuable *A History of Russian Literature.* Interesting glimpses can be obtained also from the symposium, *Through the Glass of Soviet Literature,* edited by Professor Ernest J. Simmons, 1953.

Index of Names